THE PURSUIT *of* HOCKEYNESS

Transcontinental Books
1100 René-Lévesque BoulevardWest
24th floor
Montreal (Quebec) H3B 4X9
Tel. : 514 340-3587
Toll-free 1-866-800-2500
www.livres.transcontinental.ca

Bibliothèque et Archives nationales du Québec and Library
and Archives Canada cataloguing in publication

Main entry under title :
The Pursuit of Hockeyness
At head of title: The Hockey News.

ISBN 978-0-9809924-3-4

1. Hockey - Miscellanea. 2. Hockey - Anecdotes. I. McCaig, Sam. II. Hockey
news (Montréal, Québec).

GV847.P87 2009   796.962   C2009-941707-

Project editor: Sam McCaig
Proofreading: THN staff
Photo research: Erika Vanderveer
Page design: Sutdio Andrée Robillard
Cover design: Jamie Hodgson

Printed in Canada
© Transcontinental Books, 2009
Legal deposit — 3rd quarter 2009
National Library of Quebec
National Library of Canada

We acknowledge the financial support of the Government of Canada through the Book
Publishing Industry Development Program (BPIDP) and the Government of Quebec through
the SODEC Tax Credit for our publishing activities.

For information on special rates for corporate libraries and wholesale purchases,
please call **1-866-800-2500**.

The Hockey News

Edited by Sam McCaig

THE P*of*URSUIT HOCKEYNESS

Transcontinental Books

ACKNOWLEDGEMENTS

The Pursuit of Hockeyness was a complete team effort, with the entire THN editorial staff pitching in as well as THN contributors and freelancers from across North America and around the hockey world.

THN editor-in-chief Jason Kay helped guide the project, while senior editor Sam McCaig oversaw the day-to-day process.

A sincere thank you to all of the writers, editors and fact-checkers.

THN staff: Jason Kay, Brian Costello, Ryan Kennedy, Ryan Dixon, John Grigg, Ken Campbell, Adam Proteau, Rory Boylen, Edward Fraser, Sam McCaig, Jamie Hodgson and Erika Vanderveer.

THN alumni: Mark Brender, Mike Mouat and Denis Gibbons.

THN correspondents: Larry Brooks, Luke Decock, Kevin Oklobzija, Larry Mahoney, Neil Hodge, Mike Mastovich, Nathan White and Risto Pakarinen.

THN freelancers: Chuck Brown, Matt Semansky, Alex Kunawicz, Chris Powell and Ed O'Leary.

THN interns: Anthony Murphy, Jordan Samery, Dustin Pollack, Matthew Krebs, Monika Morovan, Nikki Cook and Alan Bass.

Upper management types – THN publisher Caroline Andrews, Transcontinental book publisher Jean Pare and consultant Arnold Gosewich – provided experience, moral support and guidance.

And thank you to our communications/marketing team of Janis Davidson-Pressick and Carlie McGhee for helping spread *The Pursuit of Hockeyness.*

TABLE OF CONTENTS

INTRODUCTION

Every fan pursues hockeyness in their own unique way. Some people collect hockey cards, some like to watch kids skating around, some simply have to see an NHL game every night. And that's just the tip of the ice rink; there's a multitude of ways to express your affection for the game. Some are fun, some are frivolous, some are fearsome – but to call yourself a true-blue, hardcore hockey fan, you've got to do them all.

And that's why we decided to publish *The Pursuit Of Hockeyness* – so you, Mr. or Mrs. Hockey Fan, could use it as a handy reference guide for completing your Lifetime Achievement In The World Of Puck. Just remember to take your time and enjoy the journey.

So, what would it be? If you could do one hockey-related thing before you die, what would you decide? Skate on a frozen pond one last time? Hug the Stanley Cup? Throw an octopus on the ice at Joe Louis Arena?

What about 99 hockey-related things? What's on your own personal hockey "bucket list"? As a fan of the game, what do you just *have* to do before you die? Because...well, hate to be the bearer of bad news, but you're ultimately destined for that big rink in the sky. Hopefully not for a very, very long time, but it's true. It's inevitable; it happens to everybody. And you can't take your skates with you.

But if you can commit to *The Pursuit Of Hockeyness*, you'll experience a hockey life well lived.

Thanks for reading.

Sam McCaig
Summer 2009

1. LOVE AN NHL TEAM LIKE NO OTHER

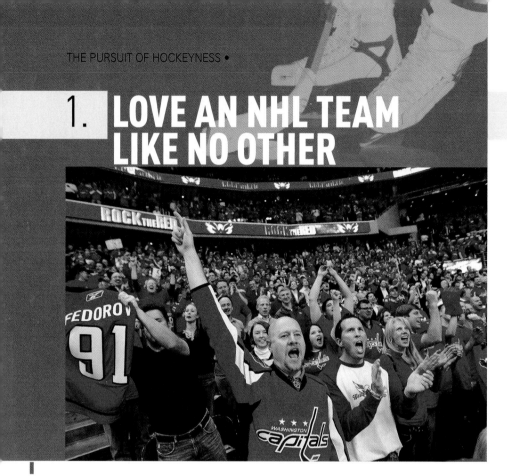

"Tis better to have loved and lost than never to have loved at all." –
Poet/hockey fan Lord Alfred Tennyson, 1850

A true fan, a real fan – not some fly-by-night wagon-hopper who became a fan some time after the age of one minute – has his team's logo tattooed on his heart and he wears that tattooed heart on the sleeve of his authentic vintage jersey, which came from either an Eaton's catalogue or was hand-knit and purchased for twice its actual value from an arena concession stand because…well, because maybe that overpriced sweater would be the nudge his team needed to grind out a big win on what some less-than-faithful, so-called fan would call a "meaningless" pre-season game.

Because that, fans from Toronto to Tampa Bay and Montreal to Manhattan (and let's not leave out Oil Country, Cow Town, the Motor City and all the hockey hotbeds from Beantown to Red Square), is what it means to be a true fan.

Hockey just isn't the same if you don't bleed black-and-gold or orange-and-blue or even teal. That devotion can be bred (some Broad Street Bullies might snipe that it's inbred in Penguins fans) or it can be learned (say, by way of a move to a hockey city from…well, what do you call a non-hockey city? Hell on earth or just purgatory?). There's no rule that dictates how you become a citizen of Isles Nation or a Carolina Caniac or how you first decide to "Rock the Red." The common denominator is simple – fans are fanatics and fanatic is a nice way of saying they are completely and totally out of their gourd.

This is the mindset you need to find if you want to wring maximum enjoyment out of this great game. This fanaticism is what made young boys growing up in Pickering or Mississauga, Ont., in the 1980s actually pretend to be Miroslav Frycer, Peter Ihnacak or Rick St. Croix in their road hockey games instead of fantasizing they were Ray Bourque or Guy Lafleur or Billy Smith – you know, decent players, but totally overrated when looking through blue-and-white-colored glasses.

It can be family, geography or whim, but anyone who has found the love of their hockey life can share one bond – they are all nuts and they love it.

Jeremy Mahar, 29, became a Penguins fan as an 11-year-old when Mario Lemieux and Jaromir Jagr were filling their trophy cases. He went to hockey school and his dad, a Leafs fan, let him wear Lemieux's No. 66.

"Even then, Dad didn't have the heart to make me a Leafs fan and for that I thank him," Mahar said.

And now he watches as Penguins chicks Sidney Crosby and Evgeni Malkin bring home Art Ross and Hart Trophies by the truckload. Mahar's not sure how and doesn't know why he learned to love Pittsburgh's flightless birds, but he does see how loyalty can cloud a fan's vision.

"I was a huge Jagr fan when he played for the Pens, I even had a No. 68 jersey," Mahar said. "After he got traded, I realized he was a complete tool."

For Islanders fan and financial consultant Dean Crandall, 41, it's all about living in the past. "Nobody can take away our dynasty years."

Or is it the future? "When John Tavares lands in Long Island, we'll start a whole new list of memories."

Well, Crandall sure ain't living in the present. Or in most people's version of reality.

Mark McCormick, 49, a structural engineer who grew up in the Canadiens corner of northern New Brunswick, is a proud supporter of *les Habitants*. He has millions of compadres across the hockey universe and they can pretty much end any argument with any other fan over which team is the best ever. Montreal has won the most Stanley Cups, by far. Argument *finis*.

Care to retort there, Hogtown? Anything? How about you, Chicago? Anaheim? Anyone? Maybe Detroit fans will someday knock the Habs down a peg, if they can peel off a dozen or so more Cups.

"I would stay overnight at my grandparents many Saturday nights to watch *Hockey Night in Canada*, sometimes on the French station when the CBC English channel had Leaf games," said McCormick of his preference for watching the Canadiens.

Ah, family bonding. Or is it corruption? Some might even say brainwashing.

But being a Canadiens fan is easy. They have the winningest tradition in hockey and have treated generations of fans to Cup parades, not like those nimrods down the road in Toronto where fans haven't even had a sniff in more than 40 years.

Case in point – the low point of a Toronto fan's existence – how about RIGHT NOW! MISSING THE PLAYOFFS FOUR STRAIGHT SEASONS! Or there's the 1980s. Or most of the '70s. And some of the '90s. The high? In living memory? There isn't one. At least not for anyone born after 1967.

Ask any Leafs fan why and the spittle and four-letter words will fly as you hear, again, about that uncalled high-sticking penalty when Wayne Gretzky clipped Doug Gilmour in the '93 Western Conference final.

A Hab fan's low point? McCormick has to think long and hard.

"When Ken Dryden retired…he left too early."

Boo friggin' hoo.

High school teacher Carol Parks, 45, learned to be a Leafs fan on her daddy's knee.

"The Toronto Maple Leafs were passed down by my dad through our special Saturday nights of Peter Puck," Parks said. "I was allowed to have ginger ale and share his snack crackers."

But those fond memories are gone. Despite attempts to improve the team via cheering, swearing and decorating the interior of her house in a Leafs motif, Parks is left with only one feeling from her years of fandom.

"I'd like to kick the Toronto GM and ownership in the ass," she said without hesitation.

And somewhere in between Toronto and Montreal lies a vast hockey wasteland/cradle – depending, again, on your view of the world – called Ottawa. Hated equally by the Leafs and Habs faithful, the Senators had an ungodly start to their existence (a paltry 10 wins in 1992-93), yet still gained a fan base.

Mike Hawkins, 40, a freelance writer and photographer, was working in Cornwall, Ont., when the Sens were born. And while the hockey world clucked about that ugly baby, he was smitten.

"It was the expansion-team blues, but I stuck with them," he said.

And Hawkins gloated prematurely when the Senators fought Anaheim for the Stanley Cup in 2007.

"Finally, after so many years of waiting, the Senators were among the best in the league," he said. "When all the other Canadian teams were playing golf, the Senators were playing hockey. All the ribbing from Leafs and Canadiens fans over the years just kind of evaporated right there."

But alas, the Sens lost. Then they swooned the following season and missed the playoffs entirely in 2008-09. Such is life as a fan. But Hawkins is ready to ride out another trip through the valley of ineptitude.

"At this point, you've just got to stay the path," he said.

Hawkins does admit, however, to something that many fans never would: He has been seduced by the temptation of all those shiny, sexy Stanley Cup rings and considered a tryst, a fling, a dalliance with the *bleu, blanc et rouge*. Ooh la la!

"I certainly do dream of cheering for another team," Hawkins said.

Had Ottawa hired John Tortorella, despicable in Hawkins' eyes, he was packing his car flags and coasters and taking up with that hot little number from *la belle province*. But they didn't, and Hawkins remained faithful.

"Dammit…still a Sens fan," he said. ■

2. GO TO AN NHL GAME FOR THE FULL FAN EXPERIENCE

High-definition television is one of the better innovations of our time, but it still doesn't do hockey justice. When it comes to the chasm between what can be viewed on the tube and the real, in-person experience, hockey is the Grand Canyon.

It may be cliche and as plain as the nose on Tim Hunter's face, but to truly absorb all that is hockey, you gotta be there. There is no sport in the world that better combines brute strength and (mostly) controlled violence, with supreme skill, artistry and grace. It's an epic that can't be fully appreciated from your couch.

The experience differs somewhat from NHL city to NHL city, but here are some suggestions and guidelines to being a full-fledged fan at a game:

• Get there early. This is a chance to see all the players in the pre-game skate, several without their helmets. (Yes, hockey players have faces and hair, too!) In many rinks, it's the best opportunity for a photo op; a chance to worm your way down to the glass, zoom in and preserve a memory – and maybe even get an autograph.

• Sport your team's colors. It amps up the mood when you dress for success. And in the playoffs, it soars to another level. Winnipeggers pioneered the white-out, a phenomenon now imitated, with variations, throughout the NHL. It serves as a unifying force for the home team, and an intimidating one for the visitors, when upwards of 20,000 people scream support with their uniform attire.

• Wear a hat. But not an expensive one. Or a personal favorite. You need to be prepared to part with your headgear in the event someone records a hat trick, that distinctly hockey tradition.

• Bring a copy of The Hockey News. Follow the teams' line combinations with our depth charts. If your THN isn't handy, buy a program. We'll forgive you.

• Sit in different sections. Granted, you may need repeat visits to accomplish this (or sleepy ushers), but try to get seats close to ice level to capture the game's speed and power; to feel the vibrations as the glass rattles; and, to hear what the players say to one another – both instructions and the trash talk. On a subsequent trip, sit high up to get the bird's-eye view. This is where you can appreciate what players do away from the puck, see how plays develop, identify the dogged backcheckers as well as those guys who simply dog it.

• Try to get on the Jumbotron. Bring a funny sign or wear a wacky wig. Be prepared to smooch the girl or guy beside you when the Kiss Cam comes your way. Have a Tic Tac first, though.

• Buy a 50/50 ticket. One way or another, the money's going to a good cause, either a worthy charity or your bank account/bar tab.

• Stay in your seat during the intermission (unless you need a bathroom break). Many rinks have fine between-periods entertainment, particularly if you enjoy laughing at the on-ice awkwardness of others. And we can't forget about those six-year-old tykes, who cruise/waddle around the big ice surface, trying to score/stand up and skate in the right direction. When the guffaws are finished, the Zambonis come out to play. There's something cathartic about a resurfaced sheet of ice, a look and feel (if you've ever played the game) that tacitly says renewal and anticipation.

• Be vocal. But not belligerent or profane. Cheer the good guys, jeer the villains, the referee or your team's inept power play. Get your money's worth.

• Stay for the three-star selection. It's a final chance to salute your heroes, or deride the rival. Call it hockey closure.

• Keep your ticket stub. Put it in a photo album or shoebox and bring it out when you tell your offspring about your first experience at an NHL game. ■

3. BUILD YOUR OWN BACKYARD RINK

Everyone else is finding shelter with a hot chocolate and a book around the fireplace on a bitter Sunday night in January. You, meanwhile, are warming your heart.

For the past two hours you've been outside under the floodlights, warding off the elements with earmuffs and thermal underwear and the empties piling up in the snowbank. The radio is cranking and the hose is pumping. You water the backyard garden where the geraniums used to be. The towel that you soaked in boiling water to get the faucet going two hours ago is frozen like a rope in the driveway. The mercury says minus-17.

Things couldn't be better.

You turn to look in through the kitchen window, grinning like a jackal. The wife returns a palms-up shoulder shrug on the way to bed, all raised eyebrows and misplaced sympathy. You blow her a kiss. And she thinks you're the crazy one. Sure, you could just let the hose run on its own, but where's the fun in that? You can't stop thinking about the time you roofed it on Jimmy McKenzie back in peewee.

This frozen-in-time feeling is why you must build a backyard rink this winter. If your lawn is uneven, flatten it. If there's a shrub where the blueline should be, cut it down. If you live in sunbelt and can't afford refrigeration pipes in your backyard, move. Even if you go broke or the weather turns balmy or you throw out your back after hours of shoveling, it will be the best thing you've ever done. If the sheet is smooth as glass for one month, or even just one week, or maybe just for one glorious afternoon shinny game with the boys that finishes under the moonlight, it will all be worth it. Because you haven't lived until you've laid out your best friend into a snowbank on your own backyard. On this rink, you will be Wayne Gretzky and Scott Stevens interchangeably as you see fit – and you never have to book the ice.

Just find some tarp and a staple gun and scour the garage for old lumber and plywood. Head down to the basement and dig out the cabinet doors from last year's kitchen reno – they'll make great sideboards. If you're a first-timer, prepare to make rookie mistakes and curse yourself for your incompetence. If the boards aren't secured properly, they will fall down. If your tarp is cheap and thin, trespassing raccoons will poke holes. Learn from your mistakes and use them to get better. With any luck it'll be a long season. And when you drag the net onto your own rink for the first time, it will be the ultimate triumph. You'll dangle like Rick Middleton and skate like Guy Lafleur.

Savor the time you have alone. Because when you build it, they will come. All of them. Within two days you'll be seeing long-lost souls from forgotten lives…people you thought were buried so deep in the past that not even The Hockey News could find them. You never knew your kids had this many friends. Hey, your kids really are alright! And when you're out alone late one night and blast a 30-foot slapshot off the crossbar and the puck shatters a giant ceramic troll in the backyard of the neighbor who complained to the city about late-night noise pollution from the rink, that's alright, too. Why?

Because you hit the crossbar. ■

4. PLAY HOCKEY NOW, PLAY HOCKEY FOREVER

A few years ago Ed Murray had a breakout rookie season...at age 55. The resident of Pembroke, Maine, digs clams for a living and always wanted to play hockey. He finally found himself a rink and a team a good 90 minutes away, across the Canada-U.S. border in Rothesay, N.B.

No matter. Murray's hockey dreams made the commute easy to take and he'd happily travel the 100 miles for his 10:15 Tuesday night ice time (hey, thanks to time zones it's only 9:15 back home in Maine).

"I can't wait to go," said the oldest rookie in the league.

Murray found the game through his son. It's not uncommon in this part of the world for American kids to cross the border into New Brunswick to play since rinks are sparse in Downeast Maine. Murray started inline skating during the summer and skating on a pond in the winter, hoping for a shot at a men's league the way Canadian kids – even some 30-year-old kids – yearn for the NHL. At one of his son's games, Murray saw a sign advertising a league for players 50 and older. He felt braver about that than other men's leagues that accept players over 35.

His introduction to Canada's game was memorable.

"I skated into a guy who was 6-foot-4 and 250 pounds if he was an ounce," Murray said. "Down I went. And he skates up to me and says, 'Ya better keep yer head up, Yank.' "

That guy – all the guys – became good friends and Murray had discovered the real reason old guys leave the comfort of the couch on those cold winter nights to sweat and sometimes bruise and bleed in front of, usually, zero fans, depending on whether the rink attendant has some sweeping to do.

"It's unreal," he said, "the fraternity-like atmosphere with those guys, it's unreal."

Ah, yes. The fraternity. The dressing room. The inner sanctum. There are thousands of them and no two are ever the same. And yet they are oh-so-similar.

The smell is a not-so-delicious blend of muscle ointment, several flavors of body odor and a hint of, good God, what is that? Turtle tank? Dead woodchuck? Trench foot?

But the characters inside chatter and joke, talk business and talk trash, oblivious to the funk that hangs thick in the air. For these oldtimers, the dressing room is as regimented as those in the NHL. The rules are simple – everyone has his special seat, if you bring Ben Gay you better have enough to share and if a conversation breaks out in the shower…keep it at eye level.

"The late nights have very little appeal," said Neil Brisley, who's sneaking up on 50 and, rumor has it, is on the short list to take over as GM of the St. Stephen Mehan's Funeral Home Blues. (Longtime GM Bruce Estey retired due to back problems over a year ago, but clings to the game by staying in the front office, a job that basically involves making sure everyone's dues are paid.)

"For me, it's hanging out with the boys," Brisley continued. "When I look around and see what other people look like at my age, I feel very good about myself. It scares me a little to think what I would look like without the two ice times per week."

Teammate Peter McCormick has serious concerns, too. So much so that he's decided off-season training might be wise. By late April, only a month removed from the Rusty Blades Hockey League season, McCormick claimed he was already ramping up the workout schedule.

"I walked past the treadmill twice today," he said.

McCormick's goal for the off-season is to trim two inches from his waist and add two inches to his inseam. He also wants to hit the weights with a focus on the upper body.

"I'm working on getting rid of these 'moobs,' " he said.

Very little – OK, none – of what they say is serious. They talk about prospects for a draft that will never happen. They discuss line combinations, like whether they should keep the McCormick-named 'Two-Headed Monster' (Larry Seabrook and Terry Moore) together or spread out the scoring. They hatch a defensive system they will never employ and they ask Seabrook about stats that no one ever records…so they make them up.

But the Blues have had a few sobering moments lately, too. In 2006, they lost teammate Rob Gullison to a heart attack. The following year, Brisley's brother, Carl, nearly lost an eye when a puck struck him during a routine clearing attempt. Several surgeries later, he's back to coaching his son, but it's doubtful he'll ever play again. He stopped by the dressing room shortly after the incident, his eye bandaged, his future unclear. He quickly defused any tension.

"Well, boys," he said when he entered the room, "it's all fun and games until…"

Since his injury, all the Blues have put on visors or full masks.

At the end of the Blues' 2008-09 season, McCormick handed out the team's end-of-season awards – which amounted to little more than a handshake for a fake photo op. Brisley was a lock as the team MVP; he's the guy who brings the cooler every game.

This is the kind of stuff that's happening in rinks across North America – just before they're locked up for the night. Murray has played other sports. He has surfed and raced motorcycles. But nothing compares to hockey, even at 10:15 on a cold winter Tuesday night with a bunch of guys whose most athletic days are decades behind them.

"It's way better than I even thought it was going to be," Murray said. "Looking at some of these guys, I've got another 10 years in me." ■

5. CHEER ON THE QUEBEC PEEWEES

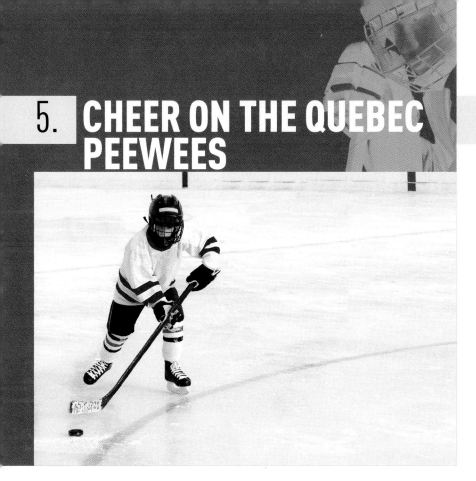

The best minor hockey tournament in the world is about so much more than sport.

Doug Yingst knows that. The longtime GM of the AHL's Hershey Bears participated in the Quebec International Peewee Hockey Tournament three times in the early 1960s, when the event was in its infancy.

A generation later, Yingst watched his two sons, Matt and Dan, and stepson, also Matt, get to feel like big-leaguers as peewee players in Quebec City. Then, in the winter of 2009, Yingst coached the Hershey Jr. Bears to victory in the International B Division as the tournament celebrated its 50th anniversary.

His grandson, Zach, just happened to be one of the players on that victorious team. Talk about sweet symmetry.

"It meant a whole lot because you treat your grandkids a little different than your kids," Yingst said. "I hate to say more leniently, but it is. Just to be able to give him a hug and be part of it was huge."

The Quebec City peewee tournament has had a huge impact on Yingst personally and the entire Hershey community. The Pennsylvania city has had a team in the event every year since 1961, which marked the second time the tournament was held. In addition to his initial participation as a player, Yingst has been a part of every team Hershey has sent for the past 30 years, usually in the role of coach.

With its passionate fans and distinct European feel, Quebec City is a very unique place for 11- and 12-year-olds to spend nearly two weeks.

"The experience in Quebec is educational, it's not just about hockey," Yingst said. "Our kids billet with French-speaking families and I've found in all my time in hockey it's one of the best-run tournaments in the world."

It's also a huge event for the city itself, as tournament GM Patrick Dom explained.

"The Quebec peewee tournament is the third-biggest event in the city after Carnival and the summer festival," said Dom, adding the hockey event usually generates about $15 million in revenue for the city.

Typically, the tournament attracts more than 2,000 kids on approximately 110 teams from upwards of 15 countries, including non-traditional hockey nations such as South Africa, Japan and China. Essentially, it is hockey's equivalent of the Little League World Series baseball tournament, held annually in Williamsport, Pa. With its combination of hockey culture and healthy competition provided by youngsters playing purely for the love of the game, the Quebec peewee tourney is an event worth witnessing first-hand at least once in your lifetime.

Every team traveling from more than 200 miles away has the option to billet with a family in Quebec City. Roughly 500 local families open their homes each year, indicating just how much the entire community embraces the tournament.

One of the biggest drawing cards for teams coming to Quebec is the opportunity to play in front of roughly 10,000 people at Le Colisee, the same arena that housed the Quebec Nordiques until they left town for Colorado in 1995.

"Usually you play in front of mom and dad, maybe 30 or 40 people," Dom said. "Here you play in front of 7,000 or 8,000 people, up to 10,000. For most of the kids, it's the first and last time they'll do that."

Each team is guaranteed at least one game on the big stage and even if they lose that contest, they have a chance to work their way back for another spin on the ice that was once home to NHL Hall of Famers such as Michel Goulet and Peter Stastny.

That's especially important because the kids tend to get a little wide-eyed during their first go as mini-pros.

"The stress can shake them up," Dom said. "So if they have a bad game, you go to the other rink, but if you keep (winning there) you can come back for the final."

Part of what makes the crowd at Le Colisee so special is its impartiality. It's almost like a sporting utopia, where team allegiances don't drive cheers so much as pure appreciation for the game itself.

"Let's say you're watching the Maple Leafs and Rangers at Air Canada Centre," Dom said. "There's 19,000 people cheering for the Leafs. Here, everybody cheers for everybody. That's the great thing."

There have been some pretty incredible players to root for over the years, beginning with Brad Park in the inaugural tournament in 1960. Since then, the likes of Guy Lafleur, Wayne Gretzky, Mario Lemieux and Eric Lindros have all passed through as peewees. In all, the tournament has hosted a total of 955 past and present NHLers.

Dom himself played in the 1979 event, a tournament dominated by future NHL defenseman Sylvain Cote, who had already sprouted into a 6-foot-2, 200-pound man-child.

"He was phenomenal," Dom recalled.

Like Yingst, Dom was fortunate enough to see the tournament experience come full circle in 2009 when his son, Anthony, took part in the event that takes place every mid-February.

Dom is one of four people employed year-round to run the event, so when it actually hits, things get pretty crazy for him. However, when his son stepped on the ice, everything else became a secondary concern.

"It was a huge feeling, I can't even describe it," Dom said. "Everybody knows me here, I'm always running around. For 120 minutes, I said, 'Don't page me, don't call, I'll be watching my son play.' It was very special.

"There were about 9,000 people in stands, and after the game he said, 'Dad, I couldn't concentrate on the game. It was amazing, the noise, the clock, the Jumbotron, the heat (in the building).' "

That kind of reaction is part of what keeps motivating Yingst to bring his Jr. Bears up from Hershey year after year.

"Collectively, for the community in Hershey and for kids aged 11 and 12, it's one of the best experiences a young boy or girl can go through," he said. ■

THE PURSUIT OF HOCKEYNESS •

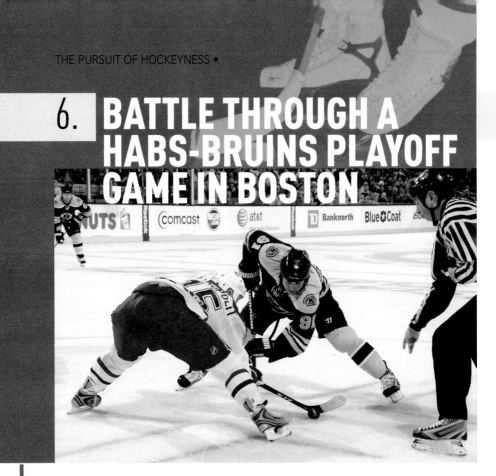

6. BATTLE THROUGH A HABS-BRUINS PLAYOFF GAME IN BOSTON

Mike Milbury has experienced the fierce rivalry between Boston and Montreal from just about every angle, so he's got a pretty good handle on why things can get a little crazy when the Habs visit Beantown.

"It starts with the fans," Milbury said. "Usually you get a whole host of people from Montreal in Boston and vice-versa."

With dissenting *bleu, blanc et rouge* supporters among the masses of black-and-gold backers, there's always the potential for conflict. Sometimes it's good-natured ribbing; other times, people go for the throat.

"It makes for a fun time that sometimes crosses the line," Milbury said. "I've seen it cross the line in the stands and on the ice. But that's why these rivalries are of intrigue. People try to stay composed, but sometimes emotions win the battle."

Milbury, who suited up for the Bruins his entire playing career, patrolled the Boston blueline with a snarl from the mid-1970s through 1987. He also coached the team for two seasons and currently takes in many B's games in his role as a TV analyst.

While New York City tends to be Boston's most natural rival on a series of fronts, including sports, Milbury believes hockey fans in his native Massachusetts get more fired up for games against the Canadiens than any other team.

"When it comes to the sport of hockey, there's no better rival for Boston than Montreal," Milbury said.

Nothing keeps a two-team competition riled like frequent playoff meetings. The Canadiens and Bruins have met four times in the post-season this decade, including Boston's four-game drubbing of the Habs in the spring of 2009. Boston and Montreal, in fact, have faced off in the NHL playoffs more often than anyone else – the B's and Habs, incredibly, have battled it out in 32 post-season series (and a total of 163 playoff games). Montreal holds a decisive all-time edge, with a 24-8 series record and 99-64 mark in playoff games versus Boston.

And while Bruins fans and players still have a healthy hate on for their northern combatants, Milbury thinks things have cooled off a bit through the years.

"It's a different game now, there's less room for craziness, the rules are called different and the rules are different themselves," he said.

Of course, back in the '70s, things were known to spiral out of control. When asked if one memory stands out from all the run-ins, Milbury cites a famous fight between Bruins tough guy Stan Jonathan and Habs heavyweight Pierre Bouchard, which occurred at the Boston Garden during Game 4 of the '78 Stanley Cup final. Despite giving up several pounds and inches to Bouchard, the 5-foot-8 Jonathan pummeled his 6-foot-2 opponent into a bloody mess, whipping the Garden faithful into a frenzy.

"Nobody who was there would forget the Jonathan-Bouchard fight that essentially ended Bouchard's career," said Milbury, whose team was nevertheless eliminated by the Habs that year.

That certainly wasn't the only time the old Garden got rocking thanks to some fisticuffs.

"There were plenty of times when I was on the ice and everybody had squared off and everybody was throwing punches, and that just isn't going to happen now," Milbury said. ▓

7. TOUCH THE STANLEY CUP

It stands nearly three feet tall and weighs almost 35 pounds. It bears the engraved names of more than 2,200 winners and the scars of almost 120 years of hockey history. Though it cost only $50 to purchase, its value can no longer be measured in dollars, but rather in the currency of blood, sweat and tears – the price that hockey players pay for the chance to lift it, the price that has led to its reputation as the most difficult trophy in pro sports to win.

Book after book could be written about the Stanley Cup and what it means to the game of hockey (and they have been). But it takes just two words for Chad King, a 13-year-old minor hockey player from Massachussetts, to describe the experience of seeing and touching the trophy for the first time.

"It's awesome."

It's a distinctly teenaged description, but hockey fans young and old feel the same sense of awe in the presence of the Stanley Cup, which spends most of its time on display at the Hockey Hall of Fame in Toronto.

The Cup is housed in the same museum-like room – the Grand Hall – with other famous NHL hardware, such as the Hart and Conn Smythe Trophies, and these individual awards are certainly inspected by visitors. But, as it is to hockey players, the Stanley Cup is by far the main attraction for hockey fans.

Phil Pritchard, vice-president and curator of the Hall of Fame – and known, thanks to a series of TV commercials, as the "Keeper of the Cup" – has seen first-hand how fans look into the silver surface of the Stanley Cup and see their most cherished hockey memories and dreams reflected back at them.

"People come up and they relive some great moments," Pritchard said. "People my age, they look for Bobby Orr's name. People that are in their early 20s look for Wayne Gretzky."

The names are indeed a huge part of the Stanley Cup's draw. They connect the fans of the present to the stars of the past, forming an unbroken line through hockey history. Tony Parsons of Paris, Ont., was just a toddler when the Toronto Maple Leafs won their last championship back in 1967, but coming to see the Cup with his father Doug and son Curtis allowed three generations of the family to bond around an experience that only Doug remembers.

For Marlowe Dejarme, a 25-year-old Edmonton resident, seeing the Cup brought back memories of getting together with his family – who adopted Canada's passion for hockey soon after emigrating from the Philippines – to watch the Oilers win the final Stanley Cup of the franchise's 1980s dynasty.

"You look at the Cup and you think, 'I remember those playoffs,' " Dejarme said.

Even for King, the connection to history was crucial. The first name the youngster searched for was Orr's, even though the legendary Boston Bruins defenseman retired two decades before King was even born.

The names are a big part of the Stanley Cup story, but the trophy itself has a rich history. It was donated by Lord Stanley of Preston (Frederick Arthur Stanley) in 1892 and was first awarded to the Montreal Amateur Athletic Association the following year; since 1926, it has been awarded exclusively to the NHL champion.

The Stanley Cup's legend grows even as the rings bearing the names of past champions are periodically removed to make room for new ones. Beginning with the 1995 New Jersey Devils, each and every member of the winning team has been allowed to spend 24 hours with the trophy – a unique tradition that has yielded dozens of unique stories. (Prior to 1995, only select members of Cup-winning clubs were given time with the trophy.)

"If the Cup could talk, it would be a best-seller, no problem," said Pritchard, who has traveled from Russian outposts to European cities to countless other corners of the world to chaperone players during their day with the Cup.

If such a book did exist, one of Pritchard's favorite chapters would concern the 2007 Stanley Cup-champion Anaheim Ducks. First, winger Brad May let his daughter eat a bowl of Cheerios out of the trophy. Then, May's teammate Teemu Selanne attempted to host a traditional Finnish sauna party with the Cup as the guest of honor.

"The Stanley Cup is silver, so we couldn't leave it in the sauna for an hour or it would melt," said Pritchard, who negotiated a compromise with Selanne. "We took it in and out a couple of times and got some pictures with Teemu and his friends."

Visitors to the Hall of Fame don't get to lift the Cup, or eat out of it, or take it into the sauna. But they can look at it and touch it and run their fingers over the surface of a trophy that Pritchard believes has no equal in the sports world.

"In the other sports they make a new trophy every year, which kind of changes the tradition and the aura and the significance," Pritchard said. "In hockey, it's the same trophy. The team that wins the Stanley Cup this year wins the same trophy that was won 100 years ago."

The famous names, the endless stories and the long history of the Stanley Cup all contribute to its singular mystique. As does the fact that anyone who has ever played so much as a game of road hockey has imagined hoisting the Cup over their head.

Chad King may have that chance one day, but until then he will accept no substitutes.

"No," said King, when asked if winning his own tournaments makes him feel like a Stanley Cup champion. "The Cup is way more important."

In fact, nothing in the game is more important than the Stanley Cup, and for hockey fans, few trips could be more memorable than a pilgrimage to see it in person. ▪

8. DRIVE THE WHL'S 'FLAT FIVE IN FIVE'

ROSS Mahoney knows his Saskatchewan geography. Knows it too well.

"Regina to Swift Current, 240 kilometers. Regina to Prince Albert, 762 kilometers. Regina to Moose Jaw…"

As director of amateur scouting for the Washington Capitals for the past 12 years, Mahoney has done the rounds in Saskatchewan hundreds of times. Based in Regina, there isn't an arena or patch of prairie highway he hasn't visited.

"I don't know if it's possible anymore to go to five WHL games in five nights in five Saskatchewan cities because they never have games on Thursdays," Mahoney said. "And you don't see too many games on Mondays. But I'm sure at some point over the years I've done it."

Don't call yourself a hardcore hockey fan unless you've done the 'Flat Five in Five,' a circuitous trip through Saskatchewan with stops in the relative metropolises of Regina and Saskatoon, the rural prairie communities of Moose Jaw and Swift Current and the scenic northern outpost of Prince Albert. It's best done in a pickup truck with snow tires. And don't forget the baseball cap and suitcase full of Pats, Blades, Warriors, Broncos and Raiders sweaters if you want to fit right in.

"No matter what town you go to in Saskatchewan," said Calgary Flames play-by-play man Peter Loubardias, "you'll find a hockey arena and curling rink. And in every hockey arena you'll find a game going on with people in the stands."

Loubardias is a Saskatoon native who cut his teeth calling Jr. A games for the Estevan Bruins and Western League games for the Pats. From the time he was a teenager to his early years as a professional in the 1980s and '90s, he was renowned for his addiction to hockey. Every night, there was a game on somewhere in the province – and he'd find it.

"I'm sure there were stretches where I'd go a few weeks having watched a game every night," Loubardias said. "I was a freak. I'd watch hockey 365 nights a year if I could."

A favorite stop of both Mahoney and Loubardias is the "crushed can" arena in Moose Jaw. The saddle-shaped roof creates a cozy atmosphere inside even though spectators in the upper rows are unable to see across to the other side of the seating area. The first row of seats are elevated so fans are virtually right on top of the players.

"It's loud and suffocating for players and media in there…it's great," Loubardias said. "When I was calling games in there, a Moose Jaw fan by the name of Kelly Rempel – he's my best friend now – used to sit in front of the press box. After the Warriors would score, he'd stand up with a group of seven guys and recite a duplicate description of the goal I had just called. It was kind of eerie at first."

The nature of the competitive WHL doesn't lend itself to Saskatchewan residents clamoring to complete the 'Flat Five in Five.' If you're a Broncos fan, why would you bother travelling to Saskatoon to watch the Blades and Raiders play? But occasionally, this hockey hotbed of a province lures fans from afar, eager to see the locales where legends such as Wendel Clark, Joe Sakic, Theoren Fleury, Mike Modano and Clark Gilies got used to the rigors of heavy travel and intense action.

During the NHL lockout in 2004-05, Michigan residents Todd Hansen and Phil Schultz went on a barnstorming trip through Western Canada specifically to watch WHL games.

"This is a chance to see cities that we've always heard about," said Schultz to the Regina *Leader-Post* in 2004.

"You see these names and there's so much hockey lore," Hansen said. "Moose Jaw, Medicine Hat, Red Deer…If we had gone to Manitoba, we would've gone to Flin Flon. We would've had to."

They rented a car and watched WHL games in 10 different communities over a two-week stretch, also stopping in Floral, Sask., the birthplace of Gordie Howe.

While Mahoney makes his trips through Saskatchewan for business purposes, he always remembers the journey is part of the adventure.

"To some people, Saskatchewan has a bad reputation because it's very flat and uneventful," Mahoney said. "But I find a certain beauty and peace in those drives. You should see the wheat fields on a breezy, sunny September afternoon or in the middle of the night when it's lit up by the lights of a farmer in his combine. And there's nothing like a prairie sunset."

The winters, well, that's another story. A prairie storm can be treacherous.

"One time Jack McCarten and I were scouting a game at Notre Dame (Wilcox, Sask.) and there was drifting snow and black ice and white-outs as we started on our way back to Regina," Mahoney said. "Jack didn't want to go because we couldn't see any patch of highway.

"I said 'Jack, don't worry, it's only 25 kilometers and the route is flat and straight. As long as we get the car going we don't have to touch the steering wheel.' Jack said, 'OK.' " ■

9. CURVE YOUR OWN BLADE

With the triple-digit price of high-end composite hockey sticks these days, parents and players are loathe to tamper with them, lest they become even more apt to "blow up" at an inopportune moment. But since the first hockey game was played more than 150 years ago, players have always had their quirks, superstitions and preferences; they like their sticks "just so."

One way to get your stick just so is to go old school ("Throwback everything!" as the TV commercial encourages) and customize your blade. The pros receive sticks that are crafted to their own specifications, but the Joe Backchecks of the hockey world usually have to make do with whatever model they like the best.

Unless, of course, they make their own model.

A time-honored tradition in blade customizing is heating or blowtorching it to a point where the curve can be manipulated. It's something everyone should try – and once you do, you may never go back to an impersonal, store-bought curve.

Curving stick blades began in the late 1950s and early '60s when Bobby Hull and Stan Mikita of the Chicago Black Hawks began shaping their curves (and revolutionizing the game). Using what would today be considered illegal curves – "banana blades" – Hull's shot in particular became the most feared in the game, both for its velocity and its unpredictable action.

"It's hard to put into words," said veteran NHL netminder Ed Giacomin of Hull's shot. "It would rise or dip. You'd pull up when you should really be ducking. It played games with your mind."

Added the legendary Jacques Plante: "You had to see it coming at you to really believe it."

Blowtorching the blade of a $300 composite stick, however, isn't something that should be done – manufacturers are constantly re-educating players on what they can and can't do with cutting-edge sticks. But a good ol' wooden blade can certainly be altered. Here's how to do it:

• Heat the blade slowly, but not too much – it shouldn't burn and you should be able to touch it for a few seconds. (Since not everyone is a welder – or arsonist – the element on your kitchen stove works just as well as a blowtorch.)

• Once the blade is pliable, gently mold it to your liking; open the toe or close it, add or take away from the heel curve, change the angle, or create a banana blade just for the fun of it. Pliers or a vice work best, but there are also curving clamps designed specifically for stick blades; they'll give you the same curve every time.

• When you've got your stick the way you like it, put the blade in a bucket of cold water. Or jam it into a snowbank – just like your dad used to do with his wooden hockey stick, and his dad before him. ▮

10. TAKE A HOCKEY HISTORY CRASH COURSE

After 90 years of NHL hockey, some history has been made.

It was inevitable, really.

And while most fans keep up to date with current events, it's always good to know how we went from Aurel Joliat to Henrik Zetterberg. Let's take a look back at the past, with a timeline of notable NHL events:

Nov. 26, 1917 The NHL is founded. The Montreal Canadiens, Montreal Wanderers, Ottawa Senators and Toronto Arenas are the first teams.

Dec. 19, 1917 Dave Ritchie of the Wanderers scores the NHL's first goal, one minute into the league's first game.

Feb. 18, 1918 Georges Vezina records the first shutout in league history.

March 20, 1918 The Toronto Arenas become first NHL team to compete for, and win, the Stanley Cup. They beat the Vancouver Millionaires three games to two.

March 30, 1919 Montreal beats Seattle 4-3 to tie the Stanley Cup final at 2-2-1, but it's the last contest of the season as the rest of the final is cancelled due to an outbreak of the Spanish flu. Several players fall ill, and Montreal's Joe Hall dies.

March 22, 1923 Foster Hewitt broadcasts his first game on radio, an intermediate play-off contest between a team from Kitchener and Toronto Parkdale's Canoe Club team.

March 30, 1925 The Victoria Cougars become the last non-NHL team to win the Stanley Cup.

Sept. 27, 1930 The NHL introduces the offside rule.

Feb. 14, 1934 The first NHL All-Star Game is held as a benefit for the injured Ace Bailey.

Sept. 24, 1937 The icing rule is introduced.

April 16, 1939 The first best-of-7 series is played. Boston beats Toronto in five games to win the Cup.

Sept. 11, 1943 The NHL approves the Hockey Hall of Fame concept.

March 28, 1945 Maurice 'Rocket' Richard becomes first player to score 50 goals.

Nov. 3, 1948 Gordie Howe makes his first of a record 23 All-Star Game appearances.

April 16, 1949 Toronto becomes the first team to win the Stanley Cup three years in a row.

Oct. 8, 1950 The NHL All-Star Game is televised for the first time.

Nov. 1, 1952 Foster Hewitt broadcasts his first NHL game on TV, from Maple Leaf Gardens in Toronto.

March 10, 1955 The Zamboni makes its NHL debut.

March 17, 1955 The Richard Riots break out in Montreal, as fans react to NHL president Clarence Campbell suspending Maurice Richard for the rest of the season and playoffs.

Jan. 18, 1958 Willie O'Ree becomes the first black player to skate in the NHL.

Nov. 2, 1959 Jacques Plante puts on a mask for the first time, and doesn't take it off.

April 14, 1960 The Montreal Canadiens become the first and only team to win the Stanley Cup five years in a row.

Aug. 26, 1961 The Hockey Hall of Fame opens.

June 5, 1963 The NHL's first amateur draft is held in Montreal. The Canadiens select Gary Monahan first overall.

March 12, 1966 Bobby Hull becomes first player to score more than 50 goals in a single season, collecting 54.

Sept. 3, 1966 Rookie Bobby Orr signs a two-year, $70,000 contract with the Bruins, making him the highest-paid player in the NHL.

May 2, 1967 The Toronto Maple Leafs beat the Montreal Canadians to win the last Stanley Cup of the Original Six era (and, of course, it's the last time the Leafs have won the Cup).

June 5, 1967 The NHL expands to 12 teams, introducing the Pittsburgh Penguins, Minnesota North Stars, Oakland Seals, Philadelphia Flyers, Los Angeles Kings and St. Louis Blues.

March 2, 1969 Phil Esposito becomes first player to score 100 points in a single season. Howe and Hull also hit the 100-point plateau in '68-69.

April 5, 1970 With 120 points in 76 games, Orr becomes the first defenseman to win the Art Ross Trophy.

May 10, 1970 Orr scores and soars to deliver Boston its first Stanley Cup since 1941.

May 22, 1970 The Vancouver Canucks and Buffalo Sabres are awarded NHL franchises.

Nov. 9, 1971 The Atlanta Flames and New York Islanders are awarded NHL franchises.

March 11, 1971 Phil Esposito scores his 59th goal and 127th point to break the NHL marks in both categories. The Bruins center racks up an astounding 76 goals and 152 points by the end of the season.

May 19, 1974 Bobby Clarke's Philadelphia Flyers become the first expansion team to win the Stanley Cup; it's the first of back-to-back titles.

June 11, 1974 The Kansas City Scouts and Washington Capitals receive NHL franchises. (The Scouts would relocate to Colorado as the Rockies before finally settling in New Jersey.)

Feb. 7, 1976 In an 11-4 win over Boston, Toronto center Darryl Sittler sets the NHL record for most points in a single game, with 10 (six goals, four assists).

April 1, 1978 Mike Bossy becomes first rookie to net 50 goals in a single season. Bossy would go on to record nine straight 50-goal campaigns, the only NHLer to accomplish the feat.

June 22, 1979 Four former World Hockey Association teams – the Edmonton Oilers, Hartford Whalers, Quebec Nordiques and Winnipeg Jets – join the NHL.

Oct. 10, 1979 Edmonton's Wayne Gretzky collects an assist in his first NHL game, a 4-2 loss to Chicago.

March 11, 1980 The Islanders obtain Butch Goring in a late-season deal, and the NHL trade deadline is born.

Feb. 24, 1982 Gretzky scores three times in the final 6:36 against Buffalo to reach 77 goals, breaking Esposito's single-season record. Gretzky amasses 92 goals by the end of the season, a league record, and 212 points, becoming the first and only NHLer to surpass 200 points.

May 17, 1983 The Islanders sweep the Oilers for New York's fourth consecutive Stanley Cup.

Jan. 28, 1984 Gretzky registers a point in his 51st consecutive game to set the NHL record for longest scoring streak.

May 19, 1984 The Oilers beat the Islanders four games to one for Edmonton's first of five Cups over seven seasons.

June 9, 1984 Pittsburgh selects Mario Lemieux No. 1 overall at the NHL entry draft. A few months later, he scores on his first shot on his first shift – and doesn't look back.

May 24, 1986 A 20-year-old rookie goalie named Patrick Roy delivers his first Stanley Cup to Montreal.

Aug. 9, 1988 The Trade: Edmonton sends Gretzky to Los Angeles for players, prospects, draft picks and $15 million. The loss is felt across Canada, and NDP house leader Nelson Riis goes as far as demanding the Canadian government block the trade.

Dec. 31, 1988 Lemieux scores five goals against New Jersey: at even strength, on the power play, shorthanded, on a penalty shot and into the empty net. He finishes the season with 85 goals and 199 points.

May 4, 1989 Alexander Mogilny defects from Russia and signs with the Buffalo Sabres.

Oct. 15, 1989 Gretzky passes Howe (1,850) for most points in NHL history. Ten years later, Gretzky would retire with 2,857 points, nearly 1,000 more than the league's No. 2 scorer (Mark Messier, 1,887).

May 9, 1990 The San Jose Sharks franchise is founded; the team begins play in 1991-92.

Dec. 16, 1991 The Ottawa Senators are awarded an NHL franchise, and, four days later, the Tampa Bay Lightning gets one, too. Both teams begin play in 1992-93.

June 22, 1991 Eric Lindros is drafted first overall and then traded – twice – by the Quebec Nordiques. On June 30, the NHL rules in favor of Quebec's deal with Philadelphia, and Lindros is sent to the Flyers in exchange for six players (including Peter Forsberg), two first round draft picks and $15 million.

Jan. 2, 1992 Toronto and Calgary consummate an NHL-record 10-player trade, featuring Doug Gilmour going to the Leafs and Gary Leeman to the Flames.

Dec. 11, 1992 Gary Bettman is named NHL commissioner.

June 7, 1993 More post-season magic from Roy, as he leads Montreal to a third straight overtime win over Los Angeles in the Stanley Cup final. Overall, it is Roy's 10th consecutive OT victory in the '93 playoffs. Two days later, the Habs claim the Cup.

June 14, 1993 The Anaheim Mighty Ducks and Florida Panthers are awarded NHL franchises; they begin play in 1993-94.

March 23, 1994 Gretzky scores his 802nd career goal, surpassing Howe's record of 801. Gretzky ends his career with 894 goals.

June 14, 1994 Messier scores the Stanley Cup winner as the Rangers beat Vancouver 3-2 in Game 7 of the final. It is the Blueshirts' first Cup in 54 years.

Jan. 11, 1995 The NHL resumes play after a lockout cancelled the first 468 games of the season; teams play a modified 48-game schedule.

May 3, 1995 Jaromir Jagr becomes first European player to lead the NHL in scoring, with 70 points in the lockout-shortened season.

April 29, 1997 Craig MacTavish retires as the last player to play without a helmet.

June 19, 1997 Buffalo's Dominik Hasek becomes the first goalie in 35 years to win the Hart Trophy as NHL MVP (Jacques Plante, 1962).

June 25, 1997 The Nashville Predators, Atlanta Thrashers, Columbus Blue Jackets and Minnesota Wild are awarded NHL franchises; the Preds begin play in 1998-99 and the Thrashers in '99-00, while the Jackets and Wild start in '00-01.

June 19, 1999 Brett Hull's foot-in-the-crease, triple-overtime winner gives Dallas its first Stanley Cup, beating Buffalo in six games.

June 26, 2004 Alex Ovechkin is drafted first overall by the Washington Capitals.

Feb. 16, 2005 Bettman announces the cancellation of the NHL regular season and playoffs, due to the lockout, and the Stanley Cup isn't awarded for the first time since 1919.

July 22, 2005 The NHL announces shootouts will be implemented to decide regular season games that remain tied after the five-minute overtime period.

July 30, 2005 Sidney Crosby is drafted first overall by the Pittsburgh Penguins.

June 6, 2007 Anaheim beats Ottawa to become the NHL's first West Coast team to win the Stanley Cup.

May 30, 2009 The Pittsburgh Penguins and Detroit Red Wings meet in the Stanley Cup final for a second year in a row, the first repeat finalists in 25 years (since the Islanders-Oilers in 1983 and '84). ■

11. SPEND A HOCKEY NIGHT IN CANADA

Saturday, October 11, 1952: A radio staple since 1933, *Hockey Night in Canada* makes its television debut with the broadcast of the third period of a Detroit Red Wings-Montreal Canadiens game from the Forum.

The action is delivered to the approximately 100,000 Canadian households that own a TV by just a handful of cameras: one following the play, one focused on either goal, and another offering a wide-angle view of the action.

The picture is snowier than the Rockies in December, and play-by-play announcer Foster Hewitt sounds like he's describing the on-ice action through a tin-can telephone. But the game – won 2-1 by the Habs on a third period goal by Billy Reay – ushers in a cherished Canadian tradition: Saturday night hockey. If you live in Canada – heck, if you've spent a weekend in Canada – you've plunked down and watched CBC's weekly winter offering.

More than 55 years and thousands of telecasts later, *HNIC* has transcended its origins as a mere TV program to become a beloved Canadian institution, celebrated in word and song, watched by movie stars and maintenance men, CEOs and subway drivers, plumbers and prime ministers.

It has delivered legendary personalities such as Hewitt, the original voice of hockey, and Danny Gallivan, who enthralled viewers with his descriptions of "cannonading" slapshots and "scintillating" saves, also giving the hockey world the "spinarama" phrase in the process. More recently, *HNIC* has been the domain of Dave Hodge, Bob Cole and Ron-and-Don – with MacLean and Cherry as famous a Canadian twosome as Wayne and Shuster or Bob and Doug. Not to mention, *HNIC*'s (former) theme song was so revered it became known as Canada's second national anthem.

HNIC has chronicled the NHL's transformation from a six-team loop to a 30-team league, and documented the entire careers of hockey immortals such as Bobby Orr, Guy Lafleur, Mario Lemieux and Wayne Gretzky. It has broadcast some of Canada's biggest hockey triumphs (the 1972 Summit Series, the 2002 Salt Lake City Olympics) and its most bitter disappointments (the 1996 World Cup, the 1998 Nagano Olympics).

It has also brought to Canadians countless legendary moments in hockey history: Orr's flying-through-the-air goal to clinch the 1970 Stanley Cup for Boston; the celebrated 1975 New Year's Eve showdown between the Canadiens and the Soviet Red Army; Darryl Sittler's 10-point night against the Bruins in 1976; Canucks coach Roger Neilson waving the white towel in the 1982 playoffs; and, the Leafs' inspiring 1993 playoff run led by Doug Gilmour, his beat-up face increasingly looking like it was stitched together from spare parts.

It is those baby-blue blazers, emblazoned with *HNIC*'s classic "puck and stick" logo; it is squeaky-voiced Howie Meeker and his telestrator, diagramming plays between periods like a five-star general planning a ground assault; it is Cherry, ranting on *Coach's Corner* about Europeans or pantywaists who refuse to drop the gloves; it is Cole's excitable "Oh, baby!"

It is Canada.

Rick Gruneau, a professor at B.C.'s Simon Fraser University and co-author of the 1994 book *Hockey Night in Canada: Sports, Identities, and Cultural Politics*, said *HNIC* – in both its radio and TV incarnations – played a vital role in forging Canada's national popular culture.

"When *Hockey Night in Canada* started on the CBC, the game became one of the foundational elements in the 'making' of an imagined national Canadian community," Gruneau said.

And renowned hockey historian Bill Fitsell, founder of the Society for International Hockey Research and author of several hockey books (including *Hockey's Captains, Colonels and Kings* and *Hockey's Hub: Three Centuries of Hockey in Kingston*), describes *HNIC* as nothing less than "a national institution."

Fitsell, who is still watching Saturday night hockey at age 85, remembers listening to *HNIC* radio broadcasts as a youngster. His family owned a dining room table with curved corners, perfect for creating a miniature Maple Leaf Gardens. Fitsell would line up his Beehive hockey cards according to the line combinations announced by Hewitt. So it was a huge thrill when TV broadcasts commenced in 1952, even if they didn't quite meet the high-definition, multi-camera standards to which modern fans have grown accustomed.

"The signals were snowy," Fitsell said. "If you could even see the blueline it was quite a thrill."

Fitsell's five daughters would also grow up watching *HNIC*, an experience replicated across the country. The program attracts some four million viewers for its Saturday telecast, although those numbers don't accurately reflect the countless numbers gathered to watch the game in bars, community centers or friends' houses across the country – from Beaver Creek in the Yukon to Cape Spear, Nfld., and from Pelee Island, Ont., to Inuvik in the Northwest Territories.

And the ratings numbers don't tell the whole story of *HNIC's* immense popularity. Meeker, a popular analyst in the 1970s and '80s, remembers one incident that underscores the program's far-flung reach.

Meeker smoked one cigar a day back then and gladly accepted what director Ron Harrison promised him was a fine stogie just as they were preparing for the show's opening.

"I lit it and on about the third drag the thing exploded," said Meeker, a spry 85-year-old who's more than 10 years removed from his Hall of Fame broadcasting career. "I said, 'You son of a bitch!' and *HNIC* then replayed the incident for viewers between periods, with commentator Brian McFarlane gleefully providing play-by-play.

"That night at a restaurant the waiter comes by and goes, 'Mr. Meeker, I've got a cigar for you,' " continued Meeker with a laugh. "I get on the airplane, the stewardess comes out and says, 'The captain and the second officer want you to come up to the flight deck to talk hockey.' Well, geez, I go up there and they say, 'Howie, I've got a cigar for you.'

"It went on for weeks. Everywhere I went, people offered me a cigar."

Meeker, who lives in Parksville, B.C., rose to prominence through his use of the telestrator ("It saved my ass," he jokes), breaking down key plays between periods. That led to one of his catchphrases: "Stop it there! Back it up!"

"When I used to say that, the director would go (crazy)," he chuckled. "Because in those days when you stopped it and backed it up, the picture broke up a lot."

Meeker was front and center for many notable on-air occurrences at *HNIC*. He was there that fateful night in 1987 when Hodge, the host, flung his pencil in disgust after CBC brass decided to cut away from a Canadiens-Flyers game that had gone to overtime for news.

"I don't blame him either," Meeker said. "He was as justified as could be."

With the advent of regional telecasts, sports specialty channels such as TSN and Sportsnet and cable packages such as Centre Ice, hockey broadcasts are ubiquitous today. But for oldtimers like Fitsell, none come close to matching the magic and mystique of those early *HNIC* Saturday night broadcasts.

"It was a treat to watch that Saturday game," he said. "You built up your hopes and dreams for that one big game." ■

12. SPEND A HOCKEY NIGHT IN RUSSIA

During the days of communist government, crowds at Russian hockey games were under strict control. Guards stationed throughout arenas made sure fans didn't become too rowdy. Canadian fans at the 1972 Summit Series in Moscow found that out quickly.

But everything changed in the early 1990s after the fall of the Berlin Wall. Russian pro teams loosened up in an effort to improve their bottom line; some started selling beer to attract fans and others actually hired strippers for intermission performances.

It's far from the norm, but a game between Ak Bars Kazan and Moscow Dynamo in 2008-09 was suspended when Dynamo fans set off flares after their team scored late in the first period. Billowing clouds of smoke filled the arena and people had to put scarves over their faces to protect themselves. Alex Ovechkin, who was in Russia to visit his ailing grandfather, was on hand to watch it all.

The Kontinental League ordered the game replayed and, at one point, considered having it take place behind locked doors with no fans. However, officials relented and spectators were allowed in.

The image of Russian hockey has been undergoing a change and there have been episodes of on-ice violence. In a game between Ak Bars Kazan and Traktor Chelyabinsk in January of 2008, a bench-clearing brawl broke out after the referee disallowed a Traktor goal in the final minute. Nearly 400 minutes in penalties were assessed in the contest and nine players received suspensions.

Thankfully, these are isolated incidents. For the most part, the KHL environment is safe and the hockey fast and highly entertaining.

Canadian goalie Ray Emery, who played in the city of Mytischi in 2008-09, said one of the big adjustments he had to make was getting used to squads of cheerleaders dancing on platforms to the sound of rock music right behind his net in some buildings.

"You kind of look up and they're right there at ice level," Emery said.

Former NHL defenseman Kevin Dallman, who played in the city of Astana, Kazakhstan, said he was pumped up for every match.

"I love our fans, they're amazing," he said. "They're 10 times louder than fans back home."

If you're attending a KHL game in Moscow, don't worry about lining up for tickets. There is so much competition for the entertainment dollar in the Russian capital of eight million that the hockey arena is rarely filled. In the KHL's inaugural season, Moscow Dynamo averaged 5,130 fans in a 7,000-seat arena; Central Red Army welcomed 4,691 in a 6,000-seat building; and, Spartak sat 4,325 in a 5,500-seat facility. Ducats are reasonably priced, at anywhere from $10 to $25.

On the other hand, in smaller cities such as Omsk and Yaroslavl, tickets are at a premium. Avangard Omsk led the KHL in attendance in '08-09 with an average of 7,881 in an 8,000-seat building.

It's not that long ago that some games, in what was then the Russian League, were played without any spectators. On more than one occasion, league games in large arenas were pre-empted by musical concerts and had to be played in rinks with no seats.

In Moscow in the mid-'70s, there were only four covered ice rinks in the city – one of which was just a sheet of ice with no seating. Today, there are dozens of them. Anybody planning a trip to Moscow is guaranteed so see a game at any time of the season. Besides the three KHL clubs based in the city itself, there are four more within an hour's drive of Red Square.

One drawback for players is the enormous distance between some venues. Dynamo Riga, the westernmost team, is more than 4,000 miles from the easternmost, Amur, which is in the city of Khabarovsk on the Japanese border.

In the old days, the famous Russian hockey song "Trus ne igrayet hokkei" (which translates to "Cowards don't play hockey") was played in every arena when the teams skated on to the ice, and some teams still continue the tradition. The uplifting tune was written by the famous Russian composer Alexandra Pakhmutova.

As Russia becomes more and more westernized, psychedelic light shows precede each game and fans often display huge 100-foot-long banners. Supporters of the Red Army club unfurled one this year with the words, "We are CSKA, we will win."

The PA announcers at KHL games inform the audience of a lot more than goals, assists and penalties. One of the regular calls in Russian is "Komanda Dynamo Moskva igryaet v pulnom sostavyeh," which translates to, "The Moscow Dynamo team is now playing at full strength," alerting fans to the end of a power play.

Russian hockey. It's the same, but different – and worth the excursion for the cultural experience. ■

13. VOICE YOUR WELL-INFORMED OPINION

Hockey fans have strong opinions. Why? Because they know the game; they're the ones watching NHL action every night and joining hockey pools and checking the Internet hourly for newsflashes and injury updates. And most fans have played hockey, too, at some level or another, and this gives them all the expertise they need.

Right?

Right.

Except, there's a problem: One fan's hockey expert is another fan's hockey fool. That is, you may believe, nay, you may *know* that Wayne Gretzky is the best player of all-time. But when you tell that well-established fact to another fan, they might laugh in your face and reply, "No, stupid, it's Gordie Howe."

Or Maurice Richard. Or Bobby Orr. Or Mario Lemieux or Patrick Roy or Guy Lafleur or…

You get the idea.

Anyhow, the important thing is to have an answer at the ready and be able to back it up. You're a hockey fan, after all, and you need a thoughtful, well-reasoned response to big-picture questions such as the game's all-time best scorer (Mike Bossy) or most vicious fighter (Donald Brashear).

Just to get you started, here's a quick thought on some of the most compelling questions facing hockey fans today:

Best player? Gretzky, for his prolific production and obliteration of the NHL record book. (Dissenting opinion: Any of the guys mentioned above, plus Jean Beliveau or Bobby Hull or Dominik Hasek or Terry Sawchuk or Doug Harvey or…)

Best goalie? Roy, for his aura of playoff invincibility. (Dissenting opinion: Hasek or Sawchuk or Martin Brodeur or Glenn Hall or Jacques Plante or Ken Dryden or…)

Best defenseman? Orr usually gets the most mentions, knees or not. (Dissenting opinion: Harvey or Ray Bourque or Larry Robinson or Nicklas Lidstrom or Denis Potvin or Eddie Shore or Paul Coffey or…)

Best coach? Scotty Bowman in Montreal, or Scotty Bowman in Pittsburgh, or Scotty Bowman in Detroit. (Dissenting opinion: Al Arbour or Toe Blake or Fred Shero or Dick Irvin or Pat Burns or Glen Sather…)

But what about best goal or best save or best hit or best fight? There are so, so many to sift through, and how to pick one Hasekian stop over another? Was Alex Ovechkin's turning-and-twisting-and-falling goal against Phoenix in 2006 the best ever? If you say yes, try convincing a Mario Lemieux fan, who has a top-10 list of goals by No. 66 that were (according to them) easily superior to Ovie's effort. Best fight? Bob Probert's people will tell you one thing, while Dave Schultz's are saying another. And Tie Domi's backers? You don't even want to get them started.

That's the challenge for some of hockey's most common questions. There's no real answer; at least, not an answer that will satisfy everybody. But that's OK; the important thing is, have an answer, any answer, as long as it's *your* answer.

As George once said to Jerry on *Seinfeld*, "Remember, it's not a lie if *you* believe it."

Cases in point: A Columbus Blue Jackets fan will look you in the eyes and earnestly inform you that Rick Nash deserves credit for scoring the most beautiful goal in NHL history. In Tampa Bay, they might try convincing you Vincent Lecavalier is the best player ever, period. Anaheim fans know Chris Pronger and Scott Niedermayer are the mightiest defense tandem in NHL history (and they might have a point on this one).

Suffice to say, the best goal from the perspective of the Dallas Stars was Brett Hull's triple-overtime Stanley Cup winner in Game 6 of the 1999 final. But they probably place a different significance on that goal in Buffalo. ■

14. SEND YOURSELF DOWN TO THE AHL

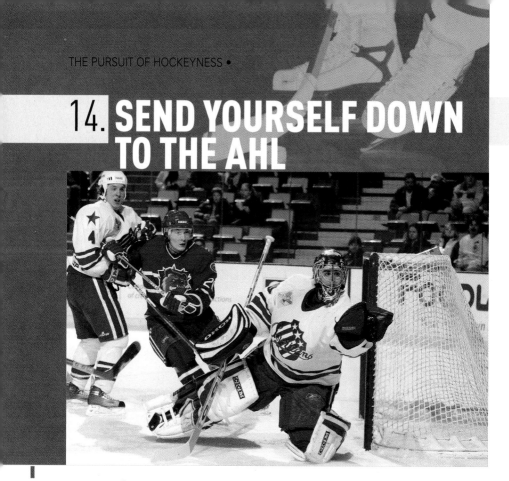

Instead of the chicken wire that once served to protect the fans, Plexiglas is now anchored atop the boards. The visiting team's basement dressing room – where the hot water usually worked and the thermostat rarely did – has been moved to the arena level. The stage at the Court Street end of the rink – a stage where visiting players on rare occasions fought with fans – no longer even exists.

But the memories of more than five decades of Rochester Americans hockey will last an eternity in the War Memorial, a building that has forever been the home of the storied American Hockey League franchise. A renovation in 1998 wiped away any resemblance to how the interior of the arena looked when Al Arbour, Don Cherry, Jim Pappin, Dick Gamble and Gerry Cheevers wore the Amerks uniform.

Unless you look skyward. And then nothing has changed.

The Calder Cup banners from 1964-65, '65-66, '67-68, '82-83, '86-87 and '95-96 still hang from the monstrous steel girders. And it's likely there are still a few champagne corks lodged somewhere overhead, too.

Despite lean years for the team since the NHL lockout ended in the summer of 2005, the Amerks remain one of the cornerstone franchises in the AHL (only the Hershey Bears have been around longer). And that's why the Americans are the perfect representative for AHL hockey, the minor-pro loop that's just one rung down from the NHL.

If fans close their eyes and let their minds drift, they can probably hear Flora Allen, the legendary anthem singer from the 1980s and '90s.

"The best I've ever heard," the late John D'Amico would say every time he came to town in his job as supervisor of officials. And having worked more than 1,900 NHL games as a linesman, D'Amico heard a lot of versions of the "Star Spangled Banner."

Season-ticket holders today say there's still an echo of the bellowing voice of diehard fan George Tyree screaming, "Hockey! Hockey! Hockey!" just before the opening faceoff.

Or maybe they'll just remember the players and coaches who brought championships to the city. Joe Crozier coached the Amerks to their first three Calder Cups in a four-year span. The Rochester squad that won the title in 1964-65 – when Cheevers played all 64 games in goal – was considered by some to be the fifth- or sixth-best team in hockey that season.

"The fifth and sixth teams in the NHL (the Rangers and Bruins) had flaws and possibly we could have at least been competitive against them," said Larry Hillman, an Americans defenseman who went on to win Stanley Cups with Detroit, Montreal and Toronto.

Cherry was a hard-nosed defenseman on Rochester's mid-'60s Calder Cup teams and remains very fond of the city. But not necessarily because of what happened to him as a player.

First, friends in the community helped Cherry find work when his playing career ended. He knew hockey and that was about it, but his construction foreman stuck with him.

Then, in 1972-73, the local ownership hired Cherry to coach a band of castoffs and discards, players no other AHL team wanted. The Amerks somehow made the playoffs and a year later Cherry was named the AHL's best coach. The Boston Bruins made Cherry their bench boss the following season and he won the Jack Adams Trophy as the NHL's coach of the year in 1975-76.

"I'll never forget Rochester," Cherry often says.

Mike Keenan also remembers. His coaching methods created chaos in his first season as a pro coach, 1980-81. But two years later, with Keenan still behind the bench, a 15-year Calder Cup drought ended in Rochester. Yvon Lambert, who was part of the Montreal Canadiens' Stanley Cup dynasty of the late 1970s, was the Amerks captain.

Early in the 1986-87 season, a Buffalo Sabres farmhand named Warren Harper was sent from Rochester to Flint (IHL). Harper was bitter about the demotion and felt disrespected. He left for Michigan with his skates and gear packed not in an equipment bag, but rather stuffed in a garbage bag.

By the springtime, though, Harper was back in the Amerks lineup and ultimately helped them win the Calder Cup.

"It was a garbage bags to riches story," Harper joked after the Game 7 triumph over the Sherbrooke Canadiens.

Alongside those title banners are banners representing the team's two retired numbers: the No. 6 of Norm 'Red' Armstrong, a rugged, heart-and-soul winger from the 1960s, and the No. 9 worn by Gamble and Jody Gage.

Gage holds every major franchise scoring record, surpassing the marks Gamble set. Management decided both should be honored in a dual ceremony in 1996.

In 1995-96, John Tortorella proved his abilities as a coach. Rochester was in last place in January, but by playoff time the Amerks were unstoppable, steamrolling their way to the Calder Cup.

In recent years, the core of today's Buffalo Sabres – goalie Ryan Miller and forwards Derek Roy, Thomas Vanek, Jason Pominville, Drew Stafford and Paul Gaustad – served their apprenticeship in Rochester.

Yeah, you could say Amerks fans have been spoiled. ■

15. COACH A KIDS' TEAM

It's Saturday morning and once again your car is parked in front of the rink. As you swing open the door of the arena, that cold, brisk sensation runs through your body. A whistle around your neck, a large double-double coffee in your left hand and a clipboard in your right. All the tools are in place for a minor hockey coach's morning routine.

As you edge closer and closer to the dressing room, you start to feel more and more energized. It's not the caffeine taking hold; it's something with a much bigger kick than a cup of coffee.

You can hear the music blasting as you approach the entrance of the room, although the music itself seems to be overpowered by the 16 high-pitched voices you've come to know so well over the past few months.

Any trace of the early morning blues has vanished and you're suddenly riding a rush. As you push the door open, you can't help but sing and laugh along with the kids and joke about their choice in music. It's loud, it's fun, everyone's talking and nobody's listening.

And for that one moment, you're a kid again.

"Coaching gives me an excitement and a zest for life from the energy of the players," said Rick Zeller, a minor hockey coach in Toronto for 14 years. "My happiest moments

THE PURSUIT OF HOCKEYNESS •

as a coach are seeing the smiles of the kids and the talk in the dressing room before and after the game. It's invigorating."

A few minutes before a game, the mood in the dressing room begins to tense. The players throw on their jerseys and the music gets turned off. All eyes turn to you as you try to do your best imitation of Kurt Russell in *Miracle*.

"After a loss in Game 3 of the league final, I felt the players were feeling down, negative and feeling too much pressure," said David Bloom, a minor hockey coach for six years.

"Before Game 4, I created a poster outlining three areas of focus that, if we executed well, would win us the game. I spoke with a lot of energy before the game and added some motivation to the poster, like photos of the team when they piled on each other after winning a tournament and a picture of the team with the trophy so they could visualize how it felt to win together.

"I think the pride in their previous accomplishments generated the extra energy and effort they needed to win."

Before you know it, the pre-game jitters in the dressing room are a thing of the past. Now it's the third period, the game is tied and the eyes of your players are darting in your direction, looking for leadership and encouragement once again. Your right foot grazes over the top of the bench, your left finger curled over your lips, trying to come up with the words to inspire them one last time.

But instead of inspiring them, they inspire you.

"One year I had a player named Jaime Besant, he was not a skilled guy at all," said Steve Simmons, another Toronto-area minor hockey coach and a columnist for the Toronto *Sun*. "He was a hard worker and played a little bit of defense and a little bit of forward. We got into a playoff series against York Mills (of the North York Hockey League) and they had a player by the name of Colin Noble. At the beginning of the series I told Jaime, 'You go where Noble goes.'

"In the final game of the series, we won 1-0. Besant intercepted a pass to Noble in the neutral zone, came in on a breakaway and scored his only goal of the season and we won 1-0 on a goal like that. That's inspirational."

The happiest moments for minor hockey coaches go far beyond winning and losing. Simply, they are the smiles, the post-game chatter and the experience of watching kids grow. When a young player who could barely skate in September is whipping by everybody in February, somewhere there's a coach taking satisfaction in a job well done. That's why they're there for all of those early morning practices, weekend road trips and weeknight house league games. That's why they deal with all the things behind the scenes. That's why they coach.

"Hockey is life and you only have to experience coaching minor hockey once to appreciate the significance of that statement," Zeller said. ■

16. LEAVE A LEGACY: THE GRETZKY FAMILY HOUSE

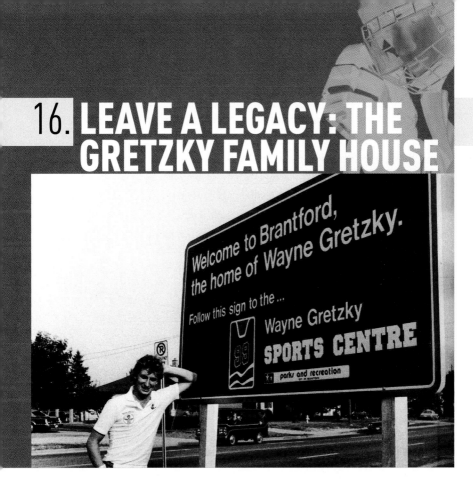

Walter Gretzky, an employee for Bell Canada in the 1980s, was following a work assignment that took him to the registry office across the street from the city hall in Brantford, Ont.

"Hey, Mr. Gretzky," called an employee to the father of Canada's greatest superstar. "I see Wayne is building you a home, eh?"

"How did you know about that?" asked Walter, who didn't let on to the woman that she had let the cat out of the bag as the elder Gretzky wasn't aware his son was planning a surprise.

When Walter arrived home from work, he informed his wife, Phyllis, of Wayne's plan and immediately phoned the NHL star.

"I understand you're building us a home and one night you're going to phone us and say, 'Your new home is ready,' " said Walter to Wayne. "But you've got to understand something, our home is our home. It may not be the biggest and fanciest home, but it's our home and we're not moving from here."

Walter and Phyllis Gretzky were married on April 23, 1960, and immediately moved into a second-story apartment in the southern section of Brantford known as Eagle Place.

Wayne, the first child, was born on Jan. 26, 1961, and they were still residing in the apartment when daughter Kim came along on May 12, 1963. After Kim's arrival, the Gretzkys discovered the apartment simply wasn't large enough for a family with two children and they went house hunting.

They settled on a three-bedroom, ranch-style home on Varadi Avenue on the northern outskirts of the city. It cost $8,500.

"This was out of town," Walter said. "That's why we got the house so cheap. There were houses on the street. It was starting to develop.

"We wanted a place that had a nice big backyard, but not because I thought of a rink at the time but because we wanted a place where the kids could play."

The Gretzkys' other children were born after the family moved to Varadi Avenue – Keith in February of 1967, Glen in August of 1969 and Brent in February of 1971.

Walter had Wayne on skates by the time he was four years old and would take him out after supper to neighborhood parks.

"I'd take him to these outdoor rinks and he'd stay for hours at a time," Walter said. "Kids never feel the cold until they come home and thaw out. Meanwhile, I'd sit in the car and gas was 18 cents a gallon and that was a lot of money. I couldn't run the car all the time so my fingers would be frozen and my toes were frozen.

"One night I came home and told Phyllis that I was going to make a rink in the backyard. Self-preservation was the only reason. I told her Wayne could go out when he wanted and stay out as long as he wanted."

Walter knew how to make a backyard rink, but it took him about two weeks to get it exactly the way he wanted it. He didn't just go out and flood a section of the backyard with a hose. He used a sprinkler to make sure the ice surface had a good base.

Unfortunately, Walter fell asleep one night with the sprinkler operating and it broke. The next morning, he sent Phyllis to the hardware store to a buy a new sprinkler. When Phyllis got to the hardware store and asked for a sprinkler, Walter remembers "the guy thought she was nuts." It was, after all, the dead middle of winter.

"Don't you ever do that to me again," Phyllis told Walter.

It was a tradition in the Gretzky household that Phyllis would go to bed early in the evening while Walter would stay up to watch the 11 o'clock news on television. One night, Walter dozed off before the news came on and remained asleep until Phyllis woke up and went downstairs.

"What is he (Wayne) still doing outside at a quarter to 12 at night," Phyllis demanded as she startled Walter out of his dreamland. "The neighbors are going to think we're crazy."

All of the Gretzky children fell in love with the backyard rink, which had homemade nets at each end. Wayne would string plastic containers inside the nets and use them as targets.

"He didn't have the hardest shot, but he was deadly accurate," Walter said. "There were times when he used to bribe kids to be his goalie in the backyard. He'd give them a nickel or something."

As Wayne became famous, so did the house in which he grew up.

When Walter and Phyllis refused to move into new accommodations, Wayne called his mother a couple of days after his chat with his father about the possibility of making renovations to the Varadi Avenue home.

"Between the two of them, my backyard rink became a swimming pool," Walter said. "The downstairs, where they played their hockey on rainy days, became a recreation room and our ranch-style home became a two-story home and a sunroom was added to the house.

"Life changed instantly, but the end result is that I'm still in my own house."

Brantfordians look at the home as "that's where the Gretzkys live." It's really no big deal and that's how the Gretzkys want it.

However, that's not the way the home is looked at by the rest of the world.

A letter arrived once that was simply addressed to "Wayne Gretzky, Canada." It was sent from "another continent," but made it safely to Varadi Avenue.

Another time, Walter noticed a car driving slowly past the front of the house. A few minutes later, the car returned and a couple of young girls jumped out and started grabbing handfuls of grass from the front lawn.

Years later, Walter was in Halifax when he was approached by someone who told him that "friends of ours" had driven past his home in Brantford, stopped and taken grass from the front lawn. The two girls had grown up, married and had children. Walter got their names and addresses and sent them each an envelope containing grass from his lawn.

On another visit to the East Coast, a young lady walked up to Walter and asked him if he knew who she was. When he hesitated, she informed him she was one of the girls who had taken the grass from his front lawn.

"I still have it at home and it's in a separate container," she told Walter.

It's not uncommon for tour buses to make a detour when they get to Brantford. Their destination could be Niagara Falls, but a knowledgeable driver will turn off Highway 24, which is also King George Road, and drive down Varadi Avenue.

"There's the house Wayne Gretzky grew up in," the driver will tell his astonished passengers.

Years ago, the basement was filled with Wayne's memorabilia along with trophies and medals won by Kim, a track star in her youth. Sometimes, strangers would come to the door and ask if they could look around the basement. Walter often took youth teams on a guided tour while they were in town for a tournament.

Finally, when Walter was in Japan to watch Team Canada play in the 1998 Winter Olympics, the police called the Gretzky home and warned "someone is casing your house."

Phyllis insisted the basement be cleaned out and Walter agreed. The Hockey Hall of Fame and Wayne Gretzky's Restaurant, both in Toronto, were the beneficiaries.

Although thousands of people, the majority of them youngsters, have been through the home, Walter insists nothing has been stolen.

"What that tells you is that people who love sports are generally honest people," Walter said.

"It goes to show you that people who care about sports have values and morals. People who aren't involved in sports, they don't have the same moral values. They just don't. I see that at the rinks with the kids. Those kids are polite when they ask for autographs."

Phyllis died of cancer in 2005, but Walter still resides in his Varadi Avenue home.

On December 29, 1999, the City of Brantford passed Bylaw 99-99 naming the Gretzky home a historical site. ■

17. GO TO THE STANLEY CUP FINAL

The Stanley Cup final.

The last barrier between an NHL team and ultimate glory, the last hurdle before fans can celebrate in the streets.

For NHL teams and players, a chance to skate in the Cup final is the reason for all those years of early-morning practices and late-night games, endless training and video sessions, weekend travel and time away from family. It's the reason for a life-time in hockey. As a player, you might only get one shot – if you're lucky – so it's a gut-checking, soul-searching series, a moment in time when you find out if your very best effort, and your team's very best effort, is enough to graduate to Stanley Cup supremacy.

For fans, the Cup final represents the climax of the season, a best-on-best battle between East and West, one series to determine league dominance. It's the NHL championship; for that reason alone, it's worth watching.

And, at least once, every hockey fan should make the trek to a Cup final contest and take in the top-end action with their very own eyes. It's not easy to get a ticket, but the experience is worth the expense.

Just ask the Morgan brothers, who grew up playing and watching as much puck as possible in Toronto in the 1980s and early '90s. Unlike the rest of southern Ontario, though, the Morgans looked beyond the Maple Leafs.

"We were force-fed the Leafs during the Harold Ballard years," said older brother Randy, a 6-foot-3, 230-pound center for the Cannons rec-league team when he isn't scouting locations for film and TV. "The Leafs sucked and our dad was a Canadiens fan…my brother and I weren't interested in either team."

Randy didn't stray too far from his geographic region, selecting the Buffalo Sabres as his favorite club.

"As a kid, I liked their old blue-and-gold uniforms, plus they had at least one televised game (in Toronto) every week on WGRZ Buffalo."

Meanwhile, younger brother Ryan wanted his own team to support. Somehow, the Minnesota North Stars rose above the rest. Was it the green uniforms or simply the fact they were in the same division as the Leafs and played Toronto a lot?

"Probably both," said Ryan, a Cannons winger. "But what I really remember is that Don Beaupre had a really cool mask."

So, it was the Buffalo Sabres and Minnesota North Stars for a couple of Toronto boys. OK, fine. It made for a fun childhood, if not a Cup-dotted one.

"You always want your team to make it to the Cup final," Randy said. "Buffalo never did…and Minnesota had a couple of runs, but never won."

Fast-forward to 1999, the year of Wayne Gretzky's retirement and Y2K doom and gloom. But some good things happened, too. Especially if your initials are R. Morgan.

For starters, the Leafs and Sabres were battling in the Eastern Conference semifinal for the right to play for the Stanley Cup.

"I was conflicted, I live in Toronto and the Leafs are my second team," Randy said. "But I was rooting for the Sabres."

Meanwhile, the North Stars had moved to Dallas in 1993 – taking Ryan's loyalties with them – and the next thing you know, it's Buffalo-Dallas in the '99 final. For the Morgans, it meant brother vs. brother, with their respective favorite teams' first Stanley Cup hanging in the balance.

At the time, Ryan was attending Dalhousie University in Halifax, while Randy was working in Toronto.

"I felt like it was destiny," Randy said. "We had to go to that final."

So Randy called Ryan and told his brother he was going to do whatever it took to get his hands on two tickets for the first game in Buffalo, Game 3.

"I told him if he could make his way from Halifax to Toronto, that I'd take care of the tickets," Randy said.

After answering a newspaper ad – "Call here for Stanley Cup tickets" – and forking over $1,000 (U.S.), Randy made good on his word. And Ryan did, too, traveling home to Toronto on a limited student budget.

On the big day, the brothers drove to Buffalo and arrived at the arena a couple hours before the game.

"There was a ton of people outside the rink," Randy said. "Fans, vendors, street performers, people selling anything and everything with a logo on it, T-shirts, hats, everything.

"The vibe in Buffalo is usually pretty depressing, but the city was floating that day. Buffalo loves its Sabres."

Inside the rink, the Morgans found their seats. Second level, right behind Sabres goalie Dominik Hasek for the first and third periods.

"Just over our left shoulder, about five rows behind us, was the ESPN booth with Darren Pang and Barry Melrose," Randy recalled. "I remember thinking it was cool that our seats were closer to the game than the NHL analysts."

Randy wore an old-school Buffalo jersey, just like the ones that drew his eye when he was an impressionable youngster. Ryan, meanwhile, had the audacity – the game was in Buffalo, remember – to show up at the Sabres' home rink in a Dallas Stars third jersey, with 'Nieuwendyk' and '25' stitched on the back, no less.

"It was a real plush jersey," Ryan laughed, "it looked good."

As they walked around the concourse before the game, Sabres fans heckled Ryan from all sides. But it was in a joking manner, not hostile.

"Don't forget, I had a pretty big brother with me," Ryan said.

During the subsequent intermissions, however, the intensity ramped up. There's more yelling, more finger-pointing and more angst – especially after the second period, as Nieuwendyk's late goal tied the game 1-1 heading into the third.

"People are getting a little more tense with Ryan's Nieuwendyk jersey," recalled Randy, who, in his Sabres sweater, was busy telling potential Buffalo vigilantes, "Don't worry, it's OK, he's my brother."

As the game goes to the third, the brothers make a bet: The loser of the game has to pay for the hotel in Buffalo that evening.

"I'm sad to report that Dallas won 2-1 and Nieuwendyk scored both goals," Randy said. "I paid for the hotel that night."

Looking back, however, it was a small price for an enduring Stanley Cup memory.

"Being a Sabres fan, it was a pinnacle moment for me, being at a Stanley Cup final game in Buffalo," Randy said.

"The fact that it ended up a loss, and they ended up losing the series, too, didn't really matter that much because the entire experience was so far above and beyond any other sporting experience that I've ever had, and I've had a few. And to be able to share it with my brother, it was like we were on a path our whole lives to get to that event.

"Winning or losing didn't matter, it was just a great day."

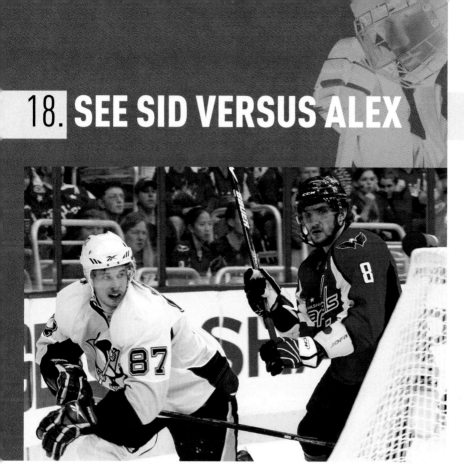

"It's gonna be sick," Alex Ovechkin beamed, invoking his adjective for all occasions to describe the Washington Capitals' 2009 Eastern Conference semifinal series against the Pittsburgh Penguins.

"Sick" is Ovechkin's ubiquitous description for anything amazing or spectacular. An unbelievable pass from a teammate is sick. A highlight-reel goal is sick. A fast car most fans can only dream of affording is sick.

By that measure, so is a Penguins-Capitals game, not to mention an entire playoff series featuring the NHL's hottest rivalry of Sidney Crosby versus Alex Ovechkin. If you're compiling your bucket list of must-do hockey experiences, watching two teams who generally dislike one another – and dueling superstars and feuding fans that express the same sentiment – in the roaring din of Washington's Verizon Center should be on your agenda.

Roughly 246 miles and chasms of cultural differences separate the cities of Pittsburgh and Washington.

Denizens of the 'Burgh would rather wrestle a Primanti Bros. sandwich than get all gussied up for a fancy sit-down at a five-star restaurant, as they surmise most do in the nation's capital. The D.C. power brokers show up at games attired in business suits, a far cry from Pens fans, a roll-up-your-sleeves lot. The Steel City crowd doesn't understand the sense of entitlement sometimes present in Washington any more than Washingtonians can grasp the blue-collar work ethic that defines the Rust Belt. Think Iron City Beer vs. this year's trendiest wine.

Losing to the Penguins is another reason hostilities run deep. Lifetime against Pittsburgh, Washington is 80-86-19. That's not too bad, but the salt in the wound is Washington's playoff record against Pittsburgh; the Penguins have taken seven of the eight all-time series between the teams, including the past five meetings.

"Every year, it seems like Pittsburgh is the one team we have to beat to get to the next level and we can't get over the hump," said Capitals fan Ray Mitten, an attorney from Arlington, Va., who has held season tickets since 1993.

"Instead, they beat us. And it's the way they beat us that's hard to swallow, whether it's losing a four-overtime game or on a bad call. It's not necessarily that the Penguins win, it's the excruciating ways they do it."

When Jaromir Jagr was traded from Pittsburgh to Washington in July of 2001, Penguins fans were livid at the measly haul the unhappy superstar fetched: three prospects that scored 13 goals in 103 career NHL games. Meanwhile, Jagr underperformed in Washington and his contract extension became an albatross around the Caps' rebuilding efforts. Both sides felt ripped off and said so.

But it boils down to this: Pittsburgh doesn't understand or like Washington. And Washingtonians feel exactly the same way.

Pittsburghers also are miffed they have trouble getting tickets to see their beloved waddlers in D.C. When Abe Pollin owned the underachieving Capitals, this wasn't an issue. Apathetic fans didn't beat down the doors at the old saddle-shaped Capital Centre in Landover, Md., and rabid Pens backers motored southeast in droves. Even when the Capitals moved into the District, a Pens-Caps game was like Steel City South for Pittsburgh fans, who were louder and rowdier than Capitals supporters.

Then, Ted Leonsis bought a majority interest in the Caps and, during the 2001 playoffs, grew tired of watching his team get outcheered. So he installed special software on the toll-free ticket-ordering phone lines that prevented folks with western Pennsylvania area codes from purchasing electronically. Now, Leonsis has enhanced software, making it difficult for folks with a ZIP code outside the Capitals' marketing area – or those whose buying history shows an allegiance to the black-and-gold – to purchase tickets to any game.

"I don't feel any shame in this, I think I'm doing exactly the right thing and I don't feel I need to apologize," said Leonsis on XM Radio.

"There are other franchises and other teams that want to sell tickets, and really don't care who they sell them to. But frankly, I do, and I think I'm doing the right thing the right way."

Lately, what excites is the promise of two high-octane offenses led by the NHL's premier scorers, Ovechkin and Crosby. Ovechkin lays Crosby out at every opportunity, while Crosby said he doesn't understand the animosity and complained about hats littering the ice when Ovechkin scored a hat trick at home. That Crosby's teammate – and fellow Ovechkin rival – Evgeni Malkin eclipsed Ovechkin for the NHL scoring title in 2008-09 only adds fuel to the fire.

"It's about the perception of who the face of the league is, too," Mitten said. "With Ovie and Crosby, there's a rivalry there, whether it's personal or not. Who's more prominent, the Canadian or the Russian?"

Each superstar's rush up the ice is precipitated by a pregnant pause, as if the jam-packed, red-clad, Caps-crazy crowd is holding its collective breath. When the home team thwarts Sid the Kid, they exhale en masse, relieved.

But if the puck finds its way onto Ovechkin's tape, the crowd inhales in anticipation. Ovechkin can be sneaky quick and his on-ice machinations demand a fan's full attention. When he snaps off a shot – or somehow miraculously manages to feather the puck past an unsuspecting netminder while sliding on his backside – the crowd erupts.

Ovechkin's goal celebrations are moments of beauty; unscripted exultations of joy punctuated by self-congratulatory chest bumps with animate (teammates) and inanimate objects (dasher boards and Plexiglass). They move in slow motion, a stark contrast to real life, and seconds seem to linger into minutes as the happy Russian and happier fans prolong a goalie's agony. Ovechkin's histrionics have inspired debate among hockey purists about the efficacy of self-expression. But you can't deny how much the home fans delight in his elation, nor the ecstasy he feels in their adulation.

"It's so genuine because it's not staged," marveled Caps fan Eric Rhew of Towson, Md., who embraced the team upon Ovechkin's arrival after the 2004-05 lockout.

"He's excited and that excites the fans. And it's not just because he's scored, but because he knows he's helped his team. It's that type of excitement that drew me to the sport."

Ovechkin isn't the only player to draw an overt reaction in D.C. One Penguin in particular – ex-Capitals defenseman Sergei Gonchar – is targeted each and every time he touches the puck. Fans let loose with a derisive catcall – a "whoop-whoop" sound something like a poorly warbling songbird – whenever the puck is on Gonchar's stick. It's a time-honored tradition in D.C., first directed at one-time Washington defenseman Larry Murphy, then at Gonchar once Murphy (who played for Washington from 1983-90 and Pittsburgh from '91-95) retired. The irreverent mocking is worn like a badge of honor by the unlucky recipient.

The Verizon Center crowd is as impressive as Ovechkin's displays. Shortly after the national anthem, a hand-held plastic horn in the upper bowl toots three times, with the masses responding, "Let's Go Caps!" on cue. If the home team needs encouragement at some point, a chap behind one of the nets cups his ear, like a preacher pleading from the pulpit, and the faithful roar the liturgy. And woe be to the unprepared when the high-definition video screen plays the movie montage. When Tom Green's character in *Road Trip* exhorts the throng to "unleash the fury," the arena literally rocks.

"It's pretty cool," Ovechkin said.

Some nights, between shifts, he sits on the bench and smiles at the crowd's antics. There's no higher form of appreciation.

19. SURVIVE A MANITOBA BLIZZARD

Steve Haddon had to be excited playing in front of his parents when they came for a visit. As a star center on the Manitoba Jr. A League's Portage Terriers, Haddon was toiling far from his southern Ontario home in Sarnia.

But Haddon's main concern wasn't how he'd fare in front of his folks. Rather, his first worry when mom and dad accompanied the team on a road trip to northern Manitoba was how they'd deal with the fan experience awaiting them in The Pas. That's where the OCN Blizzard ('OCN' stands for Opaskwayak Cree Nation), a team feverishly supported by the Native population in the area, enjoys one very intense home-ice advantage.

"I warned them that the fans all have cut-off goalie sticks and they bang them on the boards, and it's pretty loud in there," Haddon said. "For sure, OCN was the craziest place I've ever been."

But it's not the only place in Manitoba where Jr. A hockey teams are staunchly supported by a loyal, passionate small-town fan base.

Haddon, a veteran of the Ontario Jr. A and B ranks before moving to Portage for the 2004-05 season, noticed the prairie passion right away.

"Ontario is so big, it's just not as tight because there's so many teams and leagues," Haddon said. "I thought it was amazing how all these little small towns rally around their hockey teams. It's so awesome and it's really the only thing to do on a Friday or Saturday night."

Haddon, currently a 25-year-old member of the Central League's Colorado Eagles, played on a high-caliber club during his season in Portage. The Terriers won the MJHL title, then battled the Saskatchewan-based Yorkton Terriers for the right to advance to the RBC Royal Bank Cup, the national Jr. A championship tournament.

After a stirring triple-overtime win in Game 5 in Yorkton, Portage returned home with a chance to clinch a trip to the big show with a victory in Game 6. The town was gripped with Terriers fever.

"I've never seen a rink like that, just how loud it was," said Haddon of Portage's Centennial Arena. "I remember, me and my roommate, Josh Boyd, we pulled up before the game and we couldn't even get in the parking lot because it was packed. They were already tailgating.

"There's no reserved seating, you just buy your ticket and go in…everyone was sitting down already before I was even dressed. It was just plain loud inside, there were sirens going off and everything. I remember thinking, 'OK, this is going to be quite a game.' "

It certainly was, with the home side scoring a late shorthanded goal to pull off a 3-2 victory and book its ticket to the RBC Cup. When the game-winner went in, the durability of the old barn's roof was severely put to the test.

"I've never seen anything like that, not to that extent," Haddon said.

Another player who took part in that 2005 national championship was Mason Raymond, the current Vancouver Canuck and former Camrose (Alta.) Kodiak. He's one of several players – along with the likes of Phoenix Coyotes center Kyle Turris and Boston Bruins prospect Joe Colborne – who've been recent high picks from Canada's Jr. A ranks. Raymond treasured his experience – two seasons, 2003-04 and '04-05 – in the Alberta Jr. A League.

"It's one of the times of my life that I'll never forget," Raymond said. "That was where hockey really got going for me. The city of Camrose as a whole is just fantastic. It's a little city, but come playoffs, everybody was on board and cheering for you. We had great support all the way to the Royal Bank Cup. Those are years I'll always remember in my life."

The manner in which players from the West tend to play is a big part of what fuels the fans. Suffice it to say, no prairie boy in the history of hockey has ever taken the roundabout way into a corner. That hard-nosed approach, by players both big and small, jumped out to Haddon upon his arrival in Manitoba.

"I was just like, 'Who are these guys?' " Haddon laughed. "They're big-hearted guys and definitely pretty tough." ■

20. READ A BOOK

Truly understanding the game of hockey involves more than simply playing it yourself or watching it on TV. It's a game of such depth, passion and character that stats and scoresheets can't communicate why it consumes fans like few other pastimes.

Every year, another handful of titles is added to the stack of books that aims to explain the "meaning" of hockey (in fact, you're holding one right now). But we'd like to suggest two others pieces of required reading that get to the essence of what hockey is and what it says about its followers: *The Game* by Ken Dryden, possibly the most eloquent and introspective sports memoir of all-time, and *The Hockey Sweater* by Roch Carrier, the finest children's book in print about hockey.

In *The Game*, Dryden, the former Montreal Canadiens goalie, takes us through the Habs' 1978-79 season, a campaign which ultimately results in a fourth straight Stanley Cup. Dryden takes a hard and insightful look at a superstar-studded Canadiens team that outclasses the rest of the league, but is burdened by the expectation to deliver a Cup championship every season. They're so good, in fact, their only real opponents are themselves, as they compete against their arrogance, their apathy and their self-doubt.

Dryden also uses the '78-79 Habs as a jumping-off point to discuss myriad subjects within hockey, from the tragic decline of the Leafs-Canadiens rivalry, to the perks of being an NHLer in hockey-mad Montreal, to the blurring effect of life on the road. As well, he examines the role that hockey plays in defining Canadian culture, through his experience in the 1972 Summit Series and his observations as an English-speaking Montreal player during Quebec's Quiet Revolution.

During his playing career, Dryden was known as much for his intellectual pursuits as his athletic success. In fact, *The Game* takes place during the season that Dryden finalizes his decision to retire, before his 32nd birthday, in order to pursue law. Although the NHL lost one of its stars too early, the hockey world gained its finest book.

At the other end of the spectrum is the children's book *The Hockey Sweater*, which tells the simple story of a boy growing up in small-town Quebec during the height of Maurice Richard's career, when the Rocket was a hero in French Canada. Every boy in every Quebec town lives to emulate Richard, but when the main character receives a Toronto Maple Leafs sweater by mistake from the Eaton's catalogue, he feels that his life is over.

Although the book is intended for kids, the power of Carrier's story is such that it could be set in any hockey city in any era. If a player or a team has ever meant more to you than mere entertainment, then this story will ring true. The *Globe and Mail* once described *The Hockey Sweater* as "the best Canadian short story ever written" and it's a case worth making, with unforgettable images like the boy praying to God to "send a hundred million moths that would eat up my Toronto Maple Leafs sweater." So sit down with the kids and enjoy this one together.

And there you go, something for everyone, young and old. Of course, if you simply can't stand the Habs, we suggest either *Searching for Bobby Orr* by Stephen Brunt or *The Game of Our Lives* by Peter Gzowski, the late CBC favorite who writes about spending a year on the road with the 1980-81 Edmonton Oilers. Happy reading. ■

21. COLLECT HOCKEY CARDS

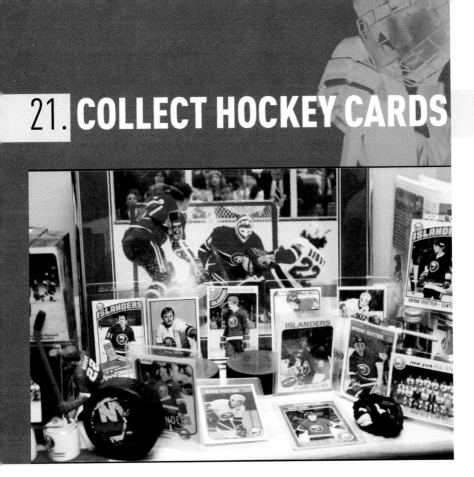

Angelo Savelli was only 10 when his parents took him on a trip to visit relatives in Boston. His eyes opened widely when he went into a variety store and noticed a stack of pictures of his baseball heroes for sale inside packages of bubblegum.

"After that, every penny I got I spent on cards," Savelli said. "Our relatives owned a casino in Framingham, Mass., and they let me try out one of the machines. I won some money and all of it went towards cards. I was throwing the wrappers out the car window on the way home."

Shortly afterwards, he discovered hockey cards in variety stores in his native Hamilton and it marked the start of North America's largest hockey card collection. Savelli doesn't know the actual number – he's never counted – and just leaves the figure at "thousands and thousands…and thousands."

The very first hockey cards were produced more than 125 years ago. In the early years of the 20th century, hockey cards were offered as inserts inside packages of cigarettes. But the first mainstream set of the modern era, the 1951-52 Parkhurst edition, is considered the grandfather of all hockey cards.

"The first Parkhurst series came out in 1951 and I was looking for Toronto Maple Leafs and Bill Barilko in particular," Savelli said. "I wanted the Barilko portrait, but all they had was the shot of him scoring the winning goal in overtime in the 1951 Stanley Cup final on Gerry McNeil of Montreal."

No. 52 in the '51-52 Parkhurst series was the only hockey card printed of Barilko. In August of 1951, the Leafs defenseman was killed in a plane crash while on a fishing trip in northern Quebec. The wreckage of the plane wasn't discovered until 11 years later near Cochrane, Ont.

Not a bad hockey player himself, Savelli was thrilled when he received a letter from one of his Leafs heroes, Ted 'Teeder' Kennedy, in 1957 inviting him to the training camp of the Jr. A Peterborough Petes. Savelli had been scouted playing for a Hamilton juvenile club and Kennedy, the former Leafs captain, was taking over as coach of the Petes. Like many boys of that era, however, Savelli yielded to pressure from his mother not to go and wound up getting a job at the Stelco steel plant, where his father and brothers worked.

His most prized possession is a card from the 1920s of Lionel 'Big Train' Conacher, another one his heroes. Conacher, who was named Canada's athlete of the first half of the 20th century, also starred in football and once played a pro football game and hockey game on the same day.

Savelli is so into collecting that he once traded a 1961 Chevrolet Impala convertible – yes, that's right, a *car* – for a box of cards from the 1950s. On another occasion, he swapped a refrigerator and stove for some coveted cards. (No word on what he got in exchange for the kitchen sink…)

As soon as Savelli had the right combination of age and years of service at Stelco, he took early retirement at age 50 and continued collecting cards full-time. Savelli wrote to companies all over North America looking for particular cards; at one time, he had complete sets from 1910 well into the 1980s.

Savelli estimates that over the years he has handled more than 50 Gordie Howe rookie cards, which were printed in 1951. He doesn't have them all now, but in mint condition the cards are listed at $3,000 apiece.

Known as the 'King of Sports Cards,' he also has an impressive collection of the famous Bee Hive photos of NHL players. (In the league's pre-expansion era, purchasers of Bee Hive corn syrup were able to obtain the photos by mailing a label and 25 cents to the company.)

In the 1950s, one company printed a set of cards in vintage blue tone from the Ontario Hockey Association's Jr. A League; Savelli still relishes the one he has of Don Cherry in the uniform of the Barrie Flyers.

While operating a sports card and memorabilia store in Hamilton in the early 1990s, Savelli sold a Hamilton Tigers NHL jersey – the last known one in existence – for $500. It has never resurfaced.

The Tigers had finished first in the NHL in 1924-25 and were set to chase the Stanley Cup in the post-season. However, when team owners told the players they wouldn't be paid extra for the playoffs, the players went on strike. The owners didn't cave in (sound familiar?), the Tigers were suspended by the NHL and the team was sold to a group of New Yorkers – through mob connections – and became the New York Americans, the first team to play in the old Madison Square Garden. In 2005, *Sports Illustrated* listed a Hamilton Tigers hockey sweater as one of the top 25 lost sports treasures.

At 72, Savelli still goes to card shows to display his collection and see what's available. He's looking for vintage hockey postcards from the 1890s, if you happen to have any extras.

"It's been my life and it's still in me," he said.

22. DON'T MISS A MINUTE OF PLAYOFF OVERTIME

The best hockey is playoff hockey. Take it a step further, and the best hockey is playoff overtime hockey.

Every fan knows it doesn't get any more intense than sudden-death, next-goal-wins overtime – preferably in a Game 7 or at least an elimination game; but really, any NHL playoff overtime will do.

As a fan, you have no control when it comes to overtime; you've just got to sit there, living and dying with every scoring chance, falling to the floor after every big save, your heart pounding as you watch every rush up the ice and every scrum in front of the net. It's agony one minute and ecstasy the next, with pure joy or abject disappointment just one shot away. Overtime is the hockey equivalent of a roller-coaster, except you never have to leave your couch.

When you come across such a contest – all tied up at the end of regulation, with Stanley Cup hopes hanging in the balance – there's only one option for any hockey fan with a conscience: Watch every period, every play, every second of that potentially endless game.

First of all, there's a chance it might be the best overtime game ever. (Hey, you never know.) Second, the game will come to an end – but when? Relatively early into the first overtime period, like the majority of playoff games that required (a little) extra time in the 2009 post-season? Or will the teams battle through the night and into the early morning hours, relentlessly skating and shooting and hustling and hitting, all the while hoping to play the hero with a goal for the ages? Because that has happened, too, plenty of times, and witnessing a marathon overtime game is a memorable experience for hockey fans; in fact, under the right circumstances, it can forge a lifelong admiration for a particular team or player.

Take the New York Islanders (…please…). OK, granted, it's been a tough couple of decades; the Isles haven't exactly had to worry about playoff overtime for a while. But the franchise has had its moments, even if you have to be Chris Chelios' age to remember them.

Bob Nystrom started New York's four-year dynasty run with an overtime goal in Game 6 of the Stanley Cup final against Philadelphia in 1980. If there's one goal that defines a franchise, it's this one. The clutch Nystrom – he has four playoff overtime markers – went to the net, as the hard-charging Islanders were known to do, and swatted a pass from John Tonelli past Flyers goalie Pete Peeters. And then the Nassau Coliseum crowd exploded, joyously cheering the team's first of four consecutive Cups, earned in the most intense of circumstances. The Isles were unstoppable over the next few years, a powerhouse that might have won six or seven Cups if not for the rise of Wayne Gretzky's Oilers in the mid-'80s. And even when New York's Stanley Cup success had subsided, the Islanders still knew what to do in overtime.

April 18, 1987. The Easter Epic. The Islanders had trailed the Washington Capitals three games to one in the first round playoff series, but fought back to force a Game 7. In the decisive contest, the Isles fell behind 1-0 after the first period and 2-1 after the second. But they kept rallying, including a Bryan Trottier backhander to tie the game 2-2 with less than five minutes remaining in the third.

After that, it was all about Kelly Hrudey and Bob Mason. The dueling goalies proved impenetrable in the first overtime period, and then the second overtime period…and then the third. Back and forth, back and forth, a goalpost here, a missed chance there. For the first time since 1951, an NHL playoff game was headed to a fourth overtime period. And with the way the goalies were playing, it looked, to steal a line from CBC commentator Bob Cole, like "it might never end!"

Finally, after 68 minutes and 47 seconds of overtime, Pat LaFontaine's turnaround slapshot from the top of the faceoff circle eluded Mason and the Isles added another chapter to their playoff legend. Hrudey stopped 73 of 75 shots (including 50 in a row after the end of the second period), while Mason blocked 54 of 57. The game had started at 7:30 p.m. and didn't end until nearly 2 o'clock in the morning. See, you never really know what you're getting into when the puck drops on overtime.

Nine years later, the Caps lost an even longer playoff game, when Pittsburgh's Petr Nedved scored at 19:15 of the fourth OT period. That's the fifth-longest overtime game ever, yet the Penguins were soon involved in an even lengthier affair. In 2000, Keith Primeau scored at 2:01 of the *fifth* overtime period – that's 92:01 of extra hockey, on top of 60 minutes of regulation play – to lead Philadelphia over Pittsburgh 2-1 in the third-longest game ever. In both of these cases, the team that lost in overtime was leading the series – but never won another game.

There have only been two longer contests in NHL history, and both were sextuple-OT affairs – that's *six* overtime periods, if you can believe it. Chances are, though, you didn't see them. And we can't blame you for that. First of all, they occurred before television was invented: Ken Doraty, after 104 minutes and 46 seconds of extra play, scored the only goal in a 1-0 win by Toronto over Boston in 1933; and, of course, old Mud Bruneteau played 116 minutes and 30 seconds of OT before scoring to lead Detroit over Montreal in 1936.

Those games might've been over a lot faster had Brian Skrudland been around. While with the Canadiens in 1986, Skrudland scored just nine seconds into overtime in Game 2 of the Stanley Cup final against Calgary.

That's the beauty of playoff overtime: You don't know if it'll last a few seconds, a few minutes or a few periods. But you can't look away, not once, or you might miss the one thing you've been watching for all along: A moment of glory, a moment to re-member forever. ■

23. SIT IN THE BLUE SEATS AT AN ISLES-RANGERS GAME

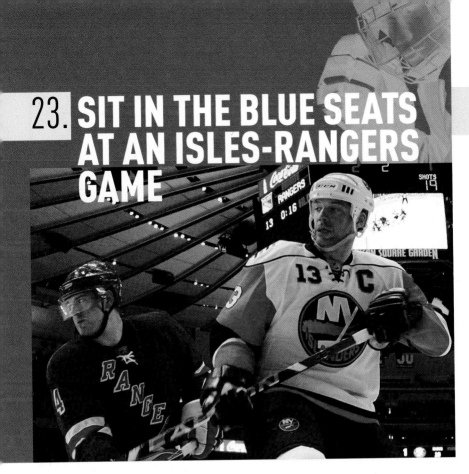

The echoes. That's what you hear as you ride the escalator to the upper tier, a place officially known as the mezzanine but more famously and notoriously known as "the blue seats."

But they're not quite blue anymore, are they? Haven't been for years, since a renovation turned the upholstery into a shade of aqua. That's when they removed a half-dozen sections from the upper tier in order to add overhanging luxury suites at the top of the Seventh and Eighth Avenue ends of Madison Square Garden.

It's known as the 'World's Most Famous Arena.' The PA announcer tells you that as he welcomes you to the building on the west side of midtown Manhattan that sits between 31st and 33rd Streets above Penn Station. You don't care about that. You're there to watch the Rangers and Islanders.

World's Most Famous Arena?

Hockey's greatest rivalry, that's all you care about, this latest installment of the Battle of New York.

The place is noisier than usual; edgier. You settle into your seat in the second row of Section 415 – used to be 419 before they tried to class up the joint with the remodeling – that's high above the net at which the Rangers will shoot twice. There are Mark Messier No. 11 jerseys to the left, Sean Avery No. 16s to the right, and even some Wayne Gretzky No. 99s sprinkled about.

But wait, what's this? A Mike Bossy No. 22 in the house?

There are enemies within; that's what makes the atmosphere come alive on this night. They came by train from Long Island, ready to root for their woebegone team that invaded the Rangers' territory in 1972 and won as many Stanley Cups from 1980 to '83 – four; in a row, no less! – as the Blueshirts have won since joining the NHL in 1926. You know that because you see the championship banners hanging from the distinctive round ceiling, the ones from 1928, 1933, 1940 and, the one that made Messier a New York legend, 1994.

They're taking warmups down below and you lean forward slightly in order to see the entire ice surface. You've got the cheapest – er, least expensive – seats in the house, but you know you've got the best view. You can see everything. And hear everything, too.

Right down below, you remember, is where Messier grabbed Jason Blake by the throat and nearly choked the Islanders pest during a brawl before the lockout. How great was that, seeing Blake's face turn crimson as 'The Captain' handled him like a mannequin, guiding him from the front of the net to the sideboards?

The Islanders are cruising through the pre-game skate at your end of the ice. Down below, the fans in Islanders jerseys – and there aren't all that many as foolhardy as the Bossy impersonator up top – are drowned out by the taunts of Blueshirts supporters.

Isn't that what it's all about, taunting the Islanders? That's what it's about in the blue seats. That's what you did in the first round of the 1994 playoffs when the Rangers swept the overmatched Isles, winning the opening two games at MSG by identical 6-0 scores. That's when the Islanders had Ron Hextall in goal – Hextall, who had already established himself as one of the Rangers' all-time opponent villains when he came into the league with the almost equally hated Flyers.

"HEK-STALLLL…HEK-STALLLL…HEK-STALL!"

Or at least that was the polite version.

You look down below. Your end of the ice, that's where J-P Parise scored just 11 seconds into overtime in Game 3 of the preliminary round in the 1975 playoffs to eliminate the Rangers. That's where the hatred was born, that night the three-year-old expansion Isles knocked Eddie Giacomin, Brad Park, Rod Gilbert, Jean Ratelle and Emile Francis into the summer.

And then you look down to your right. Warmups are over. The Zamboni is doing its work. The building is humming in anticipation. You're waiting for the first chant. Rangers fans are all waiting for the first chant. They know it well; they've been screaming it for 30 years.

It was Feb. 25, 1979, the most famous regular season game ever played between the two New York teams, one that still reverberates. For that was the game in which Islanders defenseman Denis Potvin broke Ulf Nilsson's ankle on a hipcheck along the boards just as the Swedish center caught his skate in a rut.

Did it matter that it was an accident? Not at all. Did it matter the Rangers, even without Nilsson, upset the top-seeded Islanders in six games a few months later in the semifinals? It did not.

Potvin had become Public Enemy No. 1 at Madison Square Garden.

When it began, he can't begin to tell you, but everyone knows it's still going strong.

The chant, that is.

A whistle in the stands signals the taunt that has been heard at every single Rangers home game for decades now, regardless of the opponent, but is delivered more enthusiastically and more often when the Islanders are in town.

It doesn't matter whether Potvin is in the building or not. His spirit lives. He is the ghost of disappointments past. He is the face of the Rangers' enemy, still, even 20 years after his retirement.

Ah, John Amirante has just finished belting out the national anthem. The players are lined up, waiting for the opening faceoff…and here it comes:

"Tweet, tweet, tweet-tweet-tweet, tweet, tweet, tweet-tweet-tweet…POTVIN SUCKS!…POTVIN SUCKS!…POTVIN SUCKS!"

It's the Rangers and Islanders at Madison Square Garden from the blue seats, and there's nothing else you need to know. Except to make sure, at least once, you're sitting in a blue seat when you see the game. ▪

24. GO BACK TO (PREP) SCHOOL

In the post-lockout era, a new breed of athlete has dominated the NHL. Plodding veterans have been relegated to the game's margins, pushed to the periphery by a cavalcade of younger, faster stars boasting equal amounts of exuberance and creativity.

That pro hockey has once again become a young man's game isn't by itself surprising – every few years, a new generation of skillful pups emerges to claim the old dogs' territory. But what is special about the current crop of youngsters is that so many of them have quickly assumed leadership positions on their respective teams. Sidney Crosby of the Pittsburgh Penguins and Jonathan Toews of the Chicago Blackhawks each had the captain's 'C' sewn on their jerseys before they were old enough to drink a beer in the U.S., while New Jersey's Zach Parise, 24, has become the most important forward in a Devils system that preaches conscientiousness at both ends of the ice.

Crosby, Toews and Parise aren't just great hockey players. They're baby-faces with the maturity and character to lead grown, grizzled men into battle. And it's hardly a coincidence that all three were shaped by the renowned hockey program at the Shattuck-St. Mary's prep school.

Nestled into the countryside in the town of Faribault, Minn., about 45 minutes south of Minneapolis-St. Paul, Shattuck-St. Mary's has been around since the mid-1800s. But it's only recently that the school has become synonymous with top-tier shinny.

Craig Norwich started the Shattuck-St. Mary's hockey program in the mid-1990s, seeking to generate more interest in the boarding school that prepares students for entrance into university. In barely 15 years, the program has grown to include four midget boys teams, two bantam boys teams and two women's teams, with more than 180 players per season getting their on- and off-ice education at Shattuck-St. Mary's.

Tom Ward, director of the school's hockey program and coach of its top boys prep team, has had a rinkside seat for the past 10 years. He joined the program when former NHLer Jean-Paul Parise – Zach's father – was at the helm, and has helped dozens of young players on their journey to the pros.

"We've had our share of great players wandering through our halls," said Ward, rhyming off a list of names – Crosby, Toews, Parise, Tampa Bay's Ryan Malone, Kyle Okposo of the Islanders, Los Angeles defenseman Jack Johnson – that would make any NHL GM salivate.

"And there's going to be more kids here in the next five or six years with a chance to play in the NHL and make a name for themselves."

Trying to pick out which of the youngsters skating for Shattuck-St. Mary's will go on to professional glory is just one of the reasons that hockey fans should take the opportunity to see one of the school's games up close. The top prep team doesn't play in any league, but rather creates its own independent exhibition schedule, traveling North America to test its might against top high schools and junior-level talent. Puck aficionados can track down the team on the road or pay a visit to the Shattuck-St. Mary's arena, which boasts a four-year-old ice sheet with stadium seating for 1,500 (there's also a smaller rink with a grandstand that can accommodate about 300).

While checking out the soon-to-be famous faces on the ice, attendees can also mingle with some professional bird dogs.

"We play a lot of Sunday morning games and on any given Sunday you'll have anywhere from five to 25 NHL teams represented here, five to 25 college and junior scouts, so the kids get a lot of exposure," Ward said. "There's a lot of hockey people in the building watching the kids play."

And while the scouts are watching for hockey skills, they're also counting on the school's dedication to education and the development of well-rounded individuals to churn out players who are mentally ready for stardom.

"It's a school first and there's an aptitude you need to have before you can even get in the door," Ward said. "All of the players that are marquee kinds of guys have been fantastic students. They all could have been Ivy League students."

Ward was speaking specifically of Crosby, Toews and Parise, all of whom apparently could wield a pen as effectively as a hockey stick. And Ward believes intelligence is just one of the characteristics the trio shares.

"They're all kind of the same cat…they all have the same burning desire to be great," he said. "They're hard-working and humble kids, not egotistical at all. And they'd probably be the first guys that other people would say were their good friends. They're just good guys."

Ward believes the experience of watching Shattuck-St. Mary's play is a rewarding one for hockey fans who are looking for a sneak peek at future NHL stars and leaders.

"They're out there playing hard and trying to get better and they play with a purpose," Ward said. "That's why it's so enjoyable to coach here, the kids are focused and they're hungry.

"And you never know what you'll see from one of these kids later on down the road. One of them might catch your eye, and you'll keep a game program and look at it seven years later and say, 'I saw this guy when he was 15 years old and he was a pretty good player.' "

At the very least, fans attending a Shattuck-St. Mary's game will get an education on how some of the game's students rose to the head of the NHL class. And what's more important than education?

25. FIND YOUR INNER FAN

Hockey fans are great. They can also be loud, crude and obnoxious. But the best part about them is there are so many different types.

Whether it's the fans decked out in as much team paraphernalia as possible; the beer-guzzling lunatic who screams obscenities throughout the entire contest; the businessmen out to impress clients; or, the wide-eyed youngster at his first game, hockey arenas across the globe would be empty – in more ways than one – without these individuals.

With that in mind, here are six of the more common (and entertaining) types of hockey fans. Which one are you?

1. The Bandwagon Jumpers

The "Stick with them until they lose" fan

Bandwagon jumpers are the type of fans people usually either ignore or absolutely hate. More often than not, though, they're chastised. These are the fans who come out of the woodwork when a team begins playing well (See Blackhawks, Chicago;

2008-09). They could probably afford really good tickets, but unless the team is playing well, their seat remains empty. They're the type of fan who couldn't tell you too much about the team beyond their superstar players, but probably own an abundance of team merchandise.

2. The Hometown Haters

The "Cheer for anyone but the home team" fan

It's easy to figure these ones out. They change their mind every game. It doesn't matter who is playing – as long as the home team loses, they're happy. (Or perhaps they're actually quite unhappy; thus, the reason they go against the hometown grain every game.) They like to bash the home team every chance they get. You'll never see these fans at the arena, as they can't be bothered to spend money on tickets, but they're the first to yell, "Go (insert visiting team here) Go!" when you're watching the game together on TV.

3. The Crazy Hardcore Crew

The "Dies a little inside during the playoffs" fan

These fans usually come equipped with a painted face, colored wig, team jersey and any other type of merchandise they can put on their body. They scream, cheer and jeer their way through the games. They're the ones who throw things at the TV when they think the refs made a bad call, and the first to attach a little team flag to their car window. They love to appear on the Jumbotron at games and will squash anyone who says anything negative about their beloved club. And, of course, they're inconsolable when their team loses.

4. The Dedicated

The "Never lose faith" fan

These fans could be described in another way, too: Delusional. They never give up, never stop believing. It could be the second-to-last game of the regular season, with no chance of making the playoffs, but that doesn't bother them; they'll cheer their team to the very end. They might not agree with how management is running the club, but they won't say anything bad about their team. These fans will suffer through countless seasons filled with disappointment, all the while believing that, one day, they'll see the team captain hoist the Stanley Cup above his head.

5. The Casual Joe

The "Can do with it or without it" fan

These fans usually have a team they support, but they don't go overboard doing so. It doesn't bother them if they miss a game or two – they'll just catch the highlights. When they attend a game, they may wear a jersey, but it's no big deal if they don't. You know, like, whatever…

6. The Playoff Wonders

The "Only watches the post-season" fan

Every sport has them. They're similar to the bandwagon fan, except they aren't around for the regular season. They pop their heads out of the shadows when play-off time rolls around and usually cheer for the team that has the best chance of going the distance. When their "favorite" is eliminated, they'll move on the next contender…and the next…and the next. After the Cup is awarded, they dive back down into their non-hockey holes. ■

26. HAIL THE ECHL'S CHIEFS

The Cambria County War Memorial Arena isn't among those state-of-the-art venues with expensive amenities such as big-screen video boards and lavish luxury boxes. Quite the opposite, actually. The arena was built in 1950 and seats just under 4,000 fans.

And the Johnstown Chiefs aren't one of those ECHL juggernauts that annually challenges for the Kelly Cup. Instead, the Chiefs are typically a solid, competitive bunch cheered on by a devoted and hockey-smart fan base in the Flood City.

But there are plenty of reasons for hardcore hockey fans to attend a Chiefs game in this throwback arena nestled near the confluence of three Pennsylvania rivers.

How about this scenario? The Chiefs and geographical rival Wheeling Nailers meet for the North Division playoff title.

You arrive in Johnstown a night before Game 7, which gives you plenty of time to indulge in an arm's length of the city's famous Coney Island hot dogs. These chili-laden dogs are best ingested after the midnight hour, preferably after you've sipped on a few of your favorite beverages.

On game day, you head to the rink early to watch the morning skate. A walk through the venerable arena's hallways leads past the Slap Shot Lounge, which is packed with dozens of vintage photographs from the 1977 Paul Newman movie that was filmed in Johnstown and based on the 1974-75 champion Johnstown Jets.

The lounge includes memorabilia such as tax forms filled out by extras that participated in the film (for the accountant/hockey fan that resides in us all, perhaps?) as well as signed jerseys worn by the Hanson brothers and Tim 'Dr. Hook' McCracken in the movie.

Further down the concourse is a Veterans Memorial Museum dedicated to the men and women who served the U.S. in various wars. The War Memorial Arena was built after two fundraising efforts by the area's citizens, who were determined to honor the veterans with a practical memorial that had a "useful purpose."

Since then, the arena has been home to pro teams such as the Johnstown Jets, Wings, Red Wings and Chiefs, as well as numerous high school, college and youth programs. The tribute to the veterans is impressive, with memorials to soldiers who fought in the U.S. Civil War right through to those who have served in Iraq and Afghanistan.

Once the morning skate ends, head out for a two-block walk to the intersection of Main and Market streets. Across the street from City Hall in a small grassy square stands a statue of Morley's Dog, better known to *Slap Shot* viewers as "the dog that saved Charlestown from the 1937 flood." Actually a survivor of Johnstown's catastrophic 1889 flood, Morley's Dog is a popular and sentimental attraction. Visiting hockey fans in the winter and baseball fans in the summer constantly seek out the metal brown canine for photos.

Extremely ambitious tourists also have the option of visiting the Johnstown Flood Museum or the Johnstown Heritage Discovery Center. But this is playoff hockey time, so instead go to Johnnies Restaurant, a spot players frequent for meals, especially during training camp. Johnnies is a haven for Chiefs fans in the hours leading up to the opening faceoff.

After a meal, head to Market Street and the Candy Store, where hockey jerseys, playing cards, posters and memorabilia line the tight-quartered store's walls and shelves. The owner is a friend of former Jets player and ex-Chiefs coach Steve Carlson, so there are plenty of Hanson brothers items on display. (Carlson played Steve Hanson in *Slap Shot*.) Also, this is one of the few places where you can still purchase penny candy by the piece.

Less than a block away, it's back to the War Memorial for some pre-game festivities. Chiefs and Nailers fans walk the concourse. Wheeling is only a two-hour drive, and fans from both teams usually travel to away games, sometimes taking fan buses. The three-piece Lou Stein Band plays upbeat jazz numbers, Pennsylvania polkas and patriotic tunes as patrons find their seats. As the pre-game skate nears, arena staff pulls apart the high metal barriers that form a narrow walkway for the visiting team to reach the ice without coming into contact with the home fans lined up on each side of the temporary "fence." Of course, that doesn't prevent the out-of-towners from getting an earful of colorful comments.

At the other end of the hall, lower barriers hold back the home fans, who wait for the Chiefs to exit their dressing room. Small children extend their hands as players give them a gloved high five.

The arena's intimacy is one of the unintended perks – a byproduct of the configuration of the almost 60-year-old venue.

Once the game begins, Johnstown and Wheeling play their blue-collar style, with a lot of bodychecking and maybe even a few fisticuffs. Each time the Chiefs score, the big blue horn sitting atop the aging press box blares out at length; the small size of the arena magnifies the volume to ear-piercing levels.

Popular organist Rick Oswald returned during the 2008-09 season after being away for almost a decade. His comeback, including timely musical improvisations, was well-received.

After a Chiefs win, the game's three stars skate across the ice and throw T-shirts into the stands. Selected players sit at a table outside the dressing room and sign autographs. On Sunday afternoons, the entire team participates in a post-game skate with fans.

Once outside the arena, a popular post-game pit stop sits across the street at Scott's By Dam, a bar that serves super-sized tacos (a favorite of Chiefs coach Ian Herbers and the front office staff).

The small-town touch has enabled Johnstown to survive through difficult economic times. The Chiefs are the only original member of the once five-team ECHL still playing in the same market 21 years later.

27. HOST A FANTASY POOL DRAFT

Of all the things every fan should do in the pursuit of perpetual hockeyness, hosting a fantasy draft has to be right up there.

Fantasy hockey is booming, something NHLers recognize and are dealing with on an ever-growing basis. Mike Cammalleri had the fantasy season of his life in 2008-09, setting a career high in goals (39) and points (82) while playing on the Calgary Flames' top line.

"Oh yeah," said Cammalleri when asked if his fantasy-playing friends give him the gears when he's not performing up to their standards, "they tell me I've got to pick it up when I'm not scoring."

Future fantasy stud and the NHL's No. 1 overall draft pick in 2008, Steven Stamkos, has also felt the wrath of poolie pals.

"A lot of buddies of mine and close friends are into the pools," Stamkos said. "At the beginning of the year (2008-09), I got some (complaints), but the points started to come and I didn't have any complaints (at the end of the season). It's definitely cool to be a part of that."

That's for sure.

The most publicized melding of fantasy and reality during the 2008-09 NHL season re-volved around Washington's Mike Green becoming just the eighth defenseman in NHL history to score 30 goals.

Fantasy hockey offers fans the chance to be GMs. And every fan thinks he or she has the goods to do the job. These days, pools can be as simple or as intricate as de-sired. And there's a pool out there for every type of fan, whether it's year-to-year or long-term keepers; head-to-head, rotisserie or point-based; salary-capped, or not; auction-style, draft-based or both; with or without goalies; and, with or without team-based totals such as penalty-kill percentage. If you still haven't found a suitable con-figuration, any number of websites give you the ability to shape and whittle pools into whatever you consider the ideal fantasy experience.

The Internet has made fantasy hockey more convenient and, in many ways, more virtual. "Virtual" in terms of being run online, but also virtually devoid of any real human interaction. And that's a shame, because the draft can be the most exciting day of the fantasy year.

Marc Dempsey is a 33-year-old financial advisor in Toronto. He got into fantasy hockey because, as a long-suffering Maple Leafs fan, he was looking for a way to keep NHL hockey interesting.

"Otherwise I tend to lose track of the important things in life, like who's the leading rookie goal-scorer and who's in the hunt for a playoff spot," he said.

Dempsey hit the fantasy motherlode a few years back when his friend started up a long-term keeper pool. A tradition evolved that calls for the past year's champion to host draft day. After earning bragging rights in 2008, it was Dempsey's turn to host and he offered a few helpful hints for others to make the event as festive as possible.

"Make the draft an outdoor event," he said when asked for his No. 1 tip. "This brings its own set of potential problems, namely weather. But let's be honest, even having four buddies over to watch a game can turn into a drunken barn dance. The draft is no different, and often worse.

"Make the day comfortable, controlled, problem-free and, of course, fun for everyone. I took particular pride in 'decorating' my backyard. Old hockey sticks, jerseys, pucks and any other paraphernalia I found in the garage seemed to do the trick."

And what of refreshments?

"Don't make the mistake of loading up coolers with ice and offering them to your guests," Dempsey said. "I supplied four empty coolers and one filled with ice, allow-ing my guests to put their beers into a cooler before adding the ice. Trust me, if you don't do things this way you'll end up with a bunch of warm beers sitting on a mountain of ice and a bunch of sad faces sitting around the table, which makes for a long, boring draft day."

And the best part of hosting the event?

"Welcoming everyone to the draft day I had created," Dempsey said. "I love tailgate parties and that's how I treated this event. Adding the tailgate essentials was part of the fun."

As for significant others – often the highest hurdle to clear when hosting a draft day – Dempsey did his best to include his wife, but for some reason she wasn't interested.

"I never asked her to leave the house, quite the opposite," he said. "I simply asked if she was interested in sitting around the backyard all day, eating, drinking beers, talking hockey and assigning salary values in an auction-style format to hockey players – most of whom she'd never heard of.

"She said, 'No,' and asked if it was OK if she wasn't anywhere near the house. I obliged."

All in all, hosting the draft was the highlight of Dempsey's fantasy year as his team dropped to the middle of the pool pack during the 2008-09 season.

"Draft day is one of the most important aspects of running a fun, exciting pool," he said. "It sets the tone, builds excitement and anticipation for opening day and it brings the boys together for a far too rare day of hockey, beer and camaraderie."

And, really, what else could any poolie ask for? ▪

28. GIVE THE FROZEN FOUR THE OL' COLLEGE TRY

It combines the festive atmosphere of Mardi Gras with the tension of a Stanley Cup Game 7.

The Frozen Four is a must-see for hockey fans.

For four days, the U.S. college hockey world invades an American city that has won the right to host the NCAA championship.

The two semifinal games are played on a Thursday and the winners advance to the NCAA championship game on Saturday night. On Friday, the Hobey Baker Award is presented to the best college hockey player among the 58 schools in NCAA Division I.

Fans converge on the host city from all over the U.S., and beyond, many of them wearing the sweater of their favorite school. Thousands of fans have the Frozen Four dates circled on their calendars and make the annual pilgrimage whether their team is in it or not. It's practically a rite of spring; the first Frozen Four champion was crowned more than 60 years ago in 1948, when Michigan doubled Dartmouth 8-4. (Michigan, in fact, won six of the first nine titles, and leads all NCAA schools with a total of nine Frozen Four championships.)

Tom Steele, a native of Bangor, Maine, who has attended 11 Frozen Fours, remembers the time a University of Wisconsin fan, disappointed that a particular Buffalo eatery didn't offer his beloved bratwursts, worked out a deal with the establishment's owner and had dozens of brats transported to Buffalo from Wisconsin.

"They set up some grills and cooked them right outside the restaurant," Steele recalled.

That was in 2003, and the Wisconsin Badgers didn't even make the Frozen Four that year.

"Hockey people are fun," said Steele, who renews acquaintances with many annual Frozen Four attendees.

During games, energetic bands from the four contending colleges belt out their school fight song and any other tunes that are standards at home games during the season. The crowds are raucous, with fans and alumni of all ages, and more than a few fanatics, too, with their faces and/or bodies painted in school colors. Sidewalk vendors, merchandise dealers and hockey-oriented skills competitions are also part of the festivities.

Unlike the Stanley Cup playoffs, the 16-team NCAA tournament is a single-elimination competition. There are no best-of-7 series in U.S. college hockey. Four wins is all it takes to be crowned the national champion; then again, one loss is all it takes to be sent home to start thinking about next season.

The school that wins isn't always the best team in the tournament, but NCAA champions almost always feature a hot goalie and opportunistic scoring.

Just look at what Bemidji State (Minn.) did in 2009.

Granted, the Beavers didn't win the national title, but they were the first No. 16 seed to ever reach the Frozen Four thanks to stunning upset wins over the nation's No. 2-ranked Notre Dame (5-1) and No. 9 Cornell (4-1) in the four-team Midwest Regional, one of four regionals that produces a Frozen Four finalist.

During the regular season Bemidji State played in a four-team league, College Hockey America, that is disbanding. Prior to the Beavers' magical run, CHA teams had gone 1-7 in the NCAA tournament.

It was another surprise team, Miami University in Oxford, Ohio, that ended Bemidji State's run in the semifinal, by a 4-1 score. Miami had gone 2-4-1 in its final seven games prior to the NCAA tournament, but upset Denver (4-2) and Minnesota-Duluth (2-1) in the West Regional to earn its first-ever berth in the Frozen Four.

Then, in perhaps the most dramatic finish in the history of the Frozen Four – and this is a tournament that has had its share of thrilling finales – Boston University, the nation's top-ranked team for most of the year, pulled its goalie and scored *twice* in the final minute of regulation to tie Miami and then won on a fluke overtime goal by Colby Cohen. The sophomore defenseman's shot from the left point was blocked by a sliding Kevin Roeder, but the puck went airborne and dropped softly into the net.

The 2009 Frozen Four was also notable for making its debut at the Verizon Center, home of the NHL's Washington Capitals.

"It was fabulous, we've got to try to get back to that town," said BU coach Jack Parker. "You couldn't find a better place for it. That's the best big rink I've ever been to in my life. And it was gorgeous down there. It was cherry blossom time. The venue is the thing I'll remember the most."

Parker also raved about the accommodating nature of the Capitals' front office; as the highest seed, the Terriers got to use the Caps' dressing room.

There have been many memorable semifinal and championship games, and the list of Frozen Four grads who have gone on to have exceptional NHL careers is impressive.

In an unforgettable 1991 final, Northern Michigan beat Boston University 8-7 in triple overtime on a Darryl Plandowski goal. The Terriers lineup boasted Keith Tkachuk, Shawn McEachern and Tony Amonte.

Two years later, Paul Kariya became the first and only freshman to win the Hobey Baker Award. The day after he was named the top player in U.S. college hockey, Kariya set up three Jim Montgomery goals in span of 4:35 as Maine rallied from a 4-2 deficit to top Lake Superior State 5-4 for Maine's first of two NCAA championships. Garth Snow and Mike Dunham were the Black Bears' goaltenders.

Thomas Vanek led Minnesota to the 2003 NCAA title (over New Hampshire) a year after the Gophers had rallied past Maine 4-3 in overtime. In that '02 final, Matt Koalska's goal with 52.4 seconds left forced overtime for the Gophers and Grant Potulny's power play goal won it. The game was played in St. Paul, Minn., at the Xcel Energy Center in front of a Frozen Four-record 19,324 fans.

Chris Drury helped Boston University win the 1995 NCAA title, while the 2001 Boston College championship team featured Brian Gionta, Rob Scuderi, Brooks Orpik, Krys Kolanos and Chuck Kobasew along with goalie Scott Clemmensen.

Marty Turco backstopped Michigan to two NCAA championships in a three-year span (1996 and '98), while Denver's Matt Carle led the Pioneers to back-to-back NCAA titles in '04 and '05.

"The Frozen Four is such a unique event," said University of Maine assistant coach Dan Kerluke, who played in two Frozen Fours, winning one in 1999, and has coached in two others.

"It's so tough to get to because of the single-elimination format. The odds are so stacked against you. It's one of the biggest highlights of my life. It's a festive atmosphere, the city shuts down and you have 19,000 fans and media everywhere."

ESPN provides national coverage of the Frozen Four in the U.S.

"There isn't a better stage for a hockey fan to watch hockey," Kerluke said. "You've got different cultures coming from different parts of the country."

Maine assistant coach Bob Corkum, who played in Game 7 of the 2001 Stanley Cup final for New Jersey against Colorado as well as two Frozen Fours at Maine, said a Frozen Four and a Game 7 are similar.

"Any time you are in pursuit of a championship, no matter what level it is, you're geared up and excited to play," Corkum said.

"You want to give it everything you've got. It's certainly a lasting memory."

Future venues include Ford Field in Detroit in 2010 (where the NFL's Lions play); the Xcel Energy Center in St. Paul (2011); and, the St. Pete Times Forum in Tampa Bay, home of the NHL's Lightning (2012).

Ford Field, which held more than 75,000 fans for the 2008 NCAA men's basketball Final Four, and the St. Pete Times Forum are set to be first-time hosts. And presumably, they're perfect for first-time Frozen Four fans, too, if you've got one more college road trip left in you. ▨

29. TAILGATE A PLAYOFF GAME IN CAROLINA

Along the ring road surrounding the RBC Center, a turf-covered berm separates the traffic from the arena's parking lots. Every arriving player and every visiting team bus must pass that spot on its way to the rink, and they rarely pass without notice.

There is always a barrage of signs along the road – some cute, some clever – arranged by a group of Carolina Hurricanes fans who arrive hours before the game, claim their spots in the parking lot and turn the grassy berm into an outpost of Margaritaville.

Before a typical spring playoff game on a sunny April or May afternoon, there are tens of thousands of Carolina fans in the lots – they've come to be known as "Caniacs" – drinking and grilling and tossing bean bags, and generally having a good time long before the puck is dropped.

These are the fans whom arriving players see first – and the fans know it. Starting during the 2002 playoffs, when Carolina advanced to the Stanley Cup final for the first time in franchise history, hordes of tailgaters began greeting players as they arrived. Canes defenseman Bret Hedican was the first to acknowledge them back then, but today they almost always get a honk or a wave from their arriving heroes.

The group bills its tailgate party as "Cole's Grassy Knoll Bar & Grill," a name bestowed upon it by Erik Cole himself. At an autograph session some years ago, two of the group identified themselves to Cole as "those people by the road."

"He said, 'Oh, you guys are the ones from the grassy knoll,' " said tailgater Jeff Benicase. "It stuck. We put a sign out there the next day."

During that '02 playoff/tailgate run, pre-game partying fans simply ate fast-food fried chicken out of the back of a truck. But after seven years of practice, they've raised their standards. For the first game of the 2009 playoffs, even as grey clouds threatened, Canes supporters were seen setting up full bars while grilling shrimp and filet mignon.

When Cole returned to the arena as a member of the Edmonton Oilers during the '08-09 regular season, the group hung a sign that read, "Only 242 days until free agency."

As it turned out, they didn't have to wait that long. Cole returned at the trade deadline and when two of Joe Corvo's friends visited him with a few weeks to go in the regular season, Cole and Corvo dropped them off at the grassy knoll to party until game time.

"They were treated the way a player would be treated," Corvo said. "They answered a lot of questions. They got something to eat and had a lot of fun. And they can't stop talking about it…We felt like we had to give them the full experience of a Carolina weekend game. There's no better place to drop them off."

Cole and Corvo didn't give it a second thought. They knew Corvo's friends would be well received, just as many visiting fans have been embraced by their hosts over the past few years, from the Toronto supporters who came down to watch the Eastern Conference final in 2002 to the Edmontonians who bought season tickets for the 2006-07 regular season just so they could get their hands on a ticket for the 2006 Stanley Cup final.

The one time the dynamic changes is when Buffalo – which Carolina beat in the 2006 conference final – is in town and the arena hires extra security to deal with the inevitable fights with Sabres fans before and after the game. Other than that, the biggest problem for arena staff is getting people to pay extra when they take up more than one parking spot.

"If people take more than one space, we charge them for more than one space," said arena general manager Dave Olsen. "Some people don't like paying another $10, but there are some who say, 'Yeah, sure, charge me. I'm bringing my pool and having at it.' "

That's right – he said "pool." In the heat of a Raleigh spring, where the temperature can hit 30 degrees Celsius before the first round is over, fans have been known to do some crazy things to cool off, even if that means setting up a kids' wading pool next to the grill.

When the Hurricanes and N.C. State University combined with local government to build the RBC Center on a piece of property adjacent to N.C. State's football stadium, fiscal responsibility was the order of the day. If that meant building on the outskirts of Raleigh when the prevailing national trend was to build downtown, so be it.

In its first few years, the arena sat rather forlornly next to the highway, surrounded by acres of asphalt, while downtown Raleigh's renaissance gathered pace. The arena was barely completed before it began to look like a monument to missed opportunities.

Yet that very negative has become one of its strongest assets. Those parking lots have become home to the franchise's signature fan experience, something that would never be possible downtown. And it is a fan experience not to be missed.

The tents start popping up early. The parking lots "officially" open three hours before a game, but many arrive long before that; a haze of charcoal smoke soon follows. It's a football tradition, undertaken on these same lots during N.C. State's football season, but a hockey novelty, which helps give the in-game atmosphere at the RBC Center a unique flavor.

When the arena was tagged as the NHL's loudest during the 2002 playoffs, many skeptics scoffed that it had more to do with the acoustics than the fans. But no one was saying a word during Game 7 of the 2006 Cup final, when every fan in the building stood for the entire game. (And even if someone had said a word, no one would have heard it above the noise.)

That boisterousness starts in the parking lots, among the grills and kegs and street hockey games. And the Hurricanes players know it.

"They'll be out there all day sucking back a few beers," said captain Rod Brind'Amour before Carolina's first home game of the '09 playoffs. "They'll be ready to roll."

Sociologically, it's a fascinating phenomenon. Much has been made of how the Hurricanes bring together those of varying college allegiances in the Raleigh-Durham area, known to locals as the Triangle. But the party in the parking lots takes it one step further.

Over the past 20 years, the Triangle has exploded as "northerners" have arrived seeking jobs with companies such as Cisco and IBM. The influence of the tech industry turned a sleepy southern capital into a cosmopolitan regional power, just as the banking industry fed Charlotte's growth a few hours down the road. The transition hasn't always been easy, with the inevitable collisions between locals and transplants – the subdivision-studded Raleigh suburb of Cary has been dubbed "Containment Area for Relocated Yankees" – but hockey has hastened the relationship along.

Many of those transplants were already hockey fans when the Hurricanes moved to North Carolina in 1997 and the Canes have slowly but steadily added converted southerners to their fan base. Out in the arena parking lots, those two groups merge like no place else.

The tailgating tradition is so ingrained among Hurricanes fans, they even gathered when the team wasn't playing. On what would have been the final day of the 2004-05 season, Russell Kandel's usual group set up in their usual spot just east of the arena.

On that lovely spring day, they mourned a season lost to stupidity and arrogance, yet they would only have to wait a year to experience the highest high NHL fandom has to offer – watching their team win the Stanley Cup. ■

30. WIN A HOCKEY ARGUMENT IN A BAR

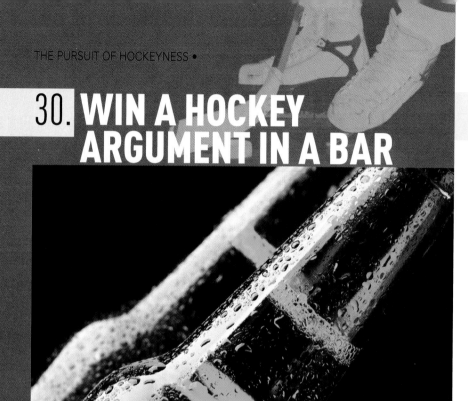

Who is the better player: Wayne Gretzky or Bobby Orr?

What about Mario Lemieux or Maurice Richard?

Does fighting belong in the game of hockey?

Wasn't that just a penalty?

There's nothing like watching a hockey game at your local watering hole, especially at a pub where hockey is king and the patrons come wearing the sweaters of their favorite teams. And you can be sure the longer you spend watching and talking hockey, the more likely it is you're going to get into a bar argument, trivial or not.

If you're going to engage in a hockey debate at a bar, make sure you come prepared and then stick to your guns – and always, *always* have a full plate of wings and a mug of ale at your disposal. You've got to make sure you're nourished and, besides, the tiffs tend to get more and more heated the longer they go on.

If you're going to argue Orr was a better player than Gretzky, for example, be sure to point out that Orr's plus-124 rating in 1970-71 is far and away the best plus-minus ever. And while everyone knows Gretzky piled up a ton of points, Orr remains the only defenseman to ever win the Art Ross Trophy as the NHL's scoring leader. (And he did it twice.)

If you're going to take Gretzky's side, simply mention the telltale fact that he has more assists (1,963) than anyone else has points. And, of course, the NHL's all-time leading playmaker just happens to be the NHL's all-time leading goal-scorer (894), too.

Here's what you *shouldn't* do: Come to the table and argue that one of them "revolutionized their position." Why not? Because they both did; really, that's why they're part of this "best player" debate in the first place.

If you can get your opponent to go on the defensive, you can set yourself up for the victory. Point out the sheer number of Stanley Cups that Gretzky won, and how he led one of the greatest sports dynasties ever in Edmonton. Or, focus on how Orr dominated and achieved things at his position that no one has accomplished before or since – or even approached – all while playing an injury-shortened 12-year career.

The later into the night it gets, the more belligerent the argument usually becomes. But like the pros who duke it out on the ice, there is sportsmanship and honor in a hockey debate; there's no need for emotions to escalate to the point where the two talking heads decide to "take it outside." What would that accomplish anyway? It would probably result in uneaten chicken wings and unfinished beer being left on the table, a crime in itself.

No, as heated as a hockey bar argument can become, it shouldn't digress into a bar fight. It's simply a case of passionate fans standing up and defending their opinions on the game. Even if the argument is futile, at least the two combatants can recognize they both love the game, a common ground for all hockey fanatics.

Ultimately, a winner is crowned when one side walks away in disgust; when one side overwhelms the other; or, as usually is the case, when one side simply becomes too inebriated. But before you go for the gloat, remember the sportsmanship and humble nature that the foundation of hockey is built on.

Winning the argument comes at a price, but it's easily affordable and enjoyable. Be sure to buy the next round of drinks if you win because no one likes a cheapskate and, besides, the late game has yet to start and a whole new battle of beliefs could kick in at any moment. ■

31. REVISIT YOUR FAVORITE OLD RINK

Tucked just off the main drag in Stratford, Ont., overlooking the scenic Avon River, is a hidden hockey gem.

On the corner of Lakeside and Morenz Drive (yes, named after Howie; more on that in a moment), you'll find the William Allman Memorial Arena, home of the Ontario Hockey Association's Jr. B Stratford Cullitons and a stomping ground for some of the game's greats for more than 85 years.

Passing through the front doors of the red-bricked front facade of the Allman, which had its name changed from the Stratford Classic Arena in 1996 to honor the building's longtime manager, is a large lobby adorned with trophy cases displaying memorabilia chronicling the city's rich hockey history.

A pair of staircases lead out of the concourse and back to the upper reaches of the arena itself. Dark-stained hardwood floors run the length of the ice and lead fans down to the two-seat wooden benches and a view of the action.

Hanging, bright lights radiate off the ice and illuminate the steel I-beams that hold an array of championship banners and create Allman's convex shape – a form that has led to its 'Old Barn' nickname.

As you file out of the arena and back into the foyer, a photo of the city's most famous player, Montreal Canadiens great Howie Morenz, looks down on you from above; a final reminder of the game's great history.

'The Stratford Streak' (or 'Mitchell Meteor,' depending on who you ask) played five years of junior and senior men's hockey in Stratford and began his Habs career the same season Allman opened, in 1923-24. While Morenz never actually skated on All-man ice, many other NHLers certainly have. George Armstrong, Bob Bailey, Hap Emms, Clarence 'Dolly' Dolson, Ray Getliffe, Joe Klukay, Danny Lewicki, Howie Meeker, Bill Touhey and Archie Wilcox are just a few of hockey's historical heavyweights who've skated through Stratford. More recently, Chris Pronger, Greg de Vries, Jeff Halpern, Ed Olczyk, Bryan Smolinski, Garth Snow and Tim Taylor have pulled on a Cullitons sweater before going on to NHL careers.

"To see the history of the players who have gone through that program and then went on further…It was great to be involved in that," said Norris Trophy winner and two-time Olympian Rob Blake, who played one season in Stratford as a 17-year-old in 1986-87.

Part of the rink's lore comes from the unparalleled success and local family connections of the Cullitons, a team born in 1975 that followed in the footsteps of the Nationals (1926-28), Majors (1938-40), Indians (1946-62), Krohlers (1946-51) and Warriors (1972-74).

The Cullitons are named after brothers Keith and George Culliton, who own a Stratford-based construction company. Up until 2007, a member of the Flanagan family acted as the team's GM, coach or both. During the 21 years Dinny Flanagan served as the club's GM – from 1975 to 1996 – the Cullitons had an overall record of 983-257-38, including 11 league championships. Dinny's son Denis' record as coach is similarly outstanding, leading the team to 11 titles and a 1,043-348-53 record over 24 years as coach (1984-2007), 11 of which were also spent as GM.

With crowds regularly exceeding 2,000 for Friday nights at the 'Old Barn,' Allman provides a unique hockey environment.

"Growing up playing in a rink like that was great," said Toronto Maple Leafs winger Boyd Devereaux, who spent two seasons with the Cullitons (1993-95). "There was always a lot of energy.

"We always had a lot of support and tradition, so there was definitely an advantage to playing at home. We were always one of the top drawing clubs, so other teams would get excited to play against us, which always added some extra intensity."

The thing Blake remembers most about games at Allman Arena is the noise.

"It's not a big building and it's got the wood seats and a low roof, so when it was filled it was nice and loud," Blake said. "The fans supported us tremendously when I was there."

If Stratford isn't a realistic trip, there are a number of other historic old arenas sure to provide a similar experience, including:

• Matthews Arena in Boston, home to Northeastern University's hockey teams. Opened in 1910.

• Hobey Baker Memorial Rink in Princeton, N.J., home to Princeton University's hockey teams. Opened in 1923.

• Yost Ice Arena in Ann Arbor, Mich., home to the University of Michigan's hockey teams. Opened in 1923.

• Galt Arena Gardens in Cambridge, Ont., home of the Jr. B's Winterhawks. Opened in 1922.

• Varsity Arena in Toronto, home to the University of Toronto's hockey teams. Opened in 1926.

• Hallenstadion in Zurich, Switzerland, home of the ZSC Lions. Opened in 1939.

Whether it's Allman or another aged barn of its ilk, and no matter if it's game of major junior or mite, when that final buzzer goes, pause for a moment before rising and take one last visual pass and one last deep, appreciative inhale of cold arena air.

A game played out on a stage of Allman's historical magnitude is more than the sum of goals; it's a tiny, but tremendously significant piece of hockey's rich history.

"It's one of those old-school rinks," Devereaux said, "it's a pretty special place."

32. STAY WARM AT A WINTER CLASSIC

Although there haven't been very many of them, the NHL's Winter Classic concept – an outdoor game at a stadium filled with tens of thousands of fans – has become an instant must-do for hockey aficionados.

Sure, the league has been blessed with ideal weather – clear and (very) crisp – for the Winter Classic games that have taken place in Edmonton, Buffalo and Chicago in recent years, but there's no guarantee Mother Nature will be so cooperative in the future.

That said, the way fans in all three cities responded to the prospect of freezing their jocks off in the stands while watching players skate in sub-arctic temperatures, it's small wonder NHL teams are lining up to stage future outdoor games in locales such as Michigan's Spartan Stadium, Boston's Fenway Park, New York's Yankee Stadium and numerous outdoor venues in Canada as well.

After playing in his first Winter Classic, former Chicago Blackhawks winger Martin Havlat understands what the fuss is all about.

"It's a lot of fun out there," said Havlat, who skated at Chicago's famed Wrigley Field on New Year's Day in 2009.

"It was cold…really, really cold. But the fans were great and you don't get to play outside all the time. I felt very lucky to be one of the guys who got to be part of something like that."

Suffice to say, fans in attendance shared Havlat's sentiments.

"To me, it was a total stroke of genius to get a game going at one of the most famous baseball stadiums there ever was," said Hawks supporter and native Chicagoan Darren Morgan, who was in attendance as the Blackhawks hosted the Detroit Red Wings. "Why they didn't think of this sooner is beyond me."

The first outdoor game, dubbed the Heritage Classic, took place in 2003 at Edmonton's Commonwealth Stadium, where the Oilers hosted the Montreal Canadiens. The spectacle immediately gave rise to one of hockey's most famous modern-day photos, as Habs goalie Jose Theodore came out clad with a Canadiens toque atop his goalie mask. Theodore's unique combination of headgear aptly exemplified the contrast of big-league shine and outdoor innocence the game embodied.

The Winter Classic has become a showpiece game for the league and represents a tantalizing taste of sporting crossover. We've already witnessed Sidney Crosby score a shootout winner in Buffalo at the same venue where Jim Kelly led the NFL's Bills to four straight Super Bowl appearances in the early 1990s. Imagine seeing Boston's Milan Lucic hammer an opponent in the shadow of the same Green Monster that Carlton Fisk's famous foul-pole homer cleared to win Game 6 of the 1975 World Series for the Boston Red Sox.

Any fan thinking of attending a future Winter Classic is advised to bundle up and prepare for the worst of weather conditions. But they also ought to bring plenty of passion – because being part of a massive spectacle demands nothing less.

"The weather is absolutely brutal, especially up here in the upper deck," said Jane Millwood, a longtime Hawks fan who also was in attendance at the Wrigley Field game. "But the wind chill isn't going to stop us from having a great time!"

33. BE A WEEKEND HOCKEY WARRIOR

Better take Monday off work, because you're not going to be in any shape to be productive.

One thing most hockey players have done at some point in their recreational league "careers" is play back-to-back games, or back-to-back-to-back, or something thereabouts.

It's the weekend hockey tournament. If you haven't played six games in three days – on a total of four hours' sleep – you haven't lived.

Attrition, the ugly stepsister of fatigue, is the name of the game in these tournaments. Attrition, not just because you played one game on Friday night, then headed to the arena bar before playing three times on Saturday and twice more on Sunday, but because you basically live at the rink for three days. Only the strong survive.

Drying your equipment in the sun if you're playing during the summer, or playing in cold, wet gear if you're not. Catching 40 winks in the car between games. Surviving on arena hot dogs and, if you're lucky, a buffet breakfast on Saturday and Sunday mornings. These are all part and parcel of the weekend warrior tourney. And they're awesome. There is simply no substitute for getting together with your boys – or girls – and leaving it all on the ice.

And then, of course, there's the fine line many walk between having a good time and having too good a time.

Brody Purser is a clean-cut, 28-year-old department manager for Fairmont Hotels by day and a brash, Billy Smith-esque goaltender for his men's league team, the Galaxy Troopers, by night.

Purser has been playing hockey for more than two decades and counts winning three provincial championships in a row during his minor hockey days as his proudest on-ice accomplishments. But championships are no longer what hockey is all about for him.

"The bonding and down time between games is what I remember most," said Purser, when asked about weekend hockey tournaments. "The poker tournaments, the bar scene, the hot tub with a beer, the 'Drunk Award' given out at the end of the night.

"The smell of your equipment in the hotel room after three days was bad enough to put the room out of commission permanently. I felt awful for the hotel maids."

So, not exactly the wholesome hockey experience he had as a youngster while winning those championships with the Mt. Brydges (Ont.) Cougars. But then again, rec-league hockey isn't about glory; it's about having a good time.

"Those crazy tournament moments become memories forever," Purser said.

In six-game, weekend-long segments, it's fair to say Purser and his pals/teammates have created many lifetime memories. One may even have cost them the tournament.

"The night before the final, our team decided to hide the other team's U-Haul, carrying all their equipment, in the woods," he said. "The look on their faces the next morning as we drove by was priceless."

Unfortunately, karma got the best of Purser's team on Sunday. The opposition found their gear, put it on, and won the championship game in overtime. It's the only time Purser's squad has ever lost that particular weekend tourney. But they'll be back again next year, pursuing weekend hockey glory once again. ■

34. ATTEND A FRANCHISE'S FIRST NHL PLAYOFF GAME

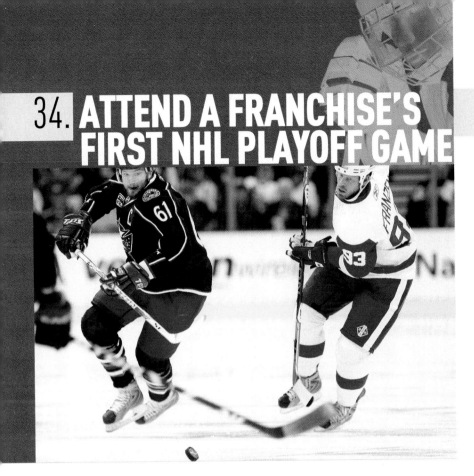

It's the hockey equivalent of that first glass of water after crossing the desert – and frothing fans of teams playing their first-ever playoff game can't wait to let the high-intensity action spill all over them.

Unless the NHL is planning to expand in the near future, the odds of being in attendance for a franchise's first post-season foray are slim indeed – especially since the Columbus Blue Jackets (a.k.a. the last current franchise to not host a post-season game) played their first one – against the mighty Detroit Red Wings – on April 21, 2009.

Nevertheless, if the opportunity ever arises, drop whatever it is you're doing, rush directly to your local ticket broker and start dropping $20 bills until you attain arena access.

It's worth the hassle. Several THN staff members were in Columbus on that fateful April evening – and even after a seven-and-a-half-hour drive, border crossing and currency exchange, each one of them would do it all over again.

Why? Well, how many other chances are you going to get to see long-suffering fans rewarded for their patronage of a team? How often will you get to hear the deafening roar of an NHL arena experiencing, for the very first time, the difference between a regular season contest and a playoff game?

Not many, and not often. And if you still don't believe how much fun a franchise's first post-season tilt can be, just ask Blue Jackets coach Ken Hitchcock.

"This (was) a huge day for this organization...and a huge day for this city," Hitchcock said. "I think there's a lot of people in this city who thought this day would never come, where we have a home playoff game.

"We're a legitimate franchise in the National Hockey League, and I don't think anybody considers you a legitimate franchise until you play in the playoffs. We're there now."

Hitchcock arrived in Columbus in November of 2006, a time when fan confidence in the foundering franchise was at an all-time low.

When the team's on-ice fortunes turned around in less than two years, however, the excitement among Columbusites – who tend to be consumed with college sports at nearby Ohio State University – returned in a hurry.

"I think everybody is happy and proud," said Hitchcock of his team's historic achievement. "The buzz in (Columbus) is that we matter again now...We're really the strong fabric of the city again, which I think is really important for us.

"We matter in this city, and we have our time of season just like Ohio State University has its time, but we matter right now, and that's the most important thing."

35. WATCH THE WOMEN PLAY

The first thing you must realize when it comes to women's hockey is that even at its highest level, the quality of play is equivalent to Jr. B. Don't let anyone tell you differently.

But you shouldn't confuse quality of play with excitement level, because when Canada and the U.S. are playing with a title on the line in the World Championship or Olympics, women's hockey is every bit as intense, competitive and chock full of compelling storylines and intrigue as a Stanley Cup final.

To put it mildly, these two teams do not like each other. The Americans think the Canadians have no class because of the way they carry on during the national anthem after they win a medal. The Canadians look down on the Americans as a bunch of college co-eds who think their sweat doesn't stink.

They play each other all year long. Canadian girls cross the border to play U.S. college hockey and American women come up to Canada after graduation to play professionally in the Canadian Women's and Western Women's Leagues. They know each other very well and they have a healthy dislike for one another.

Makes you wonder what might happen if the International Ice Hockey Federation ever saw fit to allow bodychecking in women's hockey. Of course, there is an awful lot of "incidental contact" that doesn't look so incidental a lot of the time.

You want to see puck battles? Watch Canada's Hayley Wickenheiser try to cycle the puck along the boards while Team USA defenseman Angela Ruggiero tries to steal it away. You want to see skill? Jayna Hefford of Canada and Julie Chu of the U.S. with the puck on their sticks is as good as it gets.

At the World Championship in 1997 in Kitchener, Ont., the championship final between Canada and the U.S. went into overtime. At one point during the proceedings, Shelley Looney of Team USA went down to block a shot…with her face. As it turns out, when a puck is coming off a stick from short range, it doesn't matter a whole lot that you're wearing a visor. Looney's face was busted up real good, but she missed just one shift before getting back out there, leading those in attendance to wonder whether her state of mind wasn't synonymous with her last name.

A number of countries – like, the rest of them – have a lot of work to do in order to catch up to Canada and the U.S. in women's hockey, but that might just be the key to the rivalry. If more teams forced their way into it, perhaps Canada and the U.S. might not be so focused on each other all the time. With a few notable exceptions, everyone knows the route to gold in the World Championship and the Olympics runs right through the 49th parallel. And no matter which border the gold medal crosses to get to its destination, you can count on a hard-fought contest. ■

36. SEEK OUT HOCKEY'S BIRTHPLACE

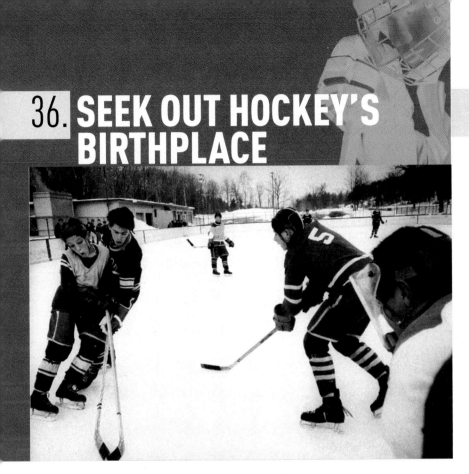

Eastern Canada has many natural sights, sounds and earthly wonders which attract thousands of tourists every year. But if you're a devoted hockey fan, there are three areas in particular you'll want to circle on your map: Kingston, Ont., Montreal and Windsor, N.S. – the three places that claim to be the cradle of the game.

Start out in Kingston, which was named the birthplace of hockey in 1943 by the Canadian Amateur Hockey Association. The first game on record in Kingston occurred in 1886 between Queen's University and Royal Military College and was contested with a rubber ball that had been crudely cut into a square. The International Hockey Hall of Fame is located in Kingston, as are the Ontario League's Frontenacs, so there's plenty to see whether you're a fan of past or present-day players.

After that, make your way east, leaving Ontario and entering Quebec, where Montreal and all its rich hockey history beckons. There, you can visit the site (Victoria Skating Rink) that the International Ice Hockey Federation recognizes as the arena where the first organized hockey game was played in 1875. This time around, the puck was wood. (Unfortunately, the location is now a parking lot, but if you head over to the Bell Centre, there are plaques celebrating the IIHF's recognition.)

Like Kingston and Montreal, Windsor is proud to point out its longstanding connection to the game. Although the Society for International Hockey Research found no evidence to support Windsor's claim that a crude form of the game originated between students of King's College School – Canada's first college – in 1800, on a frozen Nova Scotia lake called Long Pond, people from the area will be more than happy to convince you otherwise. Hockey began to take form when men who played "hurley," a game contested on a field, tried taking their sport to the ice.

The best part about being a fan touring Eastern Canada is, you don't really have to make a choice at all as to the specific geographic origin of the game. If you get out to see all three places, you can't go wrong. ■

37. OBSERVE THE ALLAN CUP TRADITION

Long johns are standard apparel for hockey fans in frigid arenas of the Canadian prairies. Supporters of the Trail (B.C.) Smoke Eaters, winners of two Allan Cups, took things a step further.

The season after the Smokies won their first Canadian senior men's championship in 1937-38, a band dressed up in long underwear, old Smoke Eaters sweaters and goofy hats and started following the team around and rocking rinks with their music.

The Al's Your Pal Underwear Band, led by team booster Al Tognotti, was particularly effective at throwing visiting teams off their game in Trail.

"There is no doubt the underwear band was the deciding factor at numerous games, both home and away," claims a story on the team website. "Over the years, they travelled throughout the Kootenays as well as Kelowna, Vancouver, Calgary, Penticton and Spokane."

The band was in attendance at five Allan Cup championships, with the most memorable occurring in 1960 when the Smokies lost to the Chatham (Ont.) Maroons. The Maroons were led by the unbeatable goaltending of Cesare Maniago, who just happened to be a native of Trail.

The highlight for the band, however, was welcoming back the Smokies in 1961 when they returned from Europe as world champions. Thousands of fans greeted the team as they were paraded around the city on a fire truck – with the underwear band leading the way, of course.

Al Tognotti died in 1985. But the band, with the help of young musicians from the Trail and Rossland school bands, continues to entertain fans at junior games today.

The Allan Cup, which was won for the first time in 1909 by the Ottawa Cliffsides, was once almost as important to Canadians living outside Quebec and Ontario as the Stanley Cup itself. It was donated by Sir H. Montague Allan, a banker and ship owner who loved sports, and became emblematic of senior men's hockey supremacy in Canada.

Allan Cup history includes a multitude of colorful incidents. Hockey historian Glen Goodhand notes that when the Hamilton Tigers and Winnipeg Selkirks clashed in the first game of the 1919 final, two gamecocks, decorated with ribbons bearing the black-and-yellow colors of the Tigers and the red-and-white of the Selkirks, commenced a competition of their own. Fortunately, the feathered mascots had been stripped of their talons and, amidst copious flying plumage, settled for a draw. The Tigers won the hockey battle to bring Hamilton its only Allan Cup.

For many years, the Allan Cup champion was selected to represent Canada at the World Championship the following season. The Penticton (B.C.) Vees distinguished themselves by shutting out the Soviet Union 5-0 in the 1955 gold medal game, restoring Canadian pride after the Soviets had humbled the Sr. B East York Lyndhursts from Toronto in the '54 final.

Connie Broden is the answer to one of the game's toughest trivia questions. The question is: Who is the only player to win a World Championship gold medal and the Stanley Cup in the same season?

Just six weeks after leading the Whitby (Ont.) Dunlops to the gold medal in Oslo, Norway, in 1958, Broden joined the Montreal Canadiens and got his named etched on Lord Stanley's mug when the Habs downed Boston in six games in the final. Broden scored 12 goals in seven games at the worlds.

Recently, the city of Belleville, Ont., marked the 50th anniversary of the Belleville McFarlands' World Championship gold medal in Prague, Czechoslovakia, in 1959.

Many of the imports recruited by the McFarlands in their drive to the '58 Allan Cup title ended up making Belleville their home. In fact, there was a time when almost every minor hockey team in the city was coached by a former Mac. Three children of team captain Floyd Crawford – Marc, Bobby and Louie – went on to play in the NHL.

Today, the Allan Cup championship is conducted under a tournament format, with the final game televised. Forty-eight Allan Cup champions have come from Ontario, with B.C. and Manitoba next on the list with 10 champs each. The United States has produced seven Allan Cup winners – four from Washington and three from Minnesota. The Spokane (Wsh.) Jets (later Chiefs) and Warroad (Minn.) Lakers competed in Canadian leagues.

Brian Sutter, of hockey's famed first family and the NHL's coach of the year in 1991, guided the 2009 Allan Cup-champion Bentley (Alta.) Generals. Similar to Trail's underwear band, Generals fans call themselves "The Army" and follow the team wherever it plays.

Don Robertson, the GM of the Dundas (Ont.) Real McCoys, who have been trying to capture the Allan Cup for the past decade, said he'd prefer to revert to the old system of having a best-of-7 final series.

"With all due respect to Hockey Canada, it (the tournament format) is a far less than perfect way to pick the best senior team in Canada," Robertson said. "To win the Cup (today), we'd have to play five games in five days. That's not the best way to showcase how good senior hockey is."

Over the years, senior clubs have loaded up with former NHL players in an attempt to bolster their roster. Shortly after competing his 10-year NHL career, goalie Don Edwards joined the Brantford (Ont.) Mott's Clamatos team and carried it to an Allan Cup title in 1987.

Former NHL star Theoren Fleury suited up for the host Steinbach (Man.) North Stars in 2009.

"Growing up on the prairies, we didn't have much contact with NHL players," Fleury said. "We looked up to the guys who played senior hockey."

The North Stars didn't make the final, but the 40-year-old Fleury, who owns a Stanley Cup ring and Olympic gold medal, led the team in scoring with two goals and seven points in four games.

"I certainly wasn't there just to put in time, that's for sure," he said.

38. BILLET A MAJOR JUNIOR PLAYER

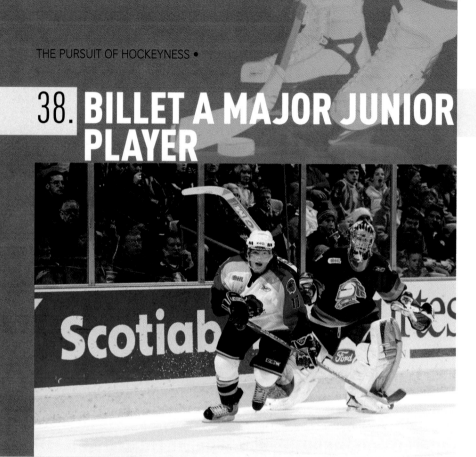

Ever answered an ad in the newspaper? How about one asking if you'll let a stranger move into your home for less than the going rate of rent? Now make that a teenaged stranger; one you'll have to cook for, monitor his studies and make sure he's home safe by curfew. Not exactly an everyday happening, but that's exactly what Rob Cowell did.

You see, Cowell and his family billet Bulls, as in the Ontario League's Belleville Bulls. And it all began with an ad in the local daily.

Each season, all 60 major junior teams in the Canadian Hockey League – consisting of the OHL, Western League and Quebec League – count on citizens to open their homes to players; it's a tradition, one the Cowells took to with some trepidation.

"My daughter was, like, 'Nope. Nope. Nope.' " Cowell said. "She was six at the time, so she was freaking out about it. We were worried because we only have the one child. You don't want to make her feel like she's been pushed aside for this other kid coming in.

"There were a lot of nerves, because you're opening your house to a kid you've never met before, plus the 19 other guys he plays with. Not all junior hockey players are angels. It was a serious, 'Do we really want to do this?' "

But that first new housemate – Matt Beleskey, an eventual Bulls team captain and a fourth round pick of Anaheim (112th overall) in 2006 – and Cowell's daughter hit it off immediately. And even though he's now an American League pro with a couple of NHL games under his belt, Beleskey still calls Cowell's daughter, who is 12, every now and again.

"He's making sure the boys aren't calling and all that stuff," Cowell said. "He's still very involved in what she's doing. We've been very fortunate with the relationship we've built with him."

But Cowell hasn't forgotten the early days, when there were worries on both sides of the equation. He remembers looking out his window the day Beleskey was due to arrive and spying a blue Suburban driving by his house a few times, "nice and slow." Later that day, Cowell met Beleskey's father, Joe, and the two began talking.

"Do you have a blue Suburban?" asked Cowell, not long into their conversation. "Were you kind of stalking my house?"

The answer was yes. The elder Beleskey was trying to get an idea of where his 16-year-old boy was going to be staying during his first extended period away from home. Beleskey ended up staying for four years, growing into a man right in the Cowell house. And, it turned out, in the house of some of their neighbors.

You see, the Cowells started a trend on their street and in their neighborhood. Before long, others around them – five in total – had been convinced to billet Bulls as well, and the Cowells' street became Ground Zero for post-game get-togethers with players, billets and parents.

"Basically, they saw the relationship we had with Matt and his parents," said Cowell of his friends and neighbors. "There were three of them we got in. And my sister, I talked her into it as well."

And it wasn't long before Saturday nights became Bull bashes, with the billets alternating as hosts.

"It was the best time ever," said Mike Murphy, a two-time OHL goalie of the year who billeted on the Cowells' street for two years. "Everyone wants to be in that area. It's a street with solid billets who all get along with each other and the players. We're all a great group of friends.

"Billets are everything. I love being at the rink, but I love being at home, too. They're great friends of mine."

Added Cowell: "The players would come back and the parents would come back. And we'd just sit around until whatever time people left or whatever time the boys had curfew. It was a unique bond."

It's that bond that has made billeting players a very special experience for the Cowells and their friends. Sure, there were instances of trouble – tomfoolery, actually, is probably a better word for it.

"Just average teenage stuff," Cowell said. "They push the limits because they know they're not at home. Sometimes there is stuff you kind of let slide a bit, but it depends on the kids and the house, I guess."

Cowell said it works the other way, too. Just as not every junior player is an angel, neither is every billet. And not everyone billets for the right reasons. But for the most part, that's not the case. Generally the kids are great, as are the homes they move into for the season.

"The experience of being with the kids and just being a part of their lives is the main thing," said Cowell when asked the best part of billeting. "It's the relationship. You see these guys away from hockey, they've graduated and they're moving on and yet they still come up and give you a great big hug. That's the good part, that's the heartwarming part."

Added Mark Simone, Murphy's billet: "You're in a parenting role, but at the same time you're kind of looking up to them because of what they're accomplishing and what they're working towards. It's a neat feeling."

Cowell remembers asking another billet, one who had been taking players in for 20 years or so, how he dealt with the kids moving on.

"He said, 'You hug 'em,' " Cowell remembered, " 'and then you cry like a baby because they're like your own kids.' "

The Cowells are still billeting, still preparing teenaged boys to succeed on the ice and off of it. Not all are destined to be NHL players; in fact, very few will be. But Cowell hopes one day, if the need arises, someone will return the favor.

"I look at it this way," he said, "if my daughter were to go somewhere, billet somewhere, to play sports or whatever…I would just want her to get to a family that was doing the same thing." ■

39. TRADE DEADLINE DAY, ALL DAY LONG

It is a day that has come to be adored by fans, and it's impossible to turn on a television without tuning into umpteen hours of consecutive coverage. From meager beginnings, it has grown into one of the most anticipated, most talked about and most overhyped days of the NHL season.

It is: Trade. Deadline. Day.

It's the last chance for NHL teams to improve their fortunes heading into the playoffs; as such, it's a day to dream for all you armchair GMs out there, from Anaheim to Edmonton and from New York to Nashville.

"I think guessing and wondering and predicting and trying to figure out how to make your favorite team better has become as popular as watching the game itself for some people," said James Duthie, the host of all things NHL on TSN, the go-to sports network for the majority of fans on deadline day.

For many of the game's followers, the late February or early March date already is an annual off-day. Even if physically at work, the 21st-century age of communication can transform any Internet-enabled cubicle into a 10-by-10 hockey hideaway, complete with streamed video and up-to-the-second trade trackers.

"In the old days, you'd go to work, come home at 5 o'clock, eat dinner and watch the 6 o'clock news to find out if there was a trade," Duthie said. "Now, people are sitting in their cubbies and hoping their boss doesn't come by because they're all watching what's going on."

To fully appreciate the deadline-day coverage, however, one must enjoy the proceedings, from start to 14-hour finish, from the comfort of their own couch, beyond the reach of any bosses' prying eyes.

If you haven't experienced an entire day of NHL wheeling and dealing, it's time you came down with a case of "puckitis" and used up one of your sick days. Heck, why not spread your newfangled disease to a couple of buddies and throw a Super Bowl-esque NHL Trade Deadline Day party?

"Like I always say on the air," Duthie said, "it's like the unofficial national Canadian holiday now."

Fans and media types aren't alone in watching all of the deadline-day drama play out on the digital stage.

"You have the TV on, you're trying to keep one eye and ear there to see what, if anything, is going on, because that's the reality for the manager," said former Tampa Bay Lightning GM Jay Feaster. "We're watching the programming just as much as anybody is."

While organizations try to notify just-traded players themselves, it's not unusual for NHLers to catch wind of the deal before their GM has had the chance to phone.

"There were a lot of rumors going around the dressing room leading up to the 2009 deadline and on the actual day, many of us gathered at the rink to watch the coverage on TV," said Phoenix Coyotes young gun Viktor Tikhonov. "The interesting thing about watching the trade deadline with all the guys is that when your team is active, anything can happen.

"Daniel Carcillo was actually in the trainer's room reading a magazine when we saw he had been dealt to Philadelphia. We yelled over to him, 'Carce, you've been traded!' So he came in and was like, 'Well, see you guys later.' "

But is the furor on deadline day mostly due to the player moves, or is it more to do the media saturation? After all, what used to be a quick update – *"Some news from the NHL as Edmonton traded Dan Lacouture to Pittsburgh for Sven Butenschon…"*

(the first trade on deadline day in 2001, as you'll surely recall) – has morphed into more coverage than most news outlets afford a national election. Canada's three cable-sports channels – TSN, Sportsnet and The Score – each offer all-day, comprehensive coverage and in-depth analysis, complete with talking heads from the media realm as well as former coaches, GMs and players. Up-to-the-minute rumors and trade speculation, report cards for all 30 NHL teams, preferred destinations for high-profile players, hired guns who are available and willing to relocate…on and on it goes. Simply put, coverage of the NHL's trade deadline has become a made-for-TV epic that addresses every last possible angle.

"That's part of it," Feaster said. "I think it's something that has grown into almost a media creation.

"Teams now feel pressure if they don't do something, they're in trouble. Your fans want to know why you didn't do anything and your ownership wants to know why you didn't make any moves."

With so much attention focused on deadline day, it has become a cure-all of sorts, a chance for teams to dispatch unwanted players and untenable contracts while bringing in young talent that will carry the franchise into a successful future.

"There's a belief that on trade deadline day, whatever problems your team has can get solved," Feaster said.

"You can find that one missing piece. And even though it's been proven 95 percent of the time that it rarely happens, it's our human nature to want to believe if you're a contending team that you're going to add the piece that's going to take you to the promised land. So, it's kind of a day for the optimists of the world."

And being a part of that madness, for just one day, is a must for even a casual fan of the game. ▪

40. EXPERIENCE THE PURITY OF POND HOCKEY

Today, anyone can play the game they love, be it in early January or late July. Technology over the decades has allowed hockey to be taken indoors and transplanted to cities such as Los Angeles and Miami, where the local residents have never seen so much as an inch of real snow on their doorstep. There is, however, one true form of hockey that has stood the test of time and transcends any other.

Pond hockey.

The first game of pond hockey between a father and son (or daughter) is an experience that shouldn't be missed and can never be forgotten. It usually happens when the child is five or six years old, but already in love with the game. He has played since he was but a few years old (knocking sticks and pucks on the ice at the local arena qualifies as playing) and he has learned how to skate, albeit hesitantly. He hasn't learned how to raise the puck, make a tape-to-tape pass or a host of other hockey habits. But he desperately wants to.

This particular weekend, his father suggests they go to the pond a few blocks from home and play a little hockey. It's a beautiful winter day and the energetic child is only too excited to get outside.

The father and son spend the first half-hour or so shoveling the ice – well, father shovels, son "helps" – and then drop a puck to begin play. It's just the two of them, but at stake is the Stanley Cup and neither is willing to lose their chance to hoist it in the bitter cold.

Years later, neither remember what was talked about, if anything. In fact, very few details of that day remain besides the big picture of it all. The child does, however, recall taking a shot and watching it go wide of the net – which consisted of two shoes on the ice, about six feet apart – and the puck bouncing over a snowbank. The son remembers climbing over the "boards" of snow that couldn't have been more than six or seven inches tall and flicking the puck to get it back into play; in doing so, he had raised it over the snow.

At that moment, the son looked up at his father, with eyes only a child doing something brilliant and magical for the first time could give, and said, "I did it, I raised the puck!" He doesn't remember his father's response, nor does it matter, but he knows that was the moment he truly became a hockey player.

Today, one can still lace 'em up on any local pond, right across the country, and skate all winter long, whether it's on the Rideau Canal in Ottawa or a coast-to-coast breakaway on the St. Lawrence River that starts in Quebec and ends in Newfoundland. The game, though, and what it has meant to countless kids, teens, and adults around the world, remains the same.

You can have your fancy multiplex arenas and heated benches all you want, but ask any father and son who have experienced a wintry afternoon skating on a frozen pond, and they'll tell you that they'll be a few blocks down the road, raising pucks over snowbanks. ■

41. MEET DON CHERRY

To some, he's a scourge to the sport, a loud-mouthed braggart with semi-hateful views. To others, he's a shining beacon and defender of all that is right and traditional about the great game of hockey.

The reality is probably somewhere in the middle.

Don Cherry is one of the most famous figures in hockey history, a living legend who was voted No. 7 on the all-time list of "Greatest Canadians" in a CBC contest in 2004 (three spots ahead of Wayne Gretzky). He was well-loved as coach of the Boston Bruins in the 1970s, but his star really took off as he carved out his legacy on Coach's Corner, the iconic first intermission show on *Hockey Night in Canada*.

Always active in the hockey community, it's actually not that difficult to find Cherry in public, or to engage the affable commentator. He attends several minor midget hockey games every week with his son in the Toronto area and makes it a point to never turn down autograph requests from children.

"I spent 22 years in the minors," Cherry said. "And nobody knew I was alive."

In deference to the kids playing on the ice, however, Cherry does tell autograph-seeking tykes to wait until a stoppage in play.

"I tell 'em, 'Wait for the whistle,' " Cherry said. "I know they can't wait for the game to end, or even the period."

In public, there are few quiet moments for the legendary personality. His trademark flashy suits, collars and ties might be absent, but it's not hard to spot the most recognizable man in Canada, even when he's in street clothes. 'Grapes' always attracts attention and he deals with it appropriately.

Because of that willingness to be accessible to his public, Cherry is almost always a hero when he comes to town, even when he was coaching a miserable Mississauga Ice Dogs team, the major junior franchise he helped found in the late 1990s. Cherry recalled his first long road trip after the team got off to a poor start one season.

"I thought the crowd was going to give it to me for sure," he recalled.

Much to Cherry's surprise, the boos and catcalls didn't come – and he would never forget that gesture from the hockey-loving public.

While his on-air hyperbole is somewhat muted 1-on-1, his convictions are as real as they come. Cherry loves talking hockey and he truly believes what he says.

Catch him on the street and he'll more than likely have at least a handshake or an autograph for you, although he doesn't like to help out collectors looking for a quick buck – Cherry personalizes signings and runs his messages into the signature so the dedication can't be erased by unscrupulous business types.

"Wayne Gretzky used to bend the hockey cards when he signed them," he laughed.

And Cherry prefers to sign rather than pose. "Something's always wrong with the camera," he said.

All in all, there are very few rules in engaging one of Canada's most engaging personalities. And meeting the man we've all watched every Saturday night is a memorable event that every hockey fan should experience. ■

42. SKATE ON NHL ICE

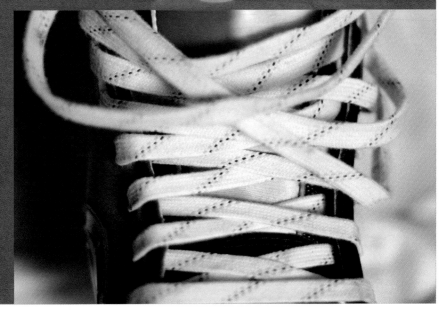

Michael Ulmer is fortunate. Why? Well, despite limited athletic ability, he's had the opportunity to skate on NHL ice surfaces a number of times in his life.

But only once did he get to wear a pro's gear while doing it.

Ulmer, a longtime hockey writer and former staff member at The Hockey News, was granted this unique opportunity during the 1999 NHL All-Star Game in Tampa Bay.

He knew that the media members covering the event traditionally get together for an early-morning shinny game at some point during the weekend, but didn't anticipate he'd be able to take part. Once he got there and realized it was something he had time for, the next hurdle was finding some equipment.

A conversation with Mats Sundin, the Toronto Maple Leafs captain at the time, solved the problem in a hurry.

"I just happened to mention it to him, just in passing, and he said, 'Why don't you use my equipment?' " recalled Ulmer, now a senior writer for Maple Leaf Sports and Entertainment. "My esteem for Mats as a person has always been high and it certainly grew that day."

After the 6-foot-5 Sundin loaned the bulk of his equipment, Ulmer – all 5-foot-11 of him – was able to piece together a few items from other sources and hit the ice. But rather than being inspired by dawning the armor of one of the NHL's best players, Ulmer was worried his everyman attributes might infect Sundin.

"My biggest fear was that my flop sweat would filter into his equipment, but he scored a goal a couple games after the All-Star Game, so thankfully that didn't happen," Ulmer chuckled.

Ulmer, it seems, underestimated his hockey ability. Another foray onto big-league ice a couple of seasons later, at a charity event, saw Ulmer have the chance to go 1-on-1 with Curtis Joseph during the goalie's first stint with the Toronto Maple Leafs. Letting little kids put pucks past him was one thing, but you have to wonder how anxious Joseph was to let a Toronto sportswriter slip one to the back of the net.

"As soon as he saw it was me, he charged right out and did the two-pad stack and, in a rare moment of athletic prowess, I put it right in the top corner," Ulmer happily recalled.

"I learned two things that day. The first was maybe I was a little better athlete than I thought and the second was, maybe Toronto was going to need a bit better goaltending in the playoffs."

While skating on the same ice surface as NHL stars is obviously a thrill – one that every hardcore fan should pursue – Ulmer said it's incredible how quickly the experience becomes about the act, not the stage.

"The biggest thing you notice is once you're playing, you really do forget where you are and just focus on the game," he said. "Once you get into the game, it's basically the same as if you were playing down at the local arena in a small town.

"The moments I notice more are when you're sitting on the bench looking around or in the visiting team's dressing room thinking, 'I wonder how many great players have stood in this shower or dressed in this stall?' "

43. FIND YOURSELF (A RIVALRY) IN EUROPE

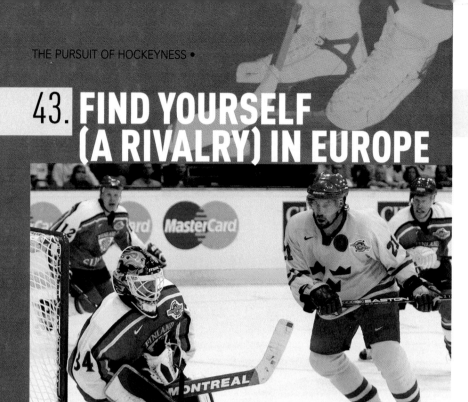

To see a derby in almost any sport anywhere in Europe is guaranteed to be good fun, for the most part, for most people. Especially for the winners.

The Swiss and the Germans have had their battles over the years, as have the Czechs and the Slovaks, but no European derby has the level of intensity or sense of purpose as the one between Finland and Sweden.

Simply put, the Finns and Swedes don't particularly like each other. Or, they do, but it's more of a love-hate relationship: The Finns love to hate the Swedes, the Swedes hate to love the Finns. And for that reason alone, it's worth the time and effort to travel to Tampere or Ornskoldsvik to take in a European rivalry for the ages.

Two hundred years ago, Finland was a part of Sweden – and Swedish remains an official language of Finland to this day. Sweden is a little bigger, better known in the world, they have more pop stars, they've had Volvo and IKEA, and they had Borje Salming, Ulf Sterner, Anders Hedberg and Kent Nilsson. And man, they had Tre Kronor, the hockey team.

The first official game the Finnish national team ever played was against Sweden in Helsinki in 1929. The score? Sweden, 8-1. In 1933, Finland's national team played its first game beyond its own borders, venturing over to Stockholm. The score? Sweden, 11-1.

It took Finland a few decades to catch up with Sweden, but by the 1970s, every game was a toss-up. Finland could go through an entire World Championship losing to the likes of East Germany, Holland, Italy and Poland, but against Sweden, they'd show up and they'd show them.

"The Swedes were always better than us, they were more skilled and played better as a team, but…you always want to beat Sweden," said Hannu Kapanen, a former national team player and Team Finland's coach at the 2002 World Junior Championship.

"Why? Oh, it's everything about them. The language, the way they feel superior…Finns always wanted to kick their royal butts."

Even the fact that Finns and Swedes battle together for the Stanley Cup in the NHL hasn't made the rivalry any easier for the players, according to Sami Kapanen, the former NHLer and Team Finland's captain at the 2009 World Championship (and, as Hannu's son, a second-generation Team Finland player).

"The Swedes are great teammates in the NHL, but of course (playing against Sweden) is a must-win game. It's especially sweet to kick them out of the World Championship."

What has made the Finns angrier, and the Swedes more confident is the fact Finland rarely seems to find a way to beat Sweden. At the 1986 World Championship, the Finns led Sweden 4-2 with a minute left in the game. For Finland, winning that last game of the tournament would have also meant winning their first-ever medal at the international level.

"We had a special play for the faceoff, but it failed completely," said Hakan Sodergren, one of the Swedes on the ice during the final minute. "However, it failed so completely that it turned into a genius play. The guy who took the faceoff, Anders Carlsson, missed what he was supposed to do and found himself wide open in front of the net."

Goal. Forty seconds left, and Finland is suddenly clinging to a 4-3 lead.

You can guess what happened next. Sweden won the center-ice faceoff, played it back to their own blueline where Robert Nordmark fired a long pass straight to the tape of Carlsson's stick, sending him in on a breakaway. Goal. It's 4-4. No medal for Finland – but a silver for Sweden.

Variations on that 1986 game have been repeated several times over the years, making the Finns desperate enough to proclaim themselves the Donald Ducks of the hockey world, the ones with the worst luck. And of course, the Swedes are the lucky-duck antagonist, the cousin who continually finds good fortune.

Finland's biggest victory on the international stage came at the 1995 World Championship, when they beat Sweden in the gold medal game – in Stockholm, no less – and stole the host country's parade. (In a show of sportsmanship, the Swedes let the Finns use their parade route and official tournament song.)

But mostly, it's been about the Swedes "keeping the family hierarchy intact," as Sodergren puts it.

In 1991, Mats Sundin tied the game against Finland, bringing Sweden back from a 4-2 deficit to a 4-4 draw. Sweden went on to win the World Championship; Finland finished fifth.

In 2003, Finland hosted the World Championship and the Finns had a 5-1 lead on Sweden in the second period of the quarterfinal. The home crowd was going wild, the stands were covered in blue-and-white flags while the blue-and-yellow Swedes sank in their seats.

But then, Sweden scored.

The arena went silent, with only one man, obviously Swedish, standing up, raising both of his arms into the air.

Then, Sweden got another one. More silence. Once again, just the lone Swede stood up, acting as a human red light for the people sitting on the opposite side from the Finnish net.

Sweden scored three more times in the third period and went on to win 6-5. Remember, the game was played in Finland, making the loss all the more bitter.

In Finland, that game is known as the "5-1 game." In Sweden, it's the "6-5 game."

After the contest, Joakim Arhammar, one of the happy Swedes in the arena, was approached by three big Finns, all wearing black leather vests and sunglasses, looking like Scandinavian Hell's Angels. Arhammar moved back slightly to let the men pass him, his smile not as wide anymore.

When the first Finn was about to pass Arhammar, he extended his hand to him, and said, in broken English, "Congratulations." (Because Finns in general simply hate studying and speaking Swedish). His two buddies followed suit.

"I think I'd better put a jacket on," Arhammar said, hiding his yellow Sweden shirt, not wanting to rub the Finns the wrong way.

Until next time. ◼

44. SEE THE MAPLE LEAFS IN MONTREAL

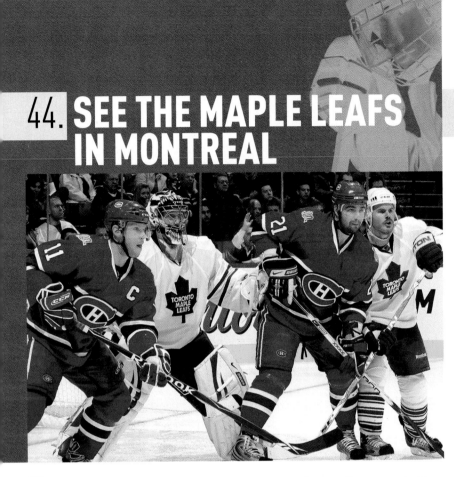

The only thing you need to know about a Maple Leafs-Canadiens game in Montreal on a Saturday night is the Leafs have historically always made the trip from the hotel to the Bell Centre using a team bus.

Which isn't really that unique in and of itself, except when you consider the Leafs stay at the Marriott Chateau Champlain, which is directly across the street from the rink.

The players aren't lazy. They just know there's no way they'd ever be able to walk across the street without getting swarmed.

"Guys used to look for fire exits to leave the hotel," said former Leafs winger Nick Kypreos. "We couldn't get from the elevator to the bus without being mobbed."

Kypreos was part of some pretty intense rivalries during his time as an NHL player – notably the Islanders-Rangers, as a Blueshirt – but said nothing compares to a game in Montreal between the Leafs and the Habs. The atmosphere in the Bell Centre is beyond raucous, largely because it's almost half-filled with Maple Leafs fans – the real ones, the ones who can't get tickets for a game in Toronto.

But it goes so far beyond that. The entire day of the game, there is almost a festival feel throughout the city, which just happens to be one of the most vibrant in Canada even in the dead of winter. There's an old saying that suggests the biggest difference between Montrealers and Torontonians is that people from Montreal can't wait for Friday night, while people from Toronto can't wait for Monday morning. But when the fans from Toronto descend on Montreal for a Saturday night game, there's no doubt they're there to embrace the *joie de vivre* that makes Montreal such a special town.

You see it everywhere. Prior to its closing in 2006, you could see Leafs sweaters in Ben's Deli on Maisonneuve or in Schwartz's on St-Laurent, depending upon your preference for a smoked meat sandwich. You could see them in places such as Chez Paree (although we have no personal experience in such a phenomenon).

Before, during and after the game is a carnival-like atmosphere. If you close your eyes during a Montreal-Toronto game on a Saturday night, you might not know whether you are in the Air Canada Centre or the Bell Centre. Check that. You'd know you're not in the ACC because the Leafs crowd is much louder in Montreal than it is in Toronto.

From the first shot on goal, the chants start and they don't let up for the entire game regardless of the score or where the teams are in the standings. Some may want to look more deeply into it and regard it as a clash of Canada's two solitudes, but really all it consists of is two hockey-mad cities with deep traditions, a devoted fan base and a long and storied rivalry.

The only problem is the two teams can never seem to synchronize their watches so they're both contending at the same time. Whenever the Leafs are on the rise, the Canadiens are struggling – and when the Habs are winning, the Leafs are missing the playoffs. It's a real shame these two teams have not met in the playoffs since 1979.

"Every game there is like Game 7 of a playoff series," Kypreos said. "It's almost like a mini-Grey Cup." ■

45. WITNESS HOCKEY HISTORY

Early-season snowstorms usually mean a day off for a baseball writer. John Kuenster, however, was asked to change on the fly when wicked weather patterns cancelled a matchup between the Chicago White Sox and Detroit Tigers in the Motor City back in the spring of 1961.

"When the hockey playoffs began, the baseball season was in progress, so I was covering the White Sox for the Chicago *Daily News*," said Kuenster, now 85. "It was a Sunday, April 16, and believe it or not there was a snowstorm that hit Detroit and Chicago. The paper called me and said, 'John, go over to Olympia and cover Game 6 of the Stanley Cup final,' because the baseball game was called off."

Instead of writing about home runs and double plays, Kuenster ended up penning a story about the Chicago Black Hawks ending a 22-year championship drought by drubbing Detroit 5-1 in the Cup-clinching game.

With young stars Bobby Hull and Stan Mikita in the mix, Chicago appeared primed for a run of titles throughout the decade. But, as any hurtin' Hawks fan can tell you, things didn't exactly work out that way. Nearly 50 years later, the team is still trying to end the longest championship dry spell in the NHL.

But the bash back in '61 was a Stanley Cup scene any fan would love to witness.

Kuenster was the last person to leave the Olympia that night after finishing his articles. He had no idea what was waiting for him when he wandered back to his hotel, which happened to be party headquarters for the Hawks.

"They couldn't fly back home because the airports were shut down in Detroit and Chicago because of the snowstorm, so what a wild party began (at the hotel)," Kuenster said. "I get on the elevator and there's a couple guys getting wild, roughing each other up, including Al Arbour, who was a defenseman for the Hawks. Somebody smacked him real hard, they were like kids playing around, and he said, 'You guys broke my $200 watch!' because, you know, he had banged it against the wall.

"We went up to the room where everybody was with the Stanley Cup. They unscrewed the bowl part and loaded it up with champagne and I don't know what else they put in there, but everybody really got drunk. What a celebration it was."

The festivities continued rollicking to the point that a couple of reporters wondered if it wasn't time to move on before things got completely out of control.

"Another writer said, 'John, why don't we get the hell out of here before we get killed?' " Kuenster recalled. "I said 'How?' and he said, 'I checked the train schedule, there's a New York Central train coming through here at 3 a.m. and we can catch that and go home,' and so that's how I got home to Chicago."

While Kuenster was a bit of a pinch-hitter covering hockey over baseball that day, it's not like he was unfamiliar with the ice. He covered the Hawks through the winter for several seasons, before switching over to the diamond in the spring. In 1969, he became the editor of *Baseball Digest*, a position he held for most of his career. He was still writing a monthly column for the publication when the 2009 baseball season began.

But hockey – and particularly those Hawks teams of the late '50s and early '60s – still holds a place in his heart.

"It was such a nice little sport to cover in those days because there were only six teams," he said. "I knew every player without even looking at them, just by their moves on the ice."

Hockey's recent revival in Chicago is reminiscent of those long ago days, when the Hawks were a focal point on the city's sports scene.

"Chicago Stadium was the place to be," Kuenster said. "In those days, everybody smoked. By the third period, there was a cloud of smoke above the ice. That had to be bad on the players' lungs."

And even when more than just the people smoked, fans' attention never wavered.

"The press box was on the west side of the stadium so we were looking directly east, and at the east end of the stadium during one game, a fire broke out where they were making popcorn," Kuenster said.

"There was a hell of a blaze going on and the fans, they didn't even pay attention. You'd think the place was going to burn down and they didn't even care, they were so (focused on the ice)." ■

46. TAKE ON THE WORLD CHAMPIONSHIP

All right, it's not the Stanley Cup playoffs. Deal with it and embrace it.

And once in your life, do yourself a favor and take in the World Championship. Had you traveled to Quebec City for the tournament in 2008, there's a good chance you would've bumped into Alexander Ovechkin or Ilya Kovalchuk in a nightclub. You would've seen some terrific hockey and watched what was once an NHL city embrace the championship with a fervor that would rival any hockey-mad city in Europe.

Once you get over the fact it's not the NHL playoffs, the World Championship is something to behold. Just because the teams are made up of players whose NHL clubs either didn't make the playoffs or were eliminated early doesn't mean they're inferior. Pretty well any North American star worth his salt has played in the tournament at one time or another and many of the European performers were there before they became stars in the NHL.

And you'd be surprised at the level of passion some players show in this event, particularly among Europeans who haven't had a lot of success in the NHL. Robert Reichel was generally regarded as a dog in the NHL – a well-earned reputation – but when it came to international events such as the World Championship, he was captain of the Czech team because he played like a demon and made his teammates accountable.

Perhaps it's the bigger ice, perhaps some players have a greater appreciation for the World Championship or maybe it's just that they feel more comfortable playing in the environment, but you can almost always count on a number of players coming up huge for their countries.

The only problem is that going to the worlds will almost certainly mean a trip to Europe since the tourney has been held in North America only once in its history. But is taking a trip to a major European city in the middle of spring such a terrible thing? Because the event is such an enormous deal in Europe, it's usually held in cities such as Prague, Vienna, St. Petersberg or Stockholm.

Despite that, the World Championship needs a better publicist because the perception problem isn't with the tournament, it's with the North American attitude toward it. In Canada, hockey fans go absolutely ga-ga over the World Junior Championship, while the rest of the hockey world reacts to one of the best hockey events going with general ambivalence.

It's the other way around with the World Championship. Ask any hockey fan in Finland, Sweden, the Czech Republic, Russia, Slovakia or Switzerland about the highlight of their season and they'll tell you it's watching their country play in the World Championship.

It's a shame fans on this side of the Atlantic don't have the same appreciation for it, but don't let that stop you from enjoying the World Championship as much as the Euros do. █

47. DRIVE THE ZAMBONI

Well *I went down to the local arena*

Asked to see the manager man

He came from his office, said, "Son can I help you?"

I looked at him and said, "Yes you can…"

Hey, I wanna drive the Zamboni

Hey, I wanna drive the Zamboni…

– "Zamboni," by the Gear Daddies

The word Zamboni is like Kleenex or Xerox; while it is, in fact, a trademarked name, it has become widely accepted as a colloquialism for any vehicle that resurfaces ice.

It was Frank J. Zamboni who, in 1949, invented the ice-resurfacing vehicle that made his name synonymous with clean sheets of ice. The operator of Iceland Skating Rink in Paramount, Calif., of all places, Frank's invention was one of necessity, not whimsy.

The Zamboni went viral a year later, when Frank sold one to Sonja Henie, an Olympic and world champion figure skater turned Hollywood actress who also starred in a traveling on-ice revue. Frank drove the machine from Paramount (where the Zamboni factory still is) to Henie – in Chicago! – and a legend was born. One that's stronger than ever, more than 50 years later.

At the Herbert Wells Ice Rink in College Park, Maryland, a couple of times a year, anybody can live every hockey fan's dream by driving the ice-resurfacing machine around the arena. At a cost of about $75, you can gain admittance into a two-night Zamboni training class and discover the industry standards for ice-scraping techniques, as well as blade changing, tank filling and vehicle storage.

"People are just fascinated by (the Zambonis)," said Russell Barrett, one of the instructors. "They line up to watch as we do cuts. The kids wave. It makes some of the guys nervous to operate it with all the people watching."

The chance to drive a Zamboni isn't limited to one location; even in a city like College Station, Texas – not exactly a hockey hotbed – you can learn about the machine as part of a $20 course (based out of Arctic Wolf Ice Center) that also allows students to get behind the Zamboni wheel and take it out for a few laps of the ice.

But if you think being a full-time Zamboni driver is the best job ever created, talk to Al Sobotka, the chief ice-resurfacer at Detroit Red Wings games. He'll set you straight.

"I'm sure a lot of people would want my job, but they don't know what comes with it," said Sobotka, whose fame has grown in recent years due to his octopi-twirling antics during Red Wings playoff games. "You can't miss deadlines getting the rink open and the ice set up."

That said, the sacrifices leading to the opportunity to drive a Zamboni are more than worthwhile to those who understand the machine's place in the game's history.

"There are very few things in life that people will stare at," said Kevin Bushey, a Zamboni operator at Yost Ice Arena in Michigan. "One of them is the Zamboni."

48. SEE THE '72 SUMMIT

Rosebud from *Citizen Kane* is (spoiler alert) a sled. Everyone knows this, even if they haven't seen the film, but knowing that fact still doesn't tell you anything about why *Citizen Kane* is so revered.

"Henderson has scored for Canada!" Every Canadian knows this call by Foster Hewitt at the end of Game 8 of the 1972 Canada-U.S.S.R. Summit Series. But like *Citizen Kane*, if you only know the ending, you have no idea why it's so important. There are a thousand reasons why this series is required watching for any hockey fan, but what makes the '72 Summit Series so compelling is its combination of history, culture, star power and blood-and-guts competition.

Put it this way: Legendary NHLer Marcel Dionne told the *Globe and Mail* in 1997 that being on Team Canada in 1972 – and not playing a single minute in any game – was the highlight of his hockey career. That's pretty high praise from a first-ballot Hall of Famer and the NHL's fifth-leading scorer of all-time.

There will never be another sporting event like the Summit Series, when two feuding cultures and political systems faced off to settle their differences. Canadians viewed the series not just as an exhibition to decide the greatest hockey nation, but as a way to prove which way of life, democratic or socialist, was superior. Although 1972 fell within the period of detente between NATO and the Eastern Bloc, Don Cherry accurately described the sentiment at the time when he bellowed, "This is war!"

There are dozens of unforgettable moments that set this series apart from any other competition in hockey history, but here's a few that stand out:

• In Game 1, you'll see the carefree expression on Team Canada's faces as they jump out to a 2-0 lead early in the first period. By the end of the game, you'll see the same Canadian players look dumbfounded at the 7-3 thrashing handed to them by the Soviets.

• Game 2 features a jaw-dropping breakaway goal by unlikely series hero Pete Mahovlich, which not only stands as the best goal of the series, but was a message to the Soviet team – and the rest of the world – that Team Canada was ready to compete with its Russian rivals.

• Game 3 opens with a haunting moment of silence, a tribute to the Israeli Olympic athletes who were taken hostage and killed in Munich the previous day. It's a chilling reminder that global conflicts can be closely connected to international sport and that the Summit Series represented far more than just bragging rights for one hockey nation over another.

• Following another loss in Game 4, the Vancouver faithful boos Team Canada as the players skate off. In an on-ice interview, Phil Esposito responds to the crowd's jeers – and calls out the rest of a disheartened nation – with the most candid off-the-cuff quote in hockey history: "We cannot believe the bad press we've got, the booing we've got in our own building," said an emotional Esposito, still sweating from the game. "I'm completely disappointed. I cannot believe it. Every one of us guys, 35 guys, we came out because we love our country. Not for any other reason. We came because we love Canada."

• The tension is palpable at the opening of Game 5, the first of the four games in Russia – at least until Esposito slips and falls during the pre-game ceremony, drawing laughs from the stoic crowd as he takes a mock bow.

• Bobby Clarke's slash to the ankle of Valeri Kharlamov in Game 6 takes the Soviet virtuoso out of Game 7 and renders him ineffective in Game 8. Yet to see it happen, the infraction doesn't seem to seriously injure Kharlamov; he doesn't even fall to the ice. Instead, he turns to face his attacker and offers a few choice words, despite the language barrier.

• In Game 7, the violent undertone of the series nearly explodes into a bench-clearing brawl when, during a shoving match between Gary Bergman and Boris Mikhailov, the Soviet captain begins kicking at Bergman with his skates. Luckily, the referees manage to diffuse the situation.

• Some of the most stirring moments of Game 8 occur before the puck even drops. During the announcement of the players for each team, the Soviet crowd cheers each of its heroes, but none more than Kharlamov, who shows up to play despite doctor's warnings. When Team Canada's players are announced, the 3,000 Canadians who traveled to support the team sound louder than the rest of the crowd put together. And when Clarke's name is called, watch him crack the slightest of smiles, which seems to say, "I know what I did…and you ain't seen nothing yet." And when Bergman is announced as the last member of Team Canada, he turns to the crowd and gives them the 'V' for victory sign.

The rest, as they say, is history. ▩

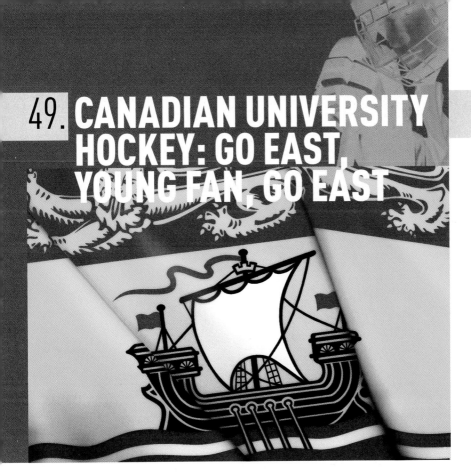

49. CANADIAN UNIVERSITY HOCKEY: GO EAST, YOUNG FAN, GO EAST

St. Thomas University is a tiny liberal arts school nestled in a quiet corner of the much larger University of New Brunswick campus in Fredericton.

But it's far from quiet when the St. Thomas Tommies take on the UNB Varsity Reds in Canadian Interuniversity Sport hockey. Whether it is in UNB's 3,673-seat Aitken Centre or down in the smaller Lady Beaverbrook Rink, the 'Battle of the Hill' has raged since 1964, when STU moved from Miramichi to share resources with UNB.

Several Canadian cities, including Montreal, Toronto, Ottawa and Halifax, have multiple CIS teams, but none share a campus. In Fredericton, opposing players sit in the same class together and often bump into each other in the city of 50,000. Former players tell stories of off-ice dust-ups and the proximity that provides personal fodder for trash-talking.

"You might know how a guy's doing in school or how a guy's doing with his girlfriend," said Shane Corston, a former STU goalie who works in North American player relations and recruitment for CMG Sports. "I remember it being hostile, not just on the ice surface, but it went beyond that."

Longtime UNB coach Don MacAdam (1977-85) recalls the animosity extending to the Fredericton fans.

"If I was ever out socializing and ran into some St. Thomas fans, I'd have to leave the establishment because they'd make it so miserable with how they were going to kick our butts the next game," said MacAdam, currently the coach of the QMJHL's Lewiston Maineiacs.

"It was not uncommon to see fights in the stands. The rivalry between the two schools was the one thing that could divide the people of Fredericton. I've heard stories about people working in the same office and there's not a problem until the week of the UNB-St. Thomas game, then they wouldn't speak to each other for that week or the week after."

Sportsnet analyst Doug MacLean, formerly the GM of the Columbus Blue Jackets, succeeded MacAdam as UNB's coach in 1985-86. Although he spent just one year in Fredericton, he remembers the pressure to beat St. Thomas.

"I've coached in the Stanley Cup final and there might have been more pressure coaching against St. Thomas," said MacLean, who guided the 1996 Florida Panthers to the NHL's championship series.

Ex-STU coach Al MacAdam, a scout for the Buffalo Sabres, agrees.

"The (university) staff had one concern with the team," he said. "That was the four times we played against UNB. (If) we were 24-4-0 but lost all our games to UNB, they'd rather us be 4-24-0 and have won all our games against UNB."

It's history that makes the games important, rather than the standings. And much of that history occurred in the Lady Beaverbrook Rink, where both teams played until the Aitken Centre was built in 1976.

The city-run community arena (capacity 1,300) was constructed in 1954 and, among myriad other events, played host to a Johnny Cash concert in the 1960s. While the Aitken Centre is more modern, the LBR is the arena that truly captures the color of the rivalry.

"You can get a seat up there (at the Aitken Centre)," said LBR rink manager Kelly Watts, "but you just don't get the action like you do here."

On a handful of nights during the season, the LBR is pure emotion and atmosphere, whether it's packed inside or lined up around the building with people waiting to buy tickets when the college rivals meet in the playoffs.

The teams sit on opposite sides of the rink, and so do their fans. The ice surface is small and a solid white wall at one end makes it feel even smaller. With no glass at that end, Corston said it "feels like a concrete pad."

When the rivalry is at its best, the rink is polarized, with fans heckling the players (including an infamous group of STU fans above the white wall known as 'Rum Row').

"It's a cage match against UNB down at the LBR," Corston said. "If you can't muster up some courage on those nights, you'd best not dress for the game."

UNB coach Gardiner MacDougall said he appreciates the atmosphere and the quirks of the LBR.

"It's a blue-collar rink," he said. "We dress in our dressing room (at the Aitken Centre), like back in the minor hockey days, with everything but skates.

"I'm not sure I'd want to practise there every day in the middle of January, but even today half the rink is UNB fans, half the rink is St. Thomas fans. It's pretty special and I certainly look forward to the games at the LBR."

Al MacAdam remembers the rivalry being "brutally emotional," while Mike Kelly, who played for UNB and later coached the Reds against MacAdam, said it had "way too much emotion" in the 1990s.

"It was not good enough to win the game, you had to win convincingly and make a statement every time you played them," said Kelly, director of hockey operations for the Saint John Sea Dogs of the QMJHL. "I wouldn't say that rivalry brought out the best in anybody."

Tommies coach Mike Eagles, a 16-season NHL veteran, said the STU-UNB sentiment has evolved into "a healthy dislike" over the past few years. There's also a lot of respect, particularly when both teams honor former players Lou Chabot (STU) and Mark Jeffrey (UNB) in annual memorial games against each other.

According to Fredericton hockey historians Ernie Fitzsimmons and Eric Drummie, UNB holds the all-time edge with a 132-62-13 record in the regular season and playoffs. The Varsity Reds have appeared in three consecutive national CIS finals (2007-09), winning two titles, and along the way have won 11 straight contests against St. Thomas in the regular season and three more in the playoffs.

While the rivalry has been lopsided recently, Eagles believes UNB's strength will make his STU program better in the long run. And with the Reds hosting the University Cup national tournament in 2011 and 2012, there'll be an extra berth available for an Atlantic-based team.

"Sometimes the greater the challenge, the greater the reward…they've set the bar so high that we're determined to get back to that level," said Eagles, a veteran of 853 NHL games who actually met his wife at a UNB-STU game when he played for the AHL's Fredericton Express in the early '80s.

"When we get that elusive next win, it's going to feel pretty awesome." ■

50. CANADIAN UNIVERSITY HOCKEY: GO NORTH, YOUNG FAN, GO NORTH

The Staals are hockey's latest golden family. With three boys playing in the NHL and a fourth working his way up, there's no arguing the genetics in this family tree. You might wonder where the kids learned their talent; to find the answer, you have to trek slightly off the beaten path.

As it turns out, Henry Staal – the father of Eric, Marc, Jordan and Jared – has his own hockey history, having cut his teeth in the late 1970s and early '80s playing Canadian university hockey with the Lakehead Norwesters in Thunder Bay, Ont. (as did Chris Pronger's father, Jim, and Sean Avery's dad, Al). While the Norwesters are a thing of the past, having disbanded in 1985, Thunder Bay remains one the most unusual hockey hotbeds you've never seen.

Thunder Bay, with a population of 110,000, is more than 800 miles northwest of Toronto, or about 16 hours away if you're brave enough to drive (follow the eastern banks of Lakes Huron and Superior, and you'll get there, eventually). The longtime logging capital is a little less than two hours by plane, but feels half-a-world away.

The blue-collar town has a well-known Canadiana connection – it was Terry Fox's last stop when the inspiring cancer fighter was forced to abandon his historic cross-country run. Thunder Bay also boasts museums and an art gallery, even a quaint little casino where visitors can pass the time. More significantly, it's the home to the Lakehead University Thunderwolves of the CIS (Canadian Interuniversity Sport), where everything you thought you knew about Canadian university hockey no longer applies.

This town loves its T-Wolves.

The Thunderwolves claim the highest average attendance in the Ontario University Athletics conference – about 3,000 fans per game at their home rink, the Fort Williams Gardens – and trail only Laval University's football team in terms of overall attendance in any CIS sport.

Maybe the fans are making up for lost time. Lakehead went without a hockey team from 1985 to 2001 after the Norwesters folded. But in 2001-02, the team was reborn with a new name and image, and the city has flocked to its games.

Henry Staal said when he played for the Norwesters from 1978-83, they received very little fan support.

"Maybe 100 or 150 fans…probably 50-60 students and then some friends and family of the team," he said, "but when they started again there was more of a business model. They did a good job of promoting it and I guess they got pretty good teams right off the get-go, which didn't hurt."

Pretty good is right. The local fans have been treated to eight consecutive playoff berths and an appearance in the 2006 CIS championship final. They've shown their support by filling the Gardens to capacity nearly every night. The CIS also showed its appreciation by selecting Thunder Bay as the host city for the 2009 national championship tournament; Lakehead appeared as the host team. (The Atlantic champions from the University of New Brunswick beat OUA champs Western Ontario in a thrilling final game to take the Cavendish Cup, emblematic of CIS supremacy.) Lakehead is set host the 2010 tournament as well.

Goaltender Chris Whitley was with the T-Wolves from 2004-05 through 2008-09 and can attest first-hand to the excitement of playing in front of a packed house.

"It's very intense, electrifying," said the native of Oshawa, Ont., just east of Toronto. "The fans in the stands are so involved and they get so excited. We feed off them."

For anyone who has never experienced CIS hockey, the reputation it carries as a league with sub-par talent will be shattered the moment you step into the rink on a game night. The buzz in Thunder Bay when Lakehead hosts arch-rival University of Western Ontario, for example, is equal to any encountered in other puck-crazy cities around the world.

Henry Staal thinks he knows why the locals have fallen in love with the school's squad.

"For the local kids growing up, maybe it's a bit corny now, but it's the way out," he said. "They feel like there's nothing owed to them, but if they work really hard they can make one of the 'big clubs down east.' We've had a lot of kids become successful from around here because they know they're going have to work to get noticed."

That's exactly what you'll notice if you ever watch Lakehead play: A group of hockey players working hard and usually winning. Especially at home.

While other programs – with equally strong, contending teams – struggle to attract 300 fans per game, attendance has not been a problem for Lakehead. The home-ice advantage, combined with the arduous travel regimen that opponents must endure just to get to Thunder Bay, is not lost on Whitley.

"It's a big advantage for us, we get to sleep in our own beds and the other team is usually flying in that day and they have little time to prep," Whitley said. "We take full advantage of that."

For all it offers in terms of atmosphere and sheer fun, a Lakehead Thunderwolves game in Thunder Bay is not to be missed. ▪

51. HAVE A HOCKEY FANTASY (CAMP)

One of the must-do's for most hockey fans – at least, for the ones who can stand up on skates without holding on to the boards – is to enroll in a "fantasy camp" and, for a few hours or a few days, spend some quality on-ice time with their childhood heroes.

Fortunately, there are more than a few hockey fantasy camps from which to choose. The most high-profile of them all is Wayne Gretzky's Fantasy Camp, which was scheduled to continue with its eighth annual camp during the 2009-10 hockey calendar year.

"It's a once-in-a-lifetime opportunity," said one 2009 camper. "It's a great experience getting to play hockey with some of the best guys in the world."

It's not cheap – the entrance fee for the experience in 2005 was $9,999 per person – but you do get to skate, train and play (both on the ice and off of it) with The Great One himself, as well as other former stars such as Lanny McDonald, Theoren Fleury and Larry Robinson.

After the fact, you're given video evidence of your time in the midst of such awesome hockey talents and can purchase official photographs from the studios of renowned NHL lensman Bruce Bennett.

The 2009 camp also included a surprise visit from Mr. Hockey himself, Gordie Howe, who mugged for the camera and palled around with the guys, even throwing a few of his patented elbows.

"Incredible," said a beaming camper in his 50s after meeting Howe. "Wow. Wow. Wow."

Somewhat cheaper, but still not exactly cheap, was the Hockey Greats Fantasy Camp put on by former Islanders star Bob Bourne in Kelowna, B.C., in 2008. For around $2,500, attendees had the opportunity to play with and against legends such as Bryan Trottier, Gilbert Perreault, Dale Hawerchuk and Billy Smith. (To see who'll be part of Bourne's next fantasy camp, visit bournevents.com.)

Some NHL teams are also getting into the fantasy camp business. The Minnesota Wild, for instance, allowed 21-year-olds with either college or high school hockey experience to take part in a day-long camp that included on-ice drills with retired NHLers Phil Housley, Darby Hendrickson and Brad Bombardir, as well as tickets to a game and a lavish dinner.

In addition, the storied Montreal Canadiens franchise has conducted a fantasy camp of its own in recent years. The price is somewhat more expensive ($5,495 per camper in 2008), but that gets you access to Hall of Famers such as Jean Beliveau, Guy Lafleur, Bob Gainey and Henri Richard, a trip to the owner's suite at the Bell Centre and a game in the Habs' home rink.

If any or all of those options sound tempting, it's because they should be for any hockey fan.

"God, I would kill to be able to afford to do that," said Syracuse, N.Y., resident Jim Johansson, a devout hockey fan who was in Toronto visiting Wayne Gretzky's restaurant when he heard of the type of fantasy camps in operation.

"I tell my son all the time that if he wins the lottery, the one thing he can spend on me is the fee they charge to let you skate with some of these superstars. I don't care if they're older and can't play anymore, either. Just to be able to hear them tell great stories, or trash talk with the opposition a little bit, that's what would make it so special."

52. SIT IN THE FIRST ROW BY THE GLASS

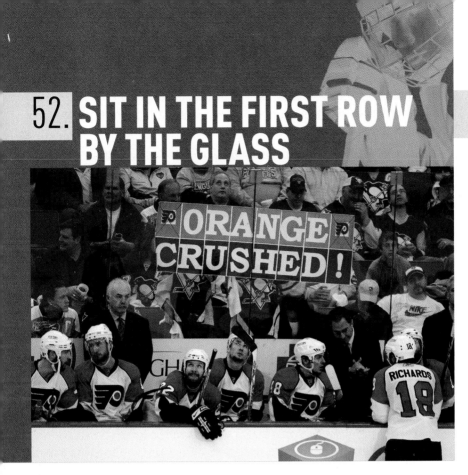

There's no telling what's going to happen when you're sitting by the glass. Being that close to the action, sometimes you've just got to seize the moment – or rather, the hockey stick.

That's what one overzealous Boston Bruins fan did to Montreal's Alexei Kovalev during the Boston-Montreal first round playoff series in 2009. Kovalev's stick found its way through the photographer's camera hole in the glass and practically landed in the guy's lap. The fan and Kovalev played a game of tug-of-war. The guy eventually had to give back the stick, but he left with a lot of up-close-and-personal memories he wouldn't have found sitting anywhere else.

The same goes for the Colorado Avalanche fan a few years back who thought it was a real rib-tickler when Steve Sullivan, then playing for Chicago, was cut on the bridge of his nose by a high stick. As a bloody Sullivan was led back to the bench by the Hawks trainer, the fan mocked him from the safety of his front-row seat. So it was sweet karma and an instant YouTube classic when an odds-defying Patrick Roy clearing shot later in the game tracked down that same fan and cut open his forehead.

That incident proved three things: One, it is still possible to get hit by a puck when sitting in the front row by the glass. Two, if you want to get noticed by taunting an NHL player while he's dripping blood, you will be successful (Sullivan skated over to give his personal regards after fate intervened). Three, sitting by the glass can be a humbling experience in more ways than one.

Because for Mr.-Cut-Nose-guy-who-gets-laughed-at-by-his-own-girlfriend-on-national-television and everyone else, never is the fan farther from the NHL than when he's sitting right there. The view by the glass provides the best vantage point to see just how good these guys have to be in order to play in the best hockey league in the world.

Longtime Colorado Avalanche beat writer Adrian Dater once had this to say after watching the third period of a Los Angeles-Colorado pre-season game by the glass: "Man, is the game different when you are that close to it. You don't realize just how fast everybody is going until you're right next to the ice."

It holds true whether you've been a fan for 50 years or are attending your first game. The following passage is from the online blog of a rookie fan who watched the warmups of his first-ever NHL game in Vancouver from behind the glass near the goal.

"The teams came out for their warmups and started flinging round, black missiles at the net. I had never been that close to an NHL slapshot. The first time one went high and hit the glass, I was pretty sure someone was going to die. It sounded like a whip cracking. That glass must be some Secret Service-approved stuff."

Here's a bigger secret, for supposed purists who believe the front-row seat offers a distorted view on the game: Sitting by the glass is the quickest way to realize there's a difference between knowing the game (fans, media, perhaps cut-nose-guy) and understanding it (players). You might see more of the ice from 25 rows up, but that doesn't mean the higher perch provides a more "real" look at what is actually going on. Once the puck drops there's only one vantage point that matters – and that's the one seen by the players on the ice. The fact that NHLers at ice level – and at full speed – can pick out the structure the rest of us only see from higher up shows how good they truly are.

Think of that all-important first pass. Everyone knows it's important, right, so let's move on to debating the merits of umbrella penalty-killing, shall we?

Not so fast, Strategyman. Look, here comes the forechecker to take off the defenseman's head. And there's nowhere to pass it anyway and no time and there's probably a neutral-zone trap out there somewhere and the defenseman is about to get creamed…and the next thing you know he's absorbing a hit and the puck is on some guy's tape breaking through a seam past the blueline. A split-second earlier and it would have been a turnover; a split-second later and it's a suicide stretch pass that lands your second-line left winger in a hospital bed.

Sitting by the glass, you can begin to understand this kind of thing a teensy-weensy bit. ▪

53. GO TO THE (HOCKEY) MOVIES

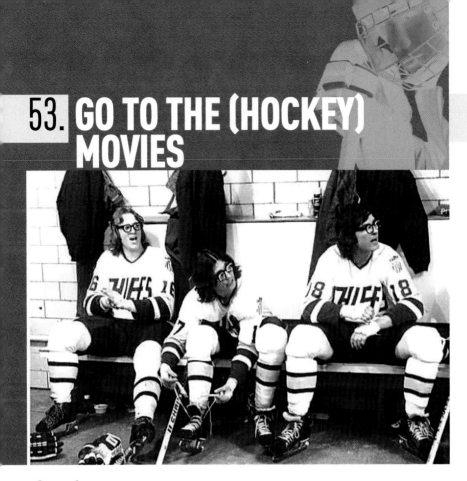

There's no shortage of not-so-well-made hockey movies. *Slap Shot 2: Breaking The Ice*, anyone? But the filmmakers who have accurately captured the thrill of being at ice level along with some of the game's greatest stories make the sport's time on the silver screen more than worthwhile.

Here are 10 top hockey movies you have to see (at least once, but probably multiple times):

1. *Slap Shot* (1977) – If you have to be convinced why this is the greatest hockey movie of all-time, you're either six years old or you've lived your entire life in a jungle-type region below the equator. Paul Newman made some unbelievably great films over the course of his career, but he'll always be Reg Dunlop to hockey fans.

2. *Miracle* (2004) – Kurt Russell's greatest role was Snake Plissken in *Escape From New York*, but a close second was his stunning portrayal of late U.S. Olympic team (and NHL) coach Herb Brooks in the tale of America's 1980 Olympic gold medal. It's worth seeing for him alone, but there's much more to like where that came from.

3. *The Rocket* (2005) – The story of legendary Canadiens superstar Maurice 'Rocket' Richard is as historically accurate and emotionally charged as hockey movies get. Be sure to look for cameos from current and former NHLers such as Vincent Lecavalier (as Jean Beliveau), Sean Avery, Ian Laperriere and Mike Ricci.

4. *Net Worth* (1995) – Another film based on real-life events, this Canadian production details former great Ted Lindsay's struggle to form a players' union and be paid fairly. The most important hockey movie ever made.

5. *The Sweater* (1980) – The most famous hockey movie ever made for kids, it's only 10 minutes long – but any Canadian who saw the tale of a young Montreal Canadiens fan who mistakenly receives a Toronto Maple Leafs jersey will never forget it. (*"One the ice…we were five Maurice Richard against five other Maurice Richard…"*)

6. *Bon Cop, Bad Cop* (2006) – This French-Canadian flick uses hockey as a relatively peripheral plot advancer. But the jokes – including thinly veiled references to NHL commissioner Gary Bettman and Wayne Gretzky, among others – have a lot of bite and satirical edge, injecting much life into the otherwise tired "mismatched police partners" genre.

7. *Les Chiefs* (2004) – This documentary on a goon-infested, semi-pro league in Quebec has a bit of everything moviegoers are looking for – drama, laughs, even a few tears. If you need proof that real life almost always is more fascinating than fiction, this movie provides it.

8. *Sudden Death* (1995) – Yeah, it's got washed-up action hero Jean-Claude Van Damme as its star and features some of the most reality-deprived, unintentionally hilarious action sequences in film history. But check out the cast list: Luc Robitaille, Markus Naslund, Bernie Nicholls, Mike Lange and, in a cameo as Player No. 2, Pat Brisson – a.k.a. Sidney Crosby's agent. That's easily the most successful cast of real-life hockey types to appear in a single film.

9. *Mystery, Alaska* (1999) – Russell Crowe, Burt Reynolds and Mike Myers appear in this hit film about an Arctic-area amateur team that takes on the New York Rangers. Look for former NHLers Phil Esposito, Jim Fox and Barry Melrose as well.

10. *Youngblood* (1986) – The acting performances here are somehow even more wooden two decades later, and any movie that foreshadowed the dramatic contributions that would be made by Rob Lowe, Keanu Reeves and Patrick Swayze is a cautionary tale for all casting agents. But in fairness, any film with the line, "Go hump your St. Bernard!" deserves a shot. ■

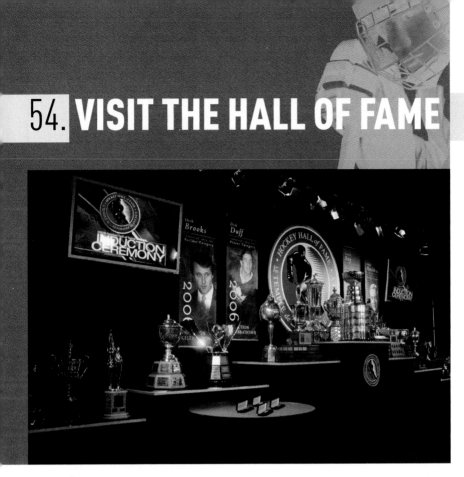

Larger-than-life statues of Ken Dryden and Fred 'Cyclone' Taylor loom over your head. Giant, blown-up photos of hockey legends such as Patrick Roy, Mike Bossy and Bernie 'Boom Boom' Geoffrion grin down at you from behind glass cases filled to the brim with game-worn sweaters, pucks from famous goals, Stanley Cup-used sticks and a plethora of other hockey memorabilia. A large screen blares a film biography of Guy Lafleur. Fans of all ages walk around admiring displays, snapping photos, pointing out favorite players and discussing records. A giant mural reads, "Welcome to the Cathedral of Hockey."

Welcome to the Hockey Hall of Fame.

Meander through the up-front exhibits and you'll soon find yourself in the Hall's outstanding interactive area. Hometown arena-like stands – concrete with blue or red wooden benches and blue rails – surround the exhibit. People hang over the boards of makeshift rinks – white plasticized surfaces that give the illusion of ice – cheering on friends and family competing against a virtual opponent. Whether you're the next

Alex Ovechkin, a retired rec-leaguer or even if you've never stepped on the ice, the Hall's interactive area lets you put your skills to the test. Try to outshoot a virtual goalie or test your own netminding skills against a cyber-sniper.

Add the sound of broadcasters' voices over the cheers, shrill whistles and clacking of sticks and pucks on the "ice" and the experience feels even more like a real hockey game. Follow the broadcasters' voices around the corner and you're in the TSN/RDS broadcast zone, which gives a nod to the history of sports broadcasting and industry greats such as Foster Hewitt and Don Cherry. Head up a staircase and you're in the broadcast pods. If you've ever seen a bad camera angle used during a pivotal on-ice moment or heard a horrendous play-by-play, here's your chance to show how you can do it better. Act as producer and editor by putting together real clips of real games, or head into the suites overlooking the interactive rink and unleash your inner commentator by calling your own play-by-play on a number of iconic hockey moments.

It's clear the Hall of Fame, which has been located in Toronto since 1958 (it moved to its current location in 1993), is not your ordinary hockey museum. Of course, there are the more traditional aspects to the Hall's exhibits, such as the trophies on display, but even the status of those awards is elevated. And this is the home of the Stanley Cup, which is displayed in the Grand Hall – a huge, dome-shaped room at the top of a marble staircase – alongside other iconic trophies such as the Conn Smythe Trophy and the Hart Trophy.

There truly is something for everyone at the Hall of Fame, regardless of age or hockey knowledge.

"The Hockey Hall of Fame combines not only the past, present and future, but it has an interactive area, films and more," said Phil Pritchard, the Hall's curator. "In today's world, that's what people like."

Get lost among exhibits ranging from the Stanley Cup Dynasty, which documents the entire history of the Cup, to the Upper Deck Collector's Corner, where you can find every collector's item under the sun – from a Wayne Gretzky lunchbox to a Montreal Canadiens alarm clock to a Chicago Blackhawks pinball machine.

The sheer volume of hockey memorabilia and information also makes the Hall of Fame stand out, not to mention the fan-friendly way in which all of it is laid out and organized. Statistics and marks such as individual goal records, goaltending milestones and all-time NHL leaders are interspersed throughout displays of memorabilia – ranging from Georges Vezina's final pair of skates; the first trophy Wayne

Gretzky ever received (most improved novice all-star player); the puck with which Gordie Howe scored his 700th career goal; and, the stick used by Patrick Roy in Game 5 of the 1986 Stanley Cup final.

Fans can also check out the replica Montreal Canadiens dressing room, made to look as it did when the Canadiens last won the Cup at the Forum in 1993. Sweaters from the team's most sought-after players – Lafleur, Maurice Richard, Jean Beliveau, Howie Morenz and others – hang from hooks above the dressing room benches, where masks, pads and skates lean.

The Hall also pays tribute to hockey from the local level to the international stage. Find out what your hometown has brought to the world arena in the 'Hometown Heroes' exhibit and pay tribute to your country's hockey heritage with the Hall's homage to the global game. If your visit to the Hall has made you feel like a hockey trivia hotshot, head back to the interactive area. Sit down in the stands and try your hand at various quizzes on TV screens.

Visitors come from far and wide – some from overseas, many from the U.S., the rest from coast-to-coast across Canada. Although the Hall gets many first-time visitors, it has its share of regulars as well.

"I've seen a few people come here many times," said Hall of Fame employee Cody McLenon. "I've seen some familiar faces."

Regardless of your reasons for being a hockey fan, the Hall of Fame is a must-see.

"Adults can relive their memories and heroes and kids can learn about those memories and heroes," Pritchard said. "For everyone who comes, they have a certain memory of hockey or a player. That can all be relived here."

55. TOSS A TEDDY BEAR

At first, it looked like just another goal.

Calgary Hitmen winger Kyle Bortis passed the puck to linemate Brandon Kozun in the slot and the shifty center ripped a shot past the glove of Brandon Wheat Kings goalie Andrew Hayes. Nothing out of the ordinary, right? But then it suddenly turned strange, as Hayes promptly dropped to the ice, curled into a ball and ducked for cover.

Usually, this would be regarded as a peculiar celebration after allowing the opening goal in a game, but Hayes had a reason for his stop-drop-and-roll reaction.

Because immediately after the goal was scored, pandemonium ensued.

The raucous Saddledome crowd of over 18,000 was worked into a frenzy, hurling…wait for it, *teddy bears* toward the ice.

Yes, teddy bears, and with that, the Calgary Hitmen's 2008 installment of their yearly tradition was underway. Since the mid-1990s, the Hitmen have held an annual Teddy Bear Toss. Once a year, the Western League team urges fans to bring at least one stuffed grizzly to the game and, after the first home goal, litter the ice with their cuddly friends.

The teddy bears are then distributed to local charities in Alberta. As well, the Hitmen players donate some of them, in person, to the Alberta Children's Hospital.

If you've never beared witness to the tossing of the bears, it's something that has to be seen to be believed.

Almost simultaneously with the puck crossing the goal line, the Saddledome horn blares and chaos reigns. Thousands of fans hurl swells of teddy bears toward the ice with reckless abandon. The playthings come pouring over the boards by the hundreds, almost as if spouted from a nozzle. Fans in the front rows are pelted repeatedly by underthrown ursines originating from the far reaches of the arena. For one night a year at the Saddledome, the ice-level seats aren't the best in the house.

After nearly five minutes of heavy downpour, it slows to a drizzle. Bears lost in aisles and under seats slowly make their way to the ice, where they're swept, bagged and lugged away.

Depending on the onslaught, games are delayed for as much as half an hour, but it's time fans are willing to concede to take part in the unique event.

In each year since its commencement, the toss has continued to grow. On Dec. 2, 2007, Hitmen fans set the world record for most teddy bears accumulated at one of these events (yes, such a record actually exists). A total of 17,341 fans pelted the ice with 26,919 teddy bears to secure bragging rights around the WHL – and the world. ■

56. TAKE THE DRAFT ROUTE TO QUEBEC

Greg Turner always knows what he's doing on the first Saturday of every June.

It's a significant time of year for him, right up there with Christmas, New Year's Eve and his wedding anniversary. The fervent fan of the Moncton Wildcats has traveled long distances to attend 11 Quebec League drafts and considers it a hockey-calendar highlight that's worth celebrating.

"Much like a hockey game where you're watching the play develop on the ice, it's the same at the draft," Turner said. "You're watching teams try to jockey for position in the selection order and there's trades made that can have a real impact on franchises.

"As a fan, you're anxious to see what strategy your team is going to take. It's also fun to look at the overall league and see what other teams are doing. It's really an exciting time, a must-see event if you're a fan."

In other words, don't call yourself a hardcore hockey fan unless you've spent six hours on a hot June day inside a rink (probably not air-conditioned), watching the 12-round QMJHL draft.

The Ontario League and Western League conduct their drafts over the Internet. In contrast, the QMJHL draft is a high-profile production with thousands of fans and hundreds of team executives, including owners, GMs, coaches, scouts and front-office staff – along with the multitude of prospects and their families and friends.

The first round is especially glitzy and takes more than two hours to unfold. It's dripping with drama. Each teenager chosen is escorted down the red carpet and there's a lively atmosphere with music playing, fans cheering and teary-eyed family members hugging while overcome with emotion. The first-rounders step onto a stage as their name is added to a huge draft board in the background. They don their new sweater, meet team officials, have photos taken and, finally, enter a media frenzy. There's usually about 75 newspaper, radio and television reporters from throughout Quebec, the Maritimes and Maine.

"Draft day is an emotional experience that changes the lives of a lot of young kids," Turner said. "It's exciting knowing that some of these young kids you're watching are going to be NHL stars, guys like Sidney Crosby, Vincent Lecavalier and Brad Richards."

The 18 QMJHL teams each have their own 12-seat table on the ice-surface floor; from there, they speak into a microphone to announce selections from the second round onwards. There are timeouts as clubs strategize and there's always a buzz in the building when officials from different teams huddle for trade talks.

The draft is conducted in English and French and it's a suit-and-tie affair with most of the prospects chosen in the first three rounds in attendance. There's typically about 3,000 fans. Glance around the stands and you'll see fans proudly decked out in jerseys, T-shirts and baseball caps of their favorite QMJHL club. Some break into a chant before it's their team's turn to pick.

"It's an exact carbon copy of the NHL draft," said QMJHL commissioner Gilles Courteau. "It's a big event for the league with a lot of exposure. It's a good exercise for the kids to experience before they go to the next step, which is the NHL draft.

"The 'Q' draft is a great opportunity for kids to meet the teams. It's important for us to make this a classy show because we want the players to see they're coming into a professional environment."

There's no question the QMJHL draft has become a bigger event over the years. First of all, there are three days of league meetings for owners, governors, GMs, coaches, athletic therapists, academic coordinators and marketing directors leading up to draft day. There's also a gala event on the day prior to the draft, in which the 18 prospects who are projected to be selected in the first round are introduced onstage. It's done in a theater with video footage of each prospect in game action. A league golf tournament is also typically part of the pre-draft festivities.

Since it's such a flagship event for the league, there are usually multiple bids to host the draft. Drummondville is the site in 2010 with bids already submitted for 2011.

"Some QMJHL teams aren't able to host the Memorial Cup tournament because their building doesn't have enough capacity," Courteau said. "But they still want to have a big event in their community, so they go after the draft."

It takes a budget of approximately $150,000 to host the draft, with teams sometimes receiving government grants. Typically, there's an influx of 1,000 visitors, providing a healthy economic impact on the local community.

The 2009 QMJHL draft in Moncton featured a special twist. The same weekend, the city also hosted Play On! 4-on-4, a giant street hockey tournament presented by CBC's Hockey Night in Canada. The concept was clear: Make these two big events coincide to create hockey fever in a mid-size hockeytown during the off-season.

Former Moncton Wildcats goalie Jean-Francois Damphousse was the fifth pick in the 1996 QMJHL draft. And he was a first-rounder in the NHL draft, too, selected 24th by New Jersey in 1997.

"To me, the Quebec League draft was even more nerve-racking," Damphousse said. "I'm from Quebec, the draft was in Victoriaville that year (near his hometown of Saint-Alexis-des-Monts) and I had a lot of family and friends there. When you're that age, a teenager, it's all about pride. You want to be drafted high. The setup for the Quebec League draft is very professional, there's an NHL dimension to it. With the experience I gained going through that in junior, I was much more relaxed at the NHL draft so I could enjoy the day instead of being nervous.

"I think it's great the Quebec League does its draft this way even though it's more expensive. It promotes the league and promotes the players more than doing it on the Internet. It creates an experience the players will never forget."

And it's a great memory for hockey fans, too, if you're able to spend a draft weekend in the Maritimes, Maine or the province that made poutine, Pepsi and Patrick Roy famous. ▪

57. SPEND A SATURDAY MORNING AT THE LOCAL RINK

It's a slice of Canadiana played out from coast to coast in every city, town or village with a rink: a crisp, early beginning to the weekend; a large, hot coffee; a fresh-ish muffin; the sound of blades, if not carving the ice, chopping away at it with gusto; and, children's laughter.

It's a Saturday morning at the local rink. And it's something everyone – hockey fan or not – should experience, just for the sheer joy of it all.

Local rinks – whether they're broken-down relics from the Cold War era or fancy new digs – and early mornings are about as grassroots as it gets in hockey. They're the places and times where you find tireless volunteers doing whatever it takes to make hockey fans out of the boys and girls they work for.

On the ice, coaches put their young charges through the paces during practice or lead the way during games; off the ice, parents huddle together, bleary-eyed and shivering, fingers raw from tightening laces, watching with bated breath as little Johnny or Janey skates – or, at least, tries to – like the puckin' wind.

And the referees? They earn a pittance, but that's OK. With the little tykes learning how to skate and having no idea of the rules, refs are more on-ice coaches than arbiters, anyway.

Is there anything cuter than two-and-a-half-foot hockey players, equipped to the max with oversized gear, chasing the puck in packs with no semblance of a system? Ever seen a five-year-old netminder play goal by collapsing to his knees in slow motion to make a pad save? Or the look of joy on a parent's face when their son or daughter scores? You can't help but smile.

Most of the kids don't know the score (it doesn't matter if it's 2-1 or 12-1, there's always one recurring question: "Who's winning?") and are just as happy mugging for the camera in mom's hands as chasing the puck "all the way down there."

Dragging yourself out of bed at some ungodly hour of the morning (in the past, perhaps you would've just been arriving home from a night of revelry), fighting through snow-covered roads before even the ploughmen are awake and entering dimly lit arenas with foggy ice surfaces, all for the kiddies.

With respect to a certain credit card company: Priceless. This is hockey in its purest form. ■

58. DISCOVER A HOCKEY DESERT OASIS

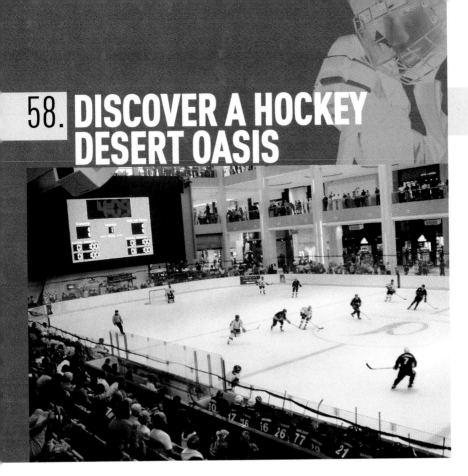

Who says hockey doesn't work in the desert? Sadly for Gary Bettman, we're not referring to Arizona. Indeed, the land in the sand where the sport is blossoming is halfway around the world: the United Arab Emirates.

While the NHL may be forced into exploring relocation – or even contraction – in the near future, fans should also note that hockey's lore is spreading around the globe in the most unlikely of places.

In the past 15 years, the oil-rich UAE has transformed itself into a hub for tourism and business.

Gleaming glass skyscrapers, palm-shaped islands and monster-sized malls are surrounded by sun, sea and sand.

Temperatures in the summer reach 45 degrees Celsius, but you'd be mistaken if you think the only ice to be found is in a tall drink by the pool.

The Emirates is embracing hockey despite having no natural history or culture of the game. There is no Thunder Bay in the UAE. Forget snow; heck, it hardly ever rains.

The sport is being pushed forward by a mixture of the indigenous Emiratis (who make up about 22 percent of the country's population of four million) as well as expats from North America and Eastern Europe.

The country has four ice sheets fit for competitive games – two in Dubai, one in the capital Abu Dhabi and one in Al Ain. The newest rink opened in early 2009 in the 440,000-square-foot Dubai Mall (which has more food outlets than Evgeni Malkin had points last season). In March, several hundred shoppers leaned over the railings and looked down to the ice – three floors below – to watch Yvan Cournoyer coach games involving Jari Kurri, Ken Linseman, Jyrki Lumme, Mats Naslund and Alexandr Yakushev, the top-scoring Soviet player from the 1972 Summit Series, plus a host of other former NHLers and locally based players.

The games were to help celebrate Canada Week, but the visit of well-known hockey players was not a one-off. In 2008, Bob Probert, Dave 'The Hammer' Schultz and Claude Lemieux were part of a (surly) traveling team that played three games in Abu Dhabi against the national team.

But while temporarily importing foreign talent in order to attract fans, inspire kids and help educate locals is a well-worn path in many countries, the UAE is also committed to nurturing homegrown talent.

The country brought over two representatives from the International Ice Hockey Federation in 2008 to help establish a domestic league and youth development program. When these are up and running, the UAE can apply to move up from associate member to full IIHF status.

The Emirates already has several well-run clubs, including the brilliantly named Dubai Mighty Camels, who've held their own invitational tournament for 15 years, and the Al Ain Vipers.

The UAE has also successfully hosted two international events in the past couple of years.

The inaugural Arab Cup of Ice Hockey was a massive success in 2008, although the four competing countries used many imports, with the UAE team having a distinctly Belarussian flavour. The Emirates beat Kuwait 4-1 in the final, and followed up that success with an even more impressive achievement in April of 2009.

Again, Abu Dhabi was the host city, this time for the second Challenge Cup of Asia, and once again the UAE triumphed.

The UAE national team's best player, Juma al Dhaheri, scored a hat trick in a 5-3 win over Thailand in the final – and then led the on-ice celebrations before a raucous crowd, which wildly waved UAE flags and scarves and chanted "Hey, hey Emirati" to the tune of Queen's "We will rock you."

But the eight-team tournament was not just about the UAE. It was about Thailand and Macau. It was about the team from India, which played on an indoor rink for the first time (they normally only see ice in the Himalayan areas of Ladakh and Himachal during the winter months). It was about Singapore sniper Iggi Ng. Who couldn't cheer for a guy with that name?

You see, as well as trying to develop hockey within its own borders, the UAE, which is one of 68 nations affiliated with the IIHF, is also helping other Eastern countries do the same.

"They certainly went above and beyond their hosting responsibilities," said Adam Sollitt of the IIHF. "They helped some of those other nations who needed a bit of extra help in getting there. And in terms of travel, equipment, finances, meals, they did an excellent job.

"Although this was only the second year of this event, we can already see it developing further and further. Hockey has a great chance to develop and grow in the UAE as it's so hot there. Virtually all sports have to be played indoors, so why not hockey?"

Why not, indeed?

"They have proven they are competitive enough to play in high-level competition," Sollitt said. "The next step is to introduce a youth program and I know they're taking steps to do this. This will start to grow their membership and get the numbers of players up. This is their priority right now and it's a good one."

In fact, the UAE has already qualified for the 2010 IIHF World Championship Division III, to be played in Athens, Greece, in April. And when the Emirates step onto the ice, guess which number Juma will have on his back? No. 99, of course. ■

59. BLOG, BABY, BLOG

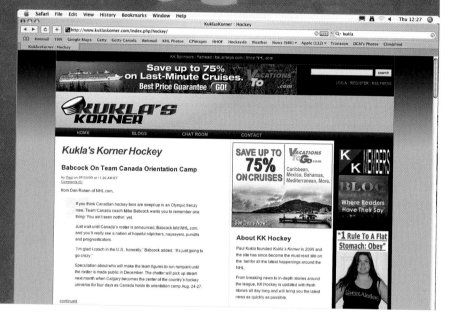

Got an opinion? Go to the 'Net.

Back in the days before the Internet existed, hockey fans aiming to make their views known, either to their favorite player or team, had few avenues by which to publicly express their feelings.

That was then, this is now. Today, technology has made it possible for fans everywhere to form allegiances with their hockey obsession – either through the magic of an online fan club or via their very own blog.

Joining up with an existing fan club – most, but not all NHL teams have them, as do many of the league's players – is one way to do it. Another is to join the cause of the NHL Fans' Association (www.nhlfa.com), a self-envisioned "union for fans" that already has more than 30,000 registered members.

Starting up a hockey website of your own also is fairly straightforward and simple: Select an available Internet address and let your imagination and creativity dictate how the site develops. News, opinion, game analysis, photos, player profiles, chat rooms, hockey history, statistics…it's all right there at your cyber fingertips.

The global hockey village allows an Anaheim supporter who idolizes Teemu Selanne to connect with a Finnish fan who saw him play as a teenager. Montreal and Boston aficionados can collide with each other on fan boards, and anybody can play the role of Toronto GM Brian Burke, laying out a plan to rebuild the Maple Leafs for all the hockey world to witness (and quite possibly, mock).

If you're hardworking and fortunate, you might eventually find yourself in the same shoes as Paul Kukla, a Detroit-area puck lover who started his website, www.kuklaskorner.com, in 2005 and has built it into one of the most popular Internet destinations in the entire hockey community.

Kukla didn't start his site as a tribute to any player, although he makes no bones about being a Red Wings supporter. Rather, he has turned it into an information service for the type of fan with whom he most identifies.

"The reason I decided to start blogging was due to the lack of information I was receiving on the (2004-05) NHL lockout," Kukla said.

"The Detroit media basically acted as if the NHL was no longer in existence and as a hockey fan, I needed and wanted as much information as possible."

Despite the great reception Kukla's web venture has received both from hockey fans and insiders, he believes it hasn't changed his relationship with the sport.

"I've always looked at myself as being just another fan of the game," Kukla said. "I try to keep my finger on the pulse of all the hockey news that I feel NHL fans would be interested in."

There you have it. A hockey blog can be as simple or as complex as you make it, with objective reporting or hard-hitting opinion – or both, and lots more. Tackle an issue, discuss a trend, pump up a favorite player, disparage Sean Avery; whatever you want, whenever you want, and for the world (wide web) to see. ■

60. TAKE A KID TO THEIR FIRST NHL GAME

The little boy had a big decision to make.

It was December, 1973, and he was cast in two roles for the Grade 2 Christmas play, including the lead part of "Pere Noel." Everything was in place when, a couple days before the production, one of his heroes, his dad, asked if he'd like to see a handful of his other idols, the Toronto Maple Leafs, live and in person for the very first time. The game against the California Golden Seals was on the same night as the play.

After as much soul-searching as a 7-year-old can muster, the wannabe Darryl Sittler decided 'The Show' must go on.

"It was actually pretty excruciating," said Jason Kay, editor-in-chief of The Hockey News. "I didn't want to let my classmates down, but the lure of my first trip to Maple Leaf Gardens was overwhelming. Who knew when the chance would come again?"

More than 35 years later, Kay has no regrets. It was simply an unforgettable experience for a young puckhead.

"The thing I remember most is the enormity and grandeur of it all," he said. "Stepping through the tunnel and into the seating area, it was a huge burst of color with all the different shades of seats. I didn't care I was only seeing the 'lowly' California Golden Seals, it was still a dream come true.

"I also remember marveling at the speed of the game compared to TV and the strength of the players. I thought it was so cool when they ringed the puck around the glass. Hey, when I was seven, it was reason to celebrate when I raised the puck."

Parents, aunts, uncles and adult friends revel in the wonderment of the innocence of the children in their lives as they absorb new experiences. When it comes to NHL hockey, the scope, size and pace of the game tends to blow away all first-time attendees, but in particular kids.

That's what NHL goalie Martin Biron carries with him as an indelible memory. His parents had season tickets to Quebec Nordiques games and he recalls sitting behind the Hartford Whalers net during warmups and being astounded by gargantuan puckstopper Mike Liut.

"I couldn't believe how the crossbar barely went above his lower back," Biron said. "He was so tall and he never bent his knees, he just played really straight up.

"At the time, I was four or five playing out in the backyard and I could fit my head under the crossbar and it was a smaller net. I couldn't believe how tall that guy was."

By the time many kids take in their first live NHL game, they have a good handle on the league and its icons thanks to the vast offering of games on TV. But that doesn't mitigate the star-struck factor. That's what Maple Leafs defenseman Luke Schenn recalls about his first trip to the Saddledome to see the Calgary Flames take on the New Jersey Devils.

"Waiting around in my seat for the players to come out for warmups…and they come out and it's like, 'Oh my gosh, that's actually…' " Schenn said.

"For me it was Jarome Iginla, Martin Brodeur and Scott Stevens and Scott Niedermayer, guys like that, seeing them in person. After watching them on TV, it was hard to believe I was actually in the rink witnessing them play."

An NHL rookie at 19 and playing in one of the game's most intense hockey markets, Schenn can still relate to the feeling of youthful joy when he looks up into the stands.

"That was me not too long ago," he said. "It's pretty cool now that kids want to get the chance to meet me and I was the same way not too long ago." ■

61. FOR GOALIES ONLY: BE SUPERSTITIOUS

Goalies are weird. Everyone knows this. If you're a goalie, you likely have a few wacky traditions or phobias. In fact, if you're a goalie who *doesn't* have at least one superstition, you're not really a goalie.

Although goaltenders have been making people scratch their heads since the first of them volunteered to stand in front of puck-shooters virtually equipmentless, a charter member of the Crazy Crease Club was Lorne Chabot, who played in the 1920s and '30s. Chabot used to make sure he shaved prior to every game, because he believed stitches were less likely to leave scars when his mug was whisker-free.

Glenn Hall is one of the greatest goalies in history – and he threw up before every game for fear that if he didn't, Chicago would lose, prompting the Black Hawks to keep a bucket close by. It worked. Hall won 407 games and played 502 consecutive games without a mask. No wonder he felt so nauseous.

Johnny Bower was no kook, but still had his quirks.

"I was very, very fussy with my equipment," Bower said. "I didn't want anybody touching my equipment or my gloves or my sticks. If anybody touched my sticks I would know it and I would get a little perturbed."

We get it, Johnny: Don't touch your stuff.

The crown prince of nutty netminders was Gilles 'Gratoony the Looney' Gratton, who played in the mid-1970s. The former New York Ranger was into meditation and was known to stand on his head in the dressing room before games.

Gratton also believed in reincarnation. He professed to be a former 12th-century sailor, a 14th-century Native American traveler, a 17th-century Spanish landlord, an 18th-century Spanish priest and a 19th-century British surgeon. But apparently being a former surgeon wasn't a cure-all for injuries, as Gratton once begged off a game because of pain from a wound sustained during the 1870-71 Franco-Prussian War.

Also in the '70s, Gary 'The Cobra' Simmons played for the California Seals, Cleveland Barons and Los Angeles Kings. (Lucky goalie, eh?) Once, on a whim, The Hockey News contacted him and asked if he had any superstitions. Within minutes, Simmons replied with a laundry list of odd items.

"I always dressed and undressed left-side first," he said. "When leaving the dressing room before games and between periods, I always tapped above the door with my catching glove. When on a winning streak, I always drove the same way to the rink. Before the game and between periods, I would whistle *The Godfather* theme to myself."

Those were just a few.

Another goalie – Erika Vanderveer, No. 37 for the Burlington Barracudas of the Canadian Women's League and a THN staffer – must eat exactly the same amount of penne before every home game, 37 pieces. If she's hungry, 74, exactly double. And she must cook it for the same length of time, every time – 10:37.

Fittingly, one of the best goalies of all-time, hot-headed Patrick Roy, was also superstitious. Two of his more famous foibles were staring down his net from the blueline before every game, trying to mentally shrink it to the size of a postage stamp, and carrying on complete conversations with his goalposts. As he said of the iron pipes: "They're my friends."

So, remember, just wearing pads and stopping pucks doesn't really mean you're a goalie. To qualify as a bona fide puckstopper, you've got to be a couple saves short of a shutout, if you catch the drift. The kind of person who's different, and not afraid to make sure everyone around them knows it.

So get yourself a superstition or three and then call yourself a goalie. ■

62. TOUR MADISON SQUARE GARDEN

It's been called the Mecca of Boxing. It's been called the Mecca of Basketball. It's known by two words.

The Garden.

There have been four of them, actually, four different incarnations of Madison Square Garden, the original built in 1874 at, well, Madison Square, which was located at Madison Avenue and 26th Street in Manhattan. The building was renovated – and without public money, imagine – in 1890.

But it didn't become *The Garden* until a new one was built on the West Side in 1925 between 49th and 50th Streets and between Eighth and Ninth Avenues. That's the building commonly referred to as "The Old Garden."

That's the smoke-filled arena in which Rocky Marciano knocked out Joe Louis, sending the beloved one-time champ into retirement. That's the arena in which the City College of New York won both the 1950 NIT and NCAA college basketball tournaments. That's the arena in which Marilyn Monroe sang (or purred) "Happy Birthday" to John F. Kennedy at a 1962 birthday party for the president of the United States.

That's the arena in which the New York Americans were the home team for the first hockey game back in 1925-26, with the Rangers coming along a year later. The Americans lasted through 1941-42 before folding. The Rangers, meanwhile, have endured.

The Old Garden? That's the one with the famous marquee on Eighth Avenue.

The new Garden opened in February of 1968, yet is somehow still the "new" Garden. It's the round building on Seventh and Eighth Avenue between 31st and 33rd Street, just across from Macy's, a few long blocks west of the Empire State Building.

It's no longer on Madison and it isn't square, yet it is Madison Square Garden, the World's Most Famous Arena.

The playing surface is on the fifth floor. The upper deck, still primarily known as "the blue seats" although they haven't been that color for years, is on the eighth floor. There's only one ring of luxury suites; they're atop the building. Somehow, the "new" Garden is the third-oldest arena in the NHL after Civic Arena in Pittsburgh and Nassau Coliseum on Long Island.

The "fight of the century" took place at the Garden, Muhammad Ali versus Joe Frazier I on March 8, 1971. Willis Reed hobbled onto the court at the Garden for Game 7 of the 1970 NBA final and led the Knicks to their first-ever championship. Banners representing every starter from that 1970 squad hang from the round ceiling: Reed's No. 19, Walt Frazier's No. 10, Dick Barnett's No. 12, Dave DeBusschere's No. 22, Bill Bradley's No. 24. They're joined by Earl Monroe's and Dick McGuire's No. 15, and by a '613' banner to commemorate the number of career victories for Red Holzman, who coached the Knicks to their only two championships, in 1970 and '73.

Ali-Frazier and Reed's Game 7 represent two of the three greatest moments in the building, the soundtrack of which was supplied for so many years by the distinctive voice of PA man John 'FX' Condon. The third moment – well, that's the night for which New York had waited 54 years.

It was June 14, 1994, and Mark Messier was lifting the Stanley Cup over his head while pandemonium reigned and rained down on the Rangers following their Game 7 victory over the Vancouver Canucks. Horns blared on Broadway. Men and women cried inside the Garden. One jubilant fan held up a sign that read, "Now I Can Die in Peace."

It's a building in midtown Manhattan, sitting above Penn Station and across the street from the city's main post office. People hurry by it on their way to or from their daily commute.

It is the Mecca of Boxing, it is the Mecca of Basketball, it is the World's Most Famous Arena.

It is, simply, The Garden. ■

63. KNOW YOUR HOCKEY TRIVIA

You've been here before; we all have – any kind of beer you want (as long as it's domestic), a diverse menu (as long as it's fried) and a wide array of sports on TV (as long as it's hockey). In a place like this, there are 10 guys for every girl – not exactly Surf City – but for any true hockey fan, a sports bar usually means you get to watch the game in the company of people as puck-crazy as yourself.

But when you put together a bunch of fans who know their hockey, inevitably you'll find someone who's sure he knows it better than you. He might be a working class old-timer who still remembers Bobby Hull raising the Stanley Cup, or a tipsy gent with a Boston twang who can tell you exactly why Don Cherry is the best coach of all-time, or maybe a college kid who's majored in NHL since kindergarten.

Few pub pastimes are more gratifying than stumping so-called hockey-know-it-alls in a no-holds-barred trivia challenge. Here are a few brain-crampers to help you leave your opponent blubbering in his brew:

Q: Who was the only No. 1 overall draft pick to win the Stanley Cup in his rookie season?

A: Rejean Houle went first overall in 1969 and won the Cup with Montreal in 1971. (See? Ken Dryden wasn't the only rookie on that team.)

Q: Name the only person to win NHL coach of the year in back-to-back seasons.

A: *Jacques Demers, with the Detroit Red Wings in 1986-87 and '87-88. (Demers almost won three times in a row, finishing as the runner-up in '85-86 while coach of the St. Louis Blues.)*

Q: Who was the last member of the Toronto Maple Leafs to be named to the NHL's first all-star team?

A: *Borje Salming, in 1976-77. (So, the Leafs haven't won the Cup since '67 and they haven't had a first-team all-star since '77.)*

Q: Who's the only player to score 500 goals with the Boston Bruins?

A: *Long-serving captain Johnny Bucyk notched 545 goals over 21 seasons as a Bruin. (Phil Esposito, the No. 2 shooter in B's history, scored 469 times during just eight-plus seasons in Boston.)*

Q: Who holds the NHL record for most points by a goaltender?

A: *Tom Barrasso, the longtime Buffalo backstop and, later, Pittsburgh champion, picked up 48 points – all assists – over 19 seasons. (That's two points more than Grant Fuhr's career total of 46, but the ex-Oiler holds the NHL single-season mark for points by a goalie: 14, all assists, in just 45 games in 1983-84.)*

Q: Which team holds the NHL record for most consecutive playoff losses?

A: *The Los Angeles Kings and Chicago Blackhawks are tied for the dubious honor with 16 losses apiece. (The Hawks, at least, also share the record for most consecutive playoff wins in the same post-season, at 11, with Pittsburgh and Montreal.)*

Q: Who was the first player to win four major awards in single season?

A: *No. 4, Bobby Orr, won the Norris, Hart, Art Ross and Conn Smythe Trophies in 1970. (And he also would've won the Pearson Award – for league MVP, as voted by the players – but it didn't exist until 1971, when it was won by Orr's teammate in Boston, Phil Esposito.)*

Q: Name the first player to score Stanley Cup-winning goals in back-to-back seasons.

A: *Mike Bossy clinched the Cup for the Islanders in both 1982 and '83. (Bossy, a natural-born scorer, fired 61 goals in 72 playoff games during the Isles' dynasty years of 1980-83.)*

Q: Which player has the most career points in the Stanley Cup final?

A: *Canadiens gentleman Jean Beliveau picked up 62 points in 64 Stanley Cup final games. (Wayne Gretzky sits in second place with 53 points in 31 Cup final games, while Gordie Howe had 50 points in 55 games.)* ■

64. SADDLE UP FOR A GAME AT THE CORRAL

Jim Peplinski is surely the first and only NHL player to register this dandy piece of distinction.

The former Calgary Flames captain must have been the only big-leaguer to have seen his home facility shrink substantially when he graduated from major junior to the NHL. The Renfrew, Ont., native remembers feeling privileged playing for three seasons in hallowed 16,300-seat Maple Leaf Gardens as a teenager for the OHA's Toronto Marlboros.

So what did he get for his hard work and graduation to the NHL? The chance to call home the tiny 6,500-seat Stampede Corral with the newly relocated Calgary Flames.

"I never thought of it in that regard, but I guess it's true," said the man Calgary fans called 'Pepper.'

"It didn't bother me at all, though. When you're 19 years old and playing in the NHL, the venue you're in is the least of your concerns. The Corral was home for me. The Corral was where I grew up."

When the Atlanta Flames were sold to Nelson Skalbania and moved to Calgary in 1980, there was no NHL-caliber arena to play in. Construction started immediately on the $100-million Saddledome, but for the first three seasons the Flames had to make do in the rinky-dink Corral, built out of cinder block and concrete for $1.2 million in 1950.

The Corral was home to the hockey Stampeders, Centennials, Cowboys and Wranglers of various pro and junior leagues over the years. But making it a home for an NHL team? That's akin to making the Rolling Stones play a gig at the local pub.

"I remember showing up for the first time in 1980 and going into the Flames' administrative office out of an Atco construction trailer," Peplinski said. "GM Cliff Fletcher had his office in a mobile home. You couldn't get in or out of the visitors' dressing room without banging your head on the concrete reverse stairs that hung over the entrance."

The Corral is anything but a dump, though, and Peplinski is the first to defend it. Its walls are filled with hundreds of vintage photos from the renaissance years of hockey in Western Canada.

"It's still an in-use arena, but it may as well be a museum," said Darryl Smith, the facilities coordinator for the Stampede Corral. "We get a lot of people coming through just to take a look at the art. We even allow people to get old photos reproduced because they find photos of their father or grandfather from 50 or 60 years ago."

That's part of what makes the Corral a must-see for hockey fans. Seating is all on one tier – some padded fold-up seats accommodate two patrons, while some sections simply have old wooden planks – a standing-room concourse rims the top of the facility and the dressing rooms are small enough to make rec-league teams complain.

Demand for ice time from September through April at the Corral is heavy. Two industrial leagues – Hoser Hockey and the Calgary Oldtimers Oilmen League – have rented ice at the Corral since 1983-84, when the Flames moved to the Saddledome.

"I've seen the same aging faces come and go through here for 25 years now," Smith said. "They tell me they love the old building, the atmosphere and the location (in Stampede Park, right next to the Saddledome.)"

Approaching 60 years old, the Corral isn't in any danger of a date with the wrecking ball. Smith said stress tests on the concrete show it to be stronger than buildings of recent construction. And the Corral has recently received upgrades to the ice plant and electrical systems and had air conditioning installed for the first time. During the summer months, the Corral was and is used for other events such as Stampede All-Star Wrestling, curling, Davis Cup tennis, consumer and auto shows, concerts and, of course, Agri Days, Rodeo Royale and livestock events during the Calgary Stampede.

A few years ago, Gordie Howe was brought to Calgary for an autograph-signing event and he specifically asked for it to be held at the Corral. Before and after the signing sessions, Howe could be seen walking the concourse looking at the old photos and reading the captions. Howe was with the World Hockey Association's Houston Aeros in the mid-1970s and would come through Calgary to play the Cowboys at the Corral.

Peplinski can relate.

"I go to the Corral a few times every year for alumni games and I find myself tempted to take down some of those old photos and bring them home with me," said the man who ranks No. 1 on the list of NHL regular season games played (117) at the Corral.

"If I could snap my fingers and play one more NHL game and it could be in either the ACC (Air Canada Centre in Toronto) or the Corral, my ego would say the ACC, but my heart would say the Corral. I wouldn't change a thing about it, either.

"I did have one complaint about the Corral, though. There would be times after a practice where we wouldn't have hot water for the showers. It would be because they were using it to clean off the bulls out back for the livestock show. Hot water for the four-legged animals, but not for the two-legged ones."

65. PLAY ROAD HOCKEY

Who says hockey isn't a year-round sport?

Instead of hitting the links when the warm weather arrives, hardcore fans take to the pavement for some road hockey.

At its grassroots level, road hockey is played by a group of neighborhood kids on the street where they live. Some old sticks, a tennis ball, a couple nets (if you're lucky) and you've got yourself a game. Intermissions aren't determined by any set clock or timed period, but instead occur when someone yells "Car!" at the first sight of an on-coming vehicle. Everyone knows that's when the ball needs to be picked up, the goalies grab their nets and everyone moves off to the side of the street to let the traffic through. And as soon as it goes by, it's "Game on!" and everyone shuffles back into position.

Of course, not everyone has access to a large group of people nearby and a road with light traffic that won't interrupt the game too much. So nowadays, the term "road hockey" is synonymous with any ball-hockey game played outdoors. Whether you're on the road or on a boarded-in paved surface, road hockey is an activity all fans have to play to get the full hockeyness experience.

Hockey is huge from coast-to-coast across Canada, of course, but it's hard to conceive just how integral the summer version of the sport is to the hungry fan's existence. For Mark McGuckin, his travels across Canada playing road hockey on his TV show *Road Hockey Rumble* opened his eyes to how such a simple sport connects such a vast nation.

"It was great going across the country," McGuckin said. "We had an inkling to how big road hockey was, but after going to all the provinces and territories and seeing all the people coming out in droves who wanted to be a part of our show and wanted to play road hockey…the common denominator was a love of road hockey.

"Especially when we went up to Nunavut and had (Nashville Predators winger) Jordin Tootoo on our show. All the towns were great. The passion up North was amazing."

What makes road hockey so accessible is how cheap and easy it is to get a game going. Unlike ice hockey, where an arena needs to be rented and expensive equipment needs to be purchased, road hockey can involve anyone who wants to join in.

Even if you're not familiar with hockey, even if you've never played the game at all and don't know the rules or the difference between a wrist shot and a slapshot, road hockey is the perfect introduction. And for those who saw ice hockey pass them by, road hockey is the perfect way to stay engaged with the sport.

"We found a lot of people who couldn't skate and just grew up playing road hockey," McGuckin said. "I played ice hockey for four years in elementary school and high school and I have the weird condition of flat feet, so when I'm on skates it gives me extreme lower back pain. So I eventually stopped playing ice hockey, but I kept playing road hockey because it doesn't give me that pain.

"We did find a lot of people who weren't too much into ice hockey. It comes down to how much money they had growing up and maybe their parents couldn't afford to pay for them to play hockey, but they loved the game and were always on the streets."

One of the most memorable moments of the show's cross-country tour occurred in British Columbia with a group of people who had obviously never played the game in their lives.

"For our demo for the show, we were down at the Vancouver art gallery and we set up mini-games throughout the day and we had a lot of Japanese tourists who never picked up a stick in their life, but they got the game right away and had a lot of fun. They were struggling to get the ball and shoot it, but you could see how much fun they were having."

McGuckin said the keys to a good game of road hockey are a smooth surface; a ball that, preferably, doesn't bounce too much so passes can be crisp; and, a healthy amount of trash talking.

To add a little spice to their games, McGuckin and his rival on the show, Calum MacLeod, have an incentive to win each showdown: Whoever loses is subject to a "punishment" that is never pleasant (and sometimes adds injury to the insults dished out when the final scores were tallied).

"We had a game in Moncton, New Brunswick," said McGuckin with a chuckle. "I won and Calum had to suffer a punishment called 'The Moncton Take-Out.'

"We were lucky to get Canadian curler and Olympic gold medalist Russ Howard to hurl his heaviest rock at Calum's nether regions. Calum was sitting on the button with just a jock on and Russ gave it all he had. As Russ said, it was the easiest double he ever threw."

After all the games and all the miles, McGuckin's best road hockey experience didn't occur on a road or a street; rather, it happened on the edge of the earth.

"We were lucky enough to go to St. John's, Newfoundland, and we played our game at the eastern-most point in North America, Cape Spear," McGuckin said. "We played our game in this parking lot that had this majestic lookout over the Atlantic." ■

66. THROW AN OCTOPUS

It is a tradition that has endured for nearly 60 years, and the act of throwing an octopus onto the ice in Detroit is performed in exactly the same manner it was the night of its maiden voyage.

On April 15, 1952, the Red Wings – led by the likes of Gordie Howe, Terry Sawchuk and Ted Lindsay – were on the verge of becoming the first team in NHL history to sweep through the Stanley Cup playoffs. At the time, the NHL was a six-team league; four teams qualified for the post-season, and it took eight wins to capture the Cup. Brothers Pete and Jerry Cusimano, owners of a fish market on the east side of Detroit, decided to throw an octopus onto the ice at Olympia Stadium. The logic being that each tentacle represented a win and it would bring good luck to the team. Little did the brothers know they were about to launch a fan-favorite tradition, one that would stand the test of time.

"When that first octopus was tossed on the ice, the fans weren't sure what it was," said Budd Lynch, the public address announcer at Joe Louis Arena. Lynch was the play-by-play voice of the Red Wings from 1949 to 1975 and called the game the night the first octopus landed on the ice. "Frank Udvari (the referee) wasn't going to touch it and I think it was Marcel Pronovost who thought it was a trout."

Pete Cusimano, the reputed original octopus thrower, once described his technique as follows: "I would fling it sidearm like a hand grenade. If you try to throw it like a baseball, you'll throw your arm out."

Good advice, and taken to heart by Adam Rice, a 19-year-old student from Franklin, Mich., who threw an octopus onto the ice prior to Game 1 of the 2008 Stanley Cup final against the Pittsburgh Penguins.

"Just as the national anthem ended, I walked down the stairs and threw it out onto the ice," Rice said. "I was about 15 rows up when I launched it like a catapult over the glass.

"Before the game myself and three friends decided to buy an octopus…I snuck it in to Joe Louis Arena in my pants and it really wasn't that hard. I had it in a plastic bag and I had my Red Wings jersey on."

The tradition has grown over the years, in part because of the twirling antics of Al Sobotka, the building operations manager at Joe Louis Arena. Sobotka's crew would clean the ice where the octopus landed, and Sobotka would walk off the playing surface while swinging the eight-legged beast over his head – to the screaming delight of 20,000 Wings fans.

"The twirling started in the early 1990s," Sobotka recalled. "I remember it was the last game of the season, I believe against Chicago. Someone threw an octopus, so I went out and grabbed it with my hands. I don't know what came over me and I just started twirling it."

His twirl rekindled the tradition and made Sobotka a celebrity. (The Wings endured some trying times in the 1960s, '70s and '80s, rarely making the playoffs and affording little opportunity for octopus-tossing.) Sobotka was featured on highlight shows from coast to coast, an octopus flailing high over his head as he walked off the ice, sending the crowd into an uproar.

"It really picked up in 1995 with the twirling and the whole octopus frenzy," he said.

"And in the 1997 playoffs against the Colorado Avalanche, I was standing by the Zamboni gate during the national anthem and all of a sudden I heard a 'Plop!' like a big piece of meat had dropped on us. I looked over and I couldn't believe the size of this one. We weighed it at 50 pounds, and I remember Claude Lemieux skating over and saying, 'You twirl *that* now.' "

It's a tradition the players have embraced as well.

"I like traditions that aren't necessarily planned and I don't think this one ever was," said Wings goalie Chris Osgood, who has had a few octopi land close to his crease. "Things that are original and just made up with the fans are great and I think the octopus is one of those that will live forever. Many, many years from now, they'll still be flying on the ice."

And what became of Rice after completing the toss? He quickly ran back up the stairs and into the concourse before security caught up with him, and then returned to his seat to watch the game.

"The crowd's reaction was the coolest part," Rice said. "The next time the Wings go far in the playoffs, I'll do it again."

67. HAVE AN ALL-STAR WEEKEND

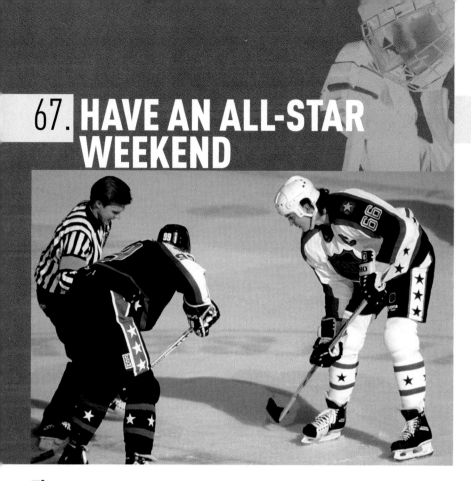

The NHL All-Star Game takes a beating on occasion from those who yearn for more intensity from hockey's best performers. And some of the players themselves have undermined the event by declining invitations or making it seem as though they're doing fans a favor by showing up.

But don't be fooled by the intermittent negativity surrounding the 60-minute game of shinny: The entire weekend offers hockey enthusiasts unique opportunities on several different levels.

Take Montreal, 2009. It was universally lauded not just for the outstanding conclusion to the main event, but also for all the peripheral happenings that cloaked the game.

"The weekend was fantastic," said New York Islanders defenseman Mark Streit, a former Canadien who appeared in his first All-Star Game. "It was a dream come true. Obviously, going back to Montreal was really emotional for me. I had three wonderful years there and the atmosphere was great, the response from the fans was unbelievable. Being part of an All-Star Game in Montreal is a once-in-a-lifetime opportunity."

From a fan perspective, the key for all-star weekend is to arrive early. If you're an out-of-towner, don't just come on the Sunday and hope to be entertained by that day's game. Get there on Thursday or Friday and start enjoying both the city you're visiting and the special events offered by the host team and NHL. Fan-friendly exhibits typically dot the areas surrounding the rink, featuring places to test your hockey skills, meet heroes of the game, view some rare collectibles and maybe even have your photo taken with the Stanley Cup.

On the Saturday, an open practice is usually held in the morning and the players tend to ham it up. It's a rare (and free!) chance to see them at ease, having fun and giving something back. Montreal was extra special in this regard. More than 20,000 excited spectators packed the Bell Centre, lifting what is usually a pedestrian happening around NHL rinks to new heights.

"I couldn't believe it," said New Jersey Devils center Zach Parise. "Not only were they there, they were excited and there was energy in the rink. That's crazy."

The evening is time for the NHL skills competition, an event that almost always delivers a "wow" moment. Chances are, a lasting memory will be created, whether it's a scruffy-looking Al Iafrate registering a then-record-breaking, 105.2-mile-per-hour slapshot (1993); Mike Gartner winning his third fastest-skater award at age 37; or, Alex Ovechkin donning sunglasses, a Tilley hat and using two sitcks during the breakaway challenge.

There are usually scores of parties in the host city frequented by players and NHL bigwigs. If you can, try to get on a guest list or score tickets to one of these shindigs. You can also rub shoulders with hockey's elite in hotel lobbies and glimpse them on their entry to the arena on the red carpet.

Naturally, the game itself has provided its share of enduring moments. Detroiters will never forget Gordie Howe's homecoming in 1980 after departing nine years earlier for the World Hockey Association. Mr. Hockey, 51 and appearing in his 23rd and final all-star show, was given one of the greatest standing ovations in league history when he was introduced to fans in the newly opened Joe Louis Arena. As his admirers continued to applaud and chant his name for several minutes, Howe exuded his typical humility, looking awkward and embarrassed as he fought back tears and fidgeted. That the same game was Wayne Gretzky's all-star debut was icing on the cake.

Much earlier in his career, in 1951, Howe engaged in something we'll never again see: an All-Star Game fight. His opponent? Who else, Maurice Richard. (Imagine Sidney Crosby and Pavel Datsyuk dropping the gloves and duking it out…in an All-Star Game, no less.) Gretzky's finest all-star moment was a four-goal, third period outburst in 1983. Not to be outdone, Mario Lemieux had points on all six of the Wales Conference's goals in 1988. Owen Nolan generated a buzz when he pulled a Babe Ruth in front of the hometown crowd in San Jose in 1997; while on a breakaway, he pointed to where he was going to shoot and then proceeded to fire one top-shelf past Dominik Hasek.

In 2003 in Florida, onlookers got their wish – the game was tied after 60 minutes. The fans cheered heartily as overtime wound down and the game was sent to the NHL's first-ever all-star shootout. Six years later in Montreal, Alex Kovalev potted the shootout winner to the delight of the home crowd in one of the most thrilling All-Star Games ever.

Due to the Olympics, there's no all-star weekend scheduled for 2010, but Phoenix is slotted to hold the party in 2011 and Chicago has its sights set on 2012. Already, Hawks president John McDonough is dreaming up ways to ensure enduring memories.

"If we're going to host an All-Star Game," McDonough said, "our ultimate goal is it to be a premier, once-in-a-lifetime event similar to the Winter Classic."

So forget the time Pavel Bure bolted the game with 10 minutes left in the third period in order to catch a flight. The vast majority of stars who participate come away with a very positive experience and do their best to put on a show.

"You want to have the best players here and hopefully everyone has that feeling as well," said Carolina Hurricanes center Eric Staal, a three-time All-Star Game participant. "I enjoy being here. I love being a part of it. To be named is an honor and it's something that I will continue to keep coming to if they ask."

68. GIVE A BOOST AND VOLUNTEER

You'll almost certainly run yourself ragged. You'll deal with over-aggressive parents who think their little Johnny is the next Pat Boutette. You'll wake up at ungodly hours. And your idea of a gourmet meal will be a half-cooked hot dog washed down with bad coffee.

And you'll have the time of your life.

Talk to anyone who has volunteered his or her time to the game and you'll find someone rich with stories and a lifetime of fulfillment. There are some horror stories to be sure, but you wouldn't see so many people coming back to do it for so many years if there wasn't something rewarding associated with doing it.

There's nothing quite like standing behind the bench during a tie game in the third period, only to have a gap-toothed youngster turn to you ask whether or not there will be post-game snacks. You haven't lived until you've seen some kid try to burp the entire alphabet. And you're truly missing out if you haven't seen the face of a young boy or girl after you've tied their skates for them.

There's an old saying that suggests we can't give our children anything more valuable than our time. That couldn't be any more true than when it comes to minor hockey. And the best thing about it is there is any number of jobs anyone can fulfill.

Not everyone can be the next Scotty Bowman – or wants to be, for that matter. But do you think the pre-season registration gets done by itself? That somehow fundraising money just magically appears out of nowhere? Do you think the time and the score of the game keep track of themselves or that little elves somehow make up the schedule each season and stage all the tournaments?

No, it's done by good-hearted volunteers, most of whom are there because their children are involved in the sport. But the funny thing is once the bug bites you, it often becomes a life-long affliction. The Ted Reeve Hockey Association in Toronto gives people who volunteer for 25 years a very impressive ring – and there are a lot of people with grey hair and rings around the rink every weekend. Their children stopped playing in the league a long time ago, but they're still there, sometimes joined in their volunteering by the same children who got them involved in the first place.

Ask any one of them and they'll tell you the smiles are as bright now as they were decades ago.

69. SOAK UP SOME U.S. COLLEGE ATMOSPHERE

U.S. college sports fans know what it means to live and die with their favorite teams. The atmosphere and energy of an NCAA hockey game is something that should be experienced by every diehard hockey fan. Imagine thousands of college students all dressed in their school colors, hyped and ready to yell and scream until the final buzzer.

For an experience such as that, look no further than the Kohl Center in Madison, Wisconsin. Home of the Wisconsin Badgers, an overwhelming sea of red engulfs the entire arena and if that isn't enough, just wait until the band begins to play. The fans have a different dance for every song and when they start to all bounce up and down in succession, be prepared for motion sickness if you choose not to join in. For a split-second, it feels like the entire building is shaking – and just for the thrill of that moment alone, it's worth checking out a Badgers game.

If you're seeking a more intimate environment, your best bet is to check out a Wolverines game at Michigan's Yost Ice Arena. With a maximum capacity of 6,603, the building comes alive as it hosts a sell-out crowd every game, building up its well-earned reputation for being one of the most intimidating rinks to play in for visiting teams. The stands are right on top of the players, and when 6,000-plus college students begin to chant and scrutinize the visitors, there is no escaping the fear factor.

But the most intimidating rinks might be the ones that house the two top teams in Minnesota university hockey: the respective homes of the Duluth Bulldogs and the Minnesota Golden Gophers. First off, the band at the Duluth Entertainment Convention Center does an over-the-top job at heckling the visiting team's goaltender, from shouting obscene cheers to continuous taunting on a first-name basis.

And be prepared for name calling, as everyone in the arena points and yells at the goalie, "Sieve! Sieve! Sieve! Sieve! Sieve! It's all your fault! It's all your fault! It's all your fault!" If you're a fan who likes to heckle, you'll fit right in at the DECC in Duluth.

And don't forget Mariucci Arena, home to the Golden Gophers. With its open-bowl atmosphere, every fan can enjoy the game from anywhere in the concourse. And if you're a fan of Minnesota hockey history, a shrine of memorabilia fills the lobby and concourse. But no great fan experience is complete without some crowd interaction; as long as the home team is scoring, the Mariucci Arena has that covered. Initiated and backed up by the school band, 10,000-plus Gophers fans sing their "Rouser" fight song after every Minnesota goal.

Or, if you're one with a luxurious taste, don't miss out on visiting the Ralph Engelstad Arena in Grand Forks, North Dakota. One of the most expensive college arenas (it cost more than $100 million), this rink is definitely worth checking out. With granite flooring throughout the concourse and leather seats filling the stands, The Ralph has been called the "finest facility of its kind in the world." And don't be fooled by its rural location, the University of North Dakota has no problem selling out its 11,640-seat arena, game in and game out.

Finally, be sure to check out the Buckeyes of The Ohio State University. The old OSU Ice Rink was built in 1961 and renovated in 1999. First home to the men's team, the women's team took over when the men moved to the newly built Value City Arena at the Jerome Schottenstein Center. Although there are only bleachers on one side of the OSU Ice Rink and it has a capacity of just 1,200, it gets loud and rowdy on most nights – especially when the OSU band makes its appearance. Add a few groups of dedicated supporters who show up for every home game and are always waiting to high-five their favorite Buckeyes as they hit the ice, and it makes for an intimate and personal experience for both the players and fans. Oh, and don't forget to bring your skates – 'Skate with the Buckeyes' and an autograph session follow every home game. ■

70. GO TO THE MEMORIAL CUP

The prevailing notion is the Memorial Cup is the most difficult trophy in hockey to win.

No argument from this corner.

Think about it, you play 68 games a year, plus playoffs, and travel through the dead of Canada's winter just to win your own league. Then you get to play three of the best teams in Canada in a tournament format that can be cruel if your timing isn't perfect.

At the 1990 Memorial Cup, the Oshawa Generals won the trophy and Eric Lindros wasn't even close to being the best player in the tournament. Some young kid by the name of Scott Niedermayer played in that one for the Kamloops Blazers, who stormed through the Western League only to fizzle out at the most crucial time.

When Bill Armstrong scored for the Generals in overtime in one of the most enter-taining games ever played – the round-robin contest between the two teams that went into double overtime was even better, if you can believe it – Oshawa goalie Fred Brathwaite skated the length of the ice to console Kitchener Rangers goalie Mike Torchia.

As the two embraced, if you looked closely enough you could see Brathwaite reach-ing around and feeling the ice until he grabbed the game-winning puck in the back of the net.

That's the kind of stuff you see at the Memorial Cup.

In 2005, Sidney Crosby was brilliant for the Rimouski Oceanic, but it wasn't enough to stop the juggernaut that was the London Knights in the final. The NHL lockout had wiped out the 2004-05 season, so this was the closest thing to a Stanley Cup final; as such, the city of London was frenetic during the week of the tournament. In 2009 in Rimouski, the Windsor Spitfires became the first team ever to win the tournament after opening with an 0-2 record in one of the most entertaining Memorial Cups in memory.

Sure, the Memorial Cup is the launching pad for future NHL stars, but that's not the beauty of the event. In fact, it's rarely the star players who supply the most lasting memories.

Perhaps that's because for the vast majority of them, this is the best it's ever going to get when it comes to hockey. Next time you go to a major junior game, look up and down each bench during the national anthem. If you see more than two or three players who end up being full-time NHLers, you've hit the jackpot.

The total is usually a little higher at the Memorial Cup, but for most of the players, the tournament represents the pinnacle of their hockey careers. Some will go on to ca-reers in the minors or Europe, while most will face the harsh reality that they're sim-ply not good enough to make a living playing hockey.

But for one week of their lives, they're on center stage and they're playing with all the passion they can muster. And that's what makes going to the Memorial Cup a must-do for any true hockey fan.

71. LIVE LIKE AN NHL PLAYER

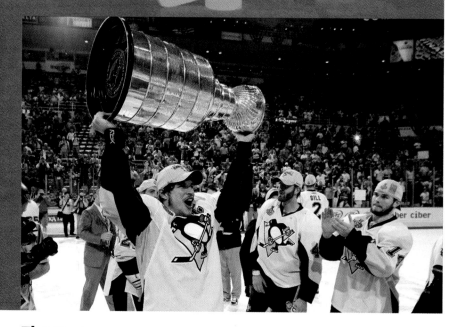

The life of an NHLer, what more could anyone ask for, right? Fame and fortune. Chartered flights. Five-star hotels. Per diems. Seven-figure salaries. Playing a game for a living. Summers off…

Ah, the good life. Wouldn't it be great to take some laps in their skates?

Well, it may be, but it's not all perks and Easy Street. In fact, being an NHLer is a year-round commitment – and sometimes a monotonous one. For all the fame and glory, there are less glamorous aspects, too.

"I eat, nap, hang around in sweatpants all day and relax, then get myself mentally prepared for the night ahead," said Minnesota Wild center James Sheppard when asked about his (not exactly exciting) game-day routine.

Sure, NHLers travel around North America in the lap of luxury, but they're on and off planes and in and out of hotels, day after day after day, for eight months a year. They live out of a suitcase. Yes, many NHLers make more money in a season than most people do in a lifetime, but everyone knows what they're paid and the pressure to perform is immense and unnerving.

Oh, and the off-season? Not as relaxing as you'd expect. It's really just time to get re-acquainted with the friends and family NHLers have been away from for more than half the year.

"I'd say yes," said St. Louis sniper Brad Boyes when asked if he's given up a lot to be an NHLer, "especially in junior, leaving home at 16. You move in with a different family, you miss your friends, parties, high school."

Added Toronto blueliner Tomas Kaberle, rather matter-of-factly, about the off-season: "I look forward to seeing my family. I go back home."

Most NHLers take a few weeks off to relax and rest any bumps and bruises incurred during the season. But then it's right back to work. This isn't your father's NHL, where players usually arrived at training camp all summer-soft and out of shape. These days, the vast majority of NHLers are physically prepared the moment camp opens. And it's trending younger and younger each year.

"I started working out at a gym when I was 15," said Los Angeles left winger Dustin Brown, when asked about his relationship with the weight room.

Many NHLers strictly adhere to training programs during the off-season. Ageless veteran Chris Chelios and the recently retired Gary Roberts are legendary for the amount of work they put in during the summers to keep their bodies in peak shape. And to be a star these days, you have to do the same to keep up.

"I have a program in the summer that involves Olympic weightlifting as well as running and sprinting," said sniper Marian Gaborik. "I also do some weightlifting during the season."

Healthy eating is another must. Chicken, fish and pasta are the staple foods for every pro, meal in and meal out, all season long and during the summer, too. With few exceptions.

"My weight usually stays the same the whole year," said Chicago center Patrick Sharp. "I do eat a little healthier in the off-season because I'm not burning off so many calories, so my diet does change a little bit. During the season you can get away with eating a bowl of ice cream here or there or bingeing a little bit."

Oh, Patrick. A whole bowl? Here and there? Don't go overboard, now. Imagine what Sharp's binges must be like. A second beer? An extra slice of thin-crust, gluten-free pizza? Lunacy, sheer lunacy.

Of course, it's not all bad. Not by any means. Playing in the NHL is a dream come true for everyone who does it and they will all tell you the sacrifices are worth it: "I wouldn't change a thing," Boyes said, despite the sacrifice. And that's a statement echoed by every NHLer.

So it's worth it, getting to the big leagues. But just don't think it's all glitz and glam, all play and no work. It's quite the opposite. Don't believe us? Then try living like an NHLer, and see how long you last. ◼

72. WATCH A GAME LIKE A SCOUT

What's it like to watch a game with a scout? Well, that depends.

If you're with a pro scout who's trying to get the skinny on other NHL teams' players, you're probably sitting high above the action in a comfortable press box chair with ample access to free popcorn and ice cream.

But if you're with an amateur scout, attempting to project which player out of a group of 16-year-olds might develop into a quality NHLer in five years, the game experience is a little different.

You might have fairly cozy conditions in a major junior rink in Red Deer or Rimouski, or you may be at a high school game in Minnesota, pasted against a wall in the corner of some tiny arena beside kids who should be doing their homework, but are instead screaming fight songs in your ear. And that's just one thing standing between you and the ability to make a shrewd assessment on a youngster who isn't even done growing yet and whose mother probably still makes his lunch.

"The coach could be the music teacher and the draft-eligible kid is playing against ninth graders," said one scout on some of the potential perils involved in evaluating high school players (who, by the way, are routinely selected in the first two rounds of the NHL draft these days).

Contrast that to, say, the Western League, where a soon-to-be drafted youngster is running up against beefy 20-year-olds and playing a very busy, NHL-like schedule.

"In major junior, you're playing against teams with 10 or 15 NHL-drafted players, you've got guys trying to jam a stick down your throat and kick (your butt) every shift, you're playing a lot of games and you're traveling thousands of miles," the scout said.

Comparing how one player performs under favorable conditions to how another functions in much more treacherous circumstances is a huge challenge for amateur scouts. And the evaluation doesn't end with the third period buzzer. Scouts need to talk to the kids and their coaches to get a genuine feel for what kind of all-around player and person may be developing.

"If you're going to draft somebody, you need to talk to them at some point," the scout said. "There's a zillion stories about teams drafting a guy and then finding out he's an idiot or likes to party. You have to talk to their coach and to the kid, get to know them, see their body language."

As for the pre-game routine, the first question a scout must answer is, "Can I possibly stomach another cold hot dog and watered-down pop for dinner?"

"I have to eat ahead of time, I can't stand arena food," said the scout, stressing he always uses the per diem his team provides to find a healthier meal than the dog-and-soda option.

If the rink happens to be a major junior facility, comprehensive information packages will be provided for all scouts in attendance. Coaches are also required to provide line combinations, so scouts can take a peek at the dry-erase board and jot down the trios and defense pairings.

The truth is, a smart scout isn't only on the lookout for the next great player. He may also have an eye toward landing his next job, given the volatile nature of the industry.

"You go to the arena, they have a designated room for us," the scout said. "The guys like to have some socializing and catching up…And for scouts, it's also a time to network. I mean, you're only as good as your last contract."

Scouting at the pro level is a bit different in that the majority of players have already developed into what they're going to be; which is to say, not many 30-year-old NHL journeymen suddenly blossom into superstars. If a player has been in the big leagues for several seasons as a third-line checker, that's probably what the player will remain.

However, that doesn't mean there aren't intangibles to consider.

Pro scouting requires a macro view. It's more about putting things in the big picture, meaning a bird dog must account for the type of team the player is on and the kinds of things he's being asked to do. If a scout is eyeing up a blueliner on a team that plays with strict adherence to defense, you may not see his complete offensive upside because he's not being encouraged to rush up the ice and join the attack. Conversely, it's important to remember a rearguard on a more offense-minded team probably has the green light to jump into the play, thus accentuating his offensive abilities and posing questions about how he may or may not fit into a more defensive approach.

"Like anything, scouting is a routine," said the scout. "You get into a system of how you do things and that system can evolve. It depends on the leagues you're scouting." ▪

73. TAKE ON THE WORLD POND HOCKEY CHAMPIONSHIP

"If you want to build it, they will come."

Remember when you were young and shoveled off the nearest creek, pond or lake with your buddies, then played puck until your mom wouldn't let you stay outside any longer?

Imagine doing so with about 500 other players from around the world, on 20 side-by-side rinks in the great outdoors, for four days – and at the end of it all, skating away with the title of World Pond Hockey Champion. It's a hockey fan's paradise.

"It's surrounded by pine trees," said Charlie Cameron, a former Jr. A and University of New Brunswick player who's now a 45-year-old policeman, as well as a member of the two-time defending champion Wheat Kings.

"You walk down and all of a sudden, especially after dark, it's all lit up and there's players playing everywhere."

"It" is Roulston Lake in Plaster Rock, N.B. – about two hours north of the provincial capital Fredericton – and "It" is quite a sight with the rinks shoveled and cordoned off.

The annual February event attracts 120 teams, each with four skaters (plus a substitute). Goalies aren't used and the puck can't be raised above the ankles – which is how high the nets are. Each team is guaranteed five games; one on Thursday, two on Friday and two on Saturday. The top 32 squads advance to Sunday's playoff round, a one-loss-and-you're-done format where the caliber of play takes a big jump.

"The tournament is like a homecoming for the people on the Tobique River," said THN correspondent and New Brunswick native Nathan White, whose wife is from the area. " 'Are you coming home for pond hockey?' is almost as common as, 'Are you coming home for Christmas?' The two are about as equally revered by the people up there."

Added Cameron: "The whole community rallies around. Like, people move out of their houses or loan people their houses."

Cameron offered one personal example of the community's involvement from a few years back. It had rained all day Friday and then the temperature dropped about 20 degrees in an hour at night, turning the rain to crusty snow almost immediately. With the rinks unplayable, all the games were cancelled for the day.

"We were sitting in the cabin playing cards, having a beer and these two ladies came to the door," Cameron said. "They said, 'Hi guys, we know it rained today. We live across the street, do you folks need any laundry done or anything dried? We'll dry it and bring it back to you.'

"That's the community there. That's the way they welcome you."

It all began in 1997, when the people from Plaster Rock decided they needed an arena to serve the community – no one wants to shovel the lake all the time. Nothing fancy (that's not the Maritime way), just a sheet of ice with a roof over it, some walls, a few dressing rooms and, maybe, a snack bar. Total cost, about $3 million; small change in the arena-building business. Unfortunately, the town's 1,200 residents didn't have that kind of capital on hand; instead, they were left to their own fundraising devices.

They did what they could, but to little avail. You can only find so many empty beer bottles or sell so many brownies. Then, in 2002, Plaster Rock began hosting the World Pond Hockey Championship, and it became the town's single-biggest fundraiser in a hurry.

"That first year we only made $6,000 or $7,000, it was a smaller-scale event than it is today," said Danny Braun, the event's manager and one of its founders. "With the feedback we got and the response, the first thing we did was trademark the name and the logo. And that took up basically all of the money we raised."

The World Pond Hockey Championship also quickly became a media darling, with its grand vision for such a grassroots side of the game. The event has been covered by THN, *Sports Illustrated* and *Hockey Night in Canada.*

Things have certainly gotten more lucrative, too. And the money is important because the community is paying down the debt on its new arena, which was built in 2007.

"The tournament has grown to the point where this year (2009) we made about $75,000 profit," Braun said. "And with some added infrastructure, we should get up to about $100,000 in 2010, with any luck."

As for tournament play, Cameron said there are all kinds of participants.

"It's just like a social setting," he said. "They have a huge tent there and people go in and sit down at a table and have a few beers and a hamburger or something.

"Some teams go with the idea of, 'I'm just going to have some fun. I'll play my five games in the round-robin and things are good, I've experienced it.' Other teams, such as us, we go to be competitive. We go to the beer tent and have a good time, but we're there to win the tournament. So there's sort of two groups."

Players and teams hail from all parts of the hockey world, from ankle-skaters to former big-leaguers. Brian Skrudland played 15 NHL seasons, winning Stanley Cups with Montreal in 1986 and Dallas in 1999. He didn't mince words about his Plaster Rock experience.

"This has been a highlight in my hockey career, honestly," he said. "This is what the game is all about. I've had a ton of fun."

Cameron echoed Skrudland's sentiments and added that simply reading about the event isn't enough.

"The atmosphere is unreal," he said "What I tell people is, 'You know what? It doesn't do it justice until you see it.' "

So if you and three friends ever find yourselves in Plaster Rock in the middle of February, looking for a pickup game or five… ▪

74. GET FIRED UP FOR THE FIRST ROUND OF THE PLAYOFFS

Optimism abounds throughout the NHL at the start of the regular season, but nothing matches the excitement generated when hockey's real season begins.

The first round of the NHL playoffs is two weeks of bliss for every type of hockey fan. People who don't pay much attention to the game all winter suddenly spend half their working day avoiding their real job in favor of rehashing overtime heroics from the previous evening.

As for the hardcore fan, the first round is almost overwhelming. The action is boiling over at every turn, with multiple games each and every night. Check that; multiple *meaningful* games each and every night. Playoff survival is on the line and NHL teams go at it shift after shift after shift, with an all-out intensity that's rarely seen in the regular season. Sixteen teams participate in the first round, so there's typically four or five games a night; on weekends, maybe a matinee, an early-evening game (or three or four) and a West Coast late-nighter.

The first round of the NHL post-season is the perfect excuse to plunk down at a neighborhood watering hole with a bunch of buddies, or see how many TVs can be stacked on top of each other and stuffed into one rec room.

Some very fortunate people, like hockey analyst Pierre McGuire, know nothing can match the vibe inside an NHL arena once the playoffs begin.

"I know people really look forward to the first round, the intrigue and the match-ups, and the potential for upsets, the intensity level's going up, the buildings are electric," McGuire said. "It's an amazing time of year for hockey fans. I love it. You become addicted the more you do it and I've been in the league since 1990, that's a long time now, but it never gets old.

"The first round of the NHL playoffs is like a drug, it's highly addictive."

As McGuire noted, the first round of the post-season is exciting based simply on the sheer volume of activity, but it's certainly not a case of quantity devoid of quality. The opening round of the playoffs traditionally features fast-paced and passionate hockey, and often produces some of the biggest upsets of the Stanley Cup derby.

Teams you've rooted against all year – or even all your life – suddenly become an adopted darling simply because they've entered the fray as a No. 8 seed and are threatening to knock off a heavyweight. Everyone loves an underdog; in Round 1, they often travel in packs.

Who could forget Chris Osgood's giveaway late in Game 7 of Detroit's first round series against San Jose in 1994? The blunder led to a Sharks goal that sealed a 3-2 win and an improbable No. 8-over-No. 1 upset. And what about unheralded rookie Ken Dryden standing on his intellectual head to help the 1971 Montreal Canadiens win a seven-gamer over the Boston Bruins, a team that finished 24 points ahead of the Habs in the standings?

For fans of teams on Cup runs, the intrigue and intensity always spikes with each successive round. But don't forget, even by Round 2, only eight clubs remain. By contrast, in Round 1, there are all of 16 teams thinking, "Hey, we're here, we have a chance." Not to mention, hordes of fans simply excited that playoff hockey has arrived, finally ending the monotony of a long regular season.

That's why, for the hockey-watching masses, no time of year rivals that first, furious playoff flurry. ■

75. MEET A MASCOT

There are very few multi-sport personalities in the history of professional athletics. To excel in one profession and be able to transfer that prowess to an entirely different sport is a characteristic few possess and even fewer are given the opportunity to implement at a high level.

Deion Sanders.

Jim Thorpe.

Bo Jackson.

Youppi!

Wait…Youpi!?

The former Montreal Expos mascot suddenly found himself out of a job after the 2004 Major League Baseball season when the team packed up and relocated to Washington. An icon of the Montreal sporting scene for 25 years, Youppi! (yes, the exclamation mark is part of his name) was beloved in the city he called home and his jovial personality never failed to brighten a room – which was important considering the many bad days the Expos had during their tenure in Montreal.

Would Youppi! just be left out in the cold?

"That would have been the ultimate insult," said Jeremy Moses, a former Montreal resident and diehard Expos and Canadiens fan. "He was the only innocence left in an age of fire sales."

But from that dark night came a white knight, the Montreal Canadiens. On Sept. 16, 2005, the Habs formally announced the lovable mascot with bright orange fur would be switching sports and don the *bleu, blanc et rouge* of Montreal's more famous, more successful pro sports team.

The first mascot in the history of hockey's most storied franchise and the first ever to switch from one pro sports league to another, Youppi! was an instant hit. And he's not the only cartoon creature to be adored by the NHL community.

There are approximately 25 NHL teams with full-time mascots. Some, like Carlton the Bear in Toronto (his name and number, 60, represents the address of the old Maple Leaf Gardens) play their roles more quietly and are left to roam the concourses entertaining children. Others, meanwhile, like Spartacat in Ottawa and Wildwing in Anaheim, take a more prominent role in the game festivities, often rappelling down from the rafters before a game and skating around on the ice to rile up the home fans.

Not all mascot stories are happy ones, though. There's the infamous "tongue incident" involving Calgary mascot Harvey the Hound and former Edmonton coach Craig MacTavish.

On Jan. 20, 2003, the Oilers were trailing the Flames 3-0 in Calgary. MacTavish, frustrated by the taunting he was receiving behind the bench from the anthropomorphic dog, gave a quick squirt of water to Harvey's face, but that failed to dissuade Harvey from his hounding ways. So, MacTavish ramped it up a notch. The Oilers coach reached back and, to everyone's shock and awe, yanked Harvey's tongue right out of the canine's mouth and tossed it into the crowd.

Although he showed up at the next game wearing a neck brace, Harvey was relatively uninjured and the incident garnered international headlines and mass outrage over the treatment of a pretend pooch. It just goes to show the love and affection a city can have for its mascot.

Youppi!, as well, still holds a very special place in the hearts of Montreal sports fans.

"He's too good a guy for anyone not to like Youppi!," Moses said. "If you don't like Youppi!, you don't like humanity." ▪

76. JOURNEY TO THE END OF THE WORLD JUNIOR CHAMPIONSHIP

There was once a time when the World Junior Championship was the hidden gem on the hockey calendar. It was a great big good time for hockey geeks, a chance to see future stars of the NHL before they got rich and jaded.

The rinks were pretty much empty with the exception of family and friends and the television pictures back home were a grainy quality that made you certain you were watching something special from some far-off, exotic place. All right, maybe not so exotic, but faraway nonetheless.

That has all changed, of course, particularly in Canada where TSN and Hockey Canada recognized a cash cow when they saw one. Everyone from the beer vendors to the cab drivers makes a killing while the players don't receive a penny for their efforts.

But it hasn't taken the luster off what is almost always an unforgettable hockey experience. And while anyone can go and be a part of the experience when the tournament is in Canada or the U.S., it requires an enormous diehard to give up two weeks at Christmastime to make the trek to Europe for the WJC.

Not that there's anything wrong with going to the tournament in North America, particularly if you're interested in being part of a hockey frenzy. But going to the tournament in Europe helps restore some of that magic that the WJC used to be before it grew up and got famous.

First, the European rinks aren't near as full as the North American ones, but you see some great things. The Swiss are hilarious. With a few notable exceptions, their team shows up at the world junior and gets beaten, but their fans spend the entire game banging on drums and singing songs. At one tournament, they were painted from head to toe and signing songs from the drop of the puck to the final shot in a thumping administered by Canada. At one point, they were singing to the tune of *Gilligan's Island*.

Go to the tournament in Russia and you can buy a hat from a policeman for a couple of bucks. Go when it's in a place such as Pardubice or Hradec Kralov in the Czech Republic and you can eat like a king for about five dollars. Go to Finland and drink with the fans, but do not, we repeat, do not try to keep up with them or you will end up with a very serious headache.

When else are you going to see Lenin's tomb? (We won't tell you the name of the hockey player who wanted to see the tomb of "John Lennon" while he was in Russia.) When else are you going to get a chance to play pickup hockey in Gorky Park with a bunch of Russian guys?

Trust us, it's worth the trip. The hockey has been, and always will be, great. But it might not even be the most memorable part of the experience. ■

77. WHERE WERE YOU WHEN?

If you were alive when something of historical consequence occurred, you probably remember exactly where you were and precisely what you were doing. Maybe you were buying a coffee on your way to work when you heard about the tragedy of 9/11, or were just finishing up your late-night beer-league game when word spread that Barack Obama had won the U.S. presidency.

But do you know where you were when hockey history was being made? Did you bear witness to an NHL moment in time, or were you upstairs putting the kids to bed when Yvon Lambert scored in overtime to eliminate Don Cherry's Bruins in 1979? Or perhaps you had fallen asleep in your easy chair shortly before Anaheim clinched the West Coast's first Stanley Cup in 2007.

The NHL has given its fans plenty of memories over the years. So, hardcore hockey fan, do you know where you were when...

...Paul Henderson scored to win the 1972 Summit Series for Canada?

...the Maple Leafs last won the Stanley Cup in 1967?

...the Blackhawks last won the Stanley Cup in 1961?

...a Canadian team last won the Stanley Cup (hint: Montreal, 1993)?

...the U.S. beat Russia en route to Olympic gold during the 'Miracle on Ice' in 1980?

...the Edmonton Oilers traded Wayne Gretzky to Los Angeles?

...Bobby Orr went flying through the air after scoring the Stanley Cup winner for the Bruins in 1970?

...Willie O'Ree became the first black NHLer in 1958?

...the World Hockey Association started up? When it folded?

...Maurice Richard surpassed Nels Stewart for most goals in NHL history? Gordie Howe surpassed Maurice Richard? Wayne Gretzky surpassed Gordie Howe?

...Wayne Gretzky surpassed Gordie Howe for most points in NHL history?

...Wayne Gretzky scored 92 goals, or 215 points, or scored his 50th goal in 39 games, or completed his 51-game point streak, or...well, where you were when Gretzky played?

...Mario Lemieux came out of retirement? The second time? The third time? (The next time?)

...the NHL announced, due to the lockout, that the 2004-05 season was cancelled?

...Nicklas Lidstrom became the first European captain to hoist the Stanley Cup, after leading Detroit to NHL supremacy in 2008?

...the Original Six expanded to 12 teams, in 1967?

...Scott Stevens flattened Eric Lindros in the 2000 playoffs? How about when Stevens ran over Slava Kozlov in '95? Paul Kariya in '03? Ron Francis and Shane Willis in '01?

...Bobby Hull and Stan Mikita turned their newly shaped "banana blades" into powerful slapshots that would change the way the game is played?

...the Canadiens tied the Soviet Red Army 3-3 on New Year's Eve, 1975, in one of the best hockey games ever played?

...NHLPA boss Alan Eagleson was found guilty of fraud and embezzlement?

...Dominik Hasek denied Canada in the 1998 Olympic semifinal, stopping all five shooters in the shootout?

...the Flyers "hosted" the Soviet Red Army in the contentious 1976 game that featured Bob Cole's memorable call: "They're goin' home! They're goin' home! Yeah, they're goin' home!"

...the Habs won their fifth consecutive Stanley Cup in 1960?

...the Oilers dumped the Islanders in the 1984 Cup final, as one dynasty took over from another?

...non-traditional hockeytown Tampa Bay won the Cup in 2004? Or Carolina in '06?

...you witnessed your first Battle of Alberta?

...Quebec bolted to Colorado? Or Winnipeg left for Phoenix?

...Florida made it to the 1996 Cup final as a third-year expansion team?

...Ottawa drafted Alexandre Daigle first overall in 1993?

...you first heard Don Cherry say, "Listen to me, all you kids out there...!"

...Bob Probert fought Tie Domi?

...Martin Brodeur overtook Patrick Roy for most all-time wins?

...Marty McSorley felled Donald Brashear? How about Todd Bertuzzi's attack on Steve Moore?

...the Stastny brothers, led by Peter, defected from Czechoslovakia and ended up in Quebec City as Nordiques?

...Alexander Mogilny defected from Russia to play for the Buffalo Sabres?

...Mark Messier led the Rangers to their first Cup in 54 years?

...Boston traded Joe Thornton to San Jose?

...they played the last game at the Montreal Forum? At Maple Leaf Gardens? The old Chicago Stadium?

...the Leafs rallied from a 3-0 series deficit, winning four straight games over Detroit to capture the 1942 Stanley Cup?

...you saw your first NHL game?

78. NHL MORNING PRACTICE MAKES PERFECT

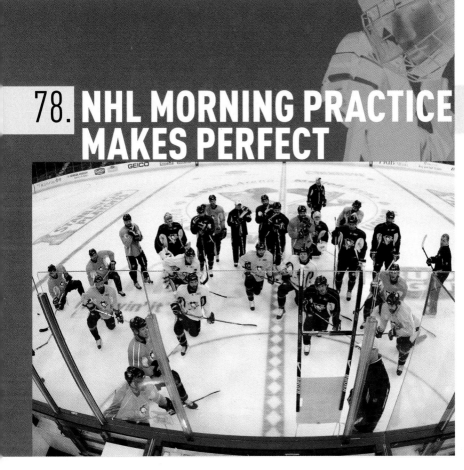

For Mike Pelino, bringing in youth teams to watch his New York Rangers practise has been a rewarding experience – with only one painful repercussion.

Pelino, an assistant coach with the Rangers since 2005, also officiates youth hockey games in his spare time. During one outing, he was served with a sharp reminder about how much attending a Blueshirts practice sticks in the mind of a youngster.

"I was out refereeing a mite game and some kid comes up to me and slashes me on the foot and says, 'You're Mike with the Rangers, we were at your practice last year,' " recalled Pelino with a chuckle.

Sore feet aside, bringing kids out to watch the Rangers skate at their beautiful facility in Tarrytown, N.Y., has been a rewarding activity for Pelino and everybody else involved.

"It's really gratifying for us, for me, for our organization, to see the awestruck looks on their faces and know we're doing something good for the kids," Pelino said.

The idea of hosting youth teams and kids with special needs at the team's big-league practice facility blossomed after Pelino brought in his son's squad and saw the team's enthusiastic reaction. The reality is, though, witnessing an NHL team's morning skate is a treat not to be missed for fans of any age.

In some ways, attending a practice session exceeds the experience of watching an actual game live, because observers get a much closer, much more intimate look at the action.

"It's incredible for them, to put it in a nutshell," Pelino said. "First of all, they're right at ice level, basically right up against the glass and to see (Rangers goalie) Henrik Lundqvist or anybody that close up is amazing.

"It's such a nice, humble environment because it's a rink without any seats."

When youth teams come to the Rangers' practice arena, they get to soak up the complete professional hockey atmosphere. In addition to watching the coaches put the players through their paces, kids tour the video room, the dressing room and often get a chance to grab a snack while socializing with some players in the team cafeteria.

"The chef usually makes them cookies or they can have Gatorade or whatever their little hearts desire," Pelino said. "And the players are great at embracing the fact there are kids around."

Then the kids get to become players themselves, hitting the ice for a team practice on the same surface the Rangers sharpen their skills on.

"When they get on the ice, I tell them we're basically running a real Rangers practice here," Pelino said, adding with a laugh, "the passing might be a little better, just not as fast."

One element that will always stand out to anybody taking in an NHL practice is the base skill level that every player in the league possesses. It's easy to stick the "scorer" and "grinder" labels on players when watching a game, but observe any group of NHLers polishing their moves during practice shootouts or any kind of puck drill and it's immediately obvious even fourth-liners are blessed with incredible natural abilities.

"Colton Orr is as good as anybody coming in on Henrik Lundqvist," said Pelino of the NHL tough guy. "The kids get inspired by that, to see even the so-called 'worst' NHLer, how good they have to be." ◾

79. SKATE IN RED SQUARE

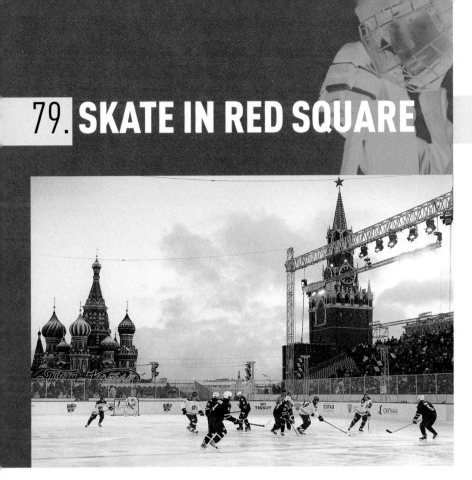

Alfresco hockey is a staple of the sport and about as grassroots as a game of snow and ice can get. Typically, though, the act of gathering a group of people to play a game of shinny outdoors is accompanied by a background of pine trees, a snow-covered park or a nearby chalet to recover warmth in.

It goes without saying that initiating a game of outdoor hockey should be on every fan's bucket list. But to add to the truly liberating experience, how about taking that outdoor game and slapping it in the middle of Moscow's Red Square?

Formerly the center of a universe cut off to the Western world, Red Square is now open for any tourist to see up close. Trying to get a hockey game going there, though, is still a daunting task. However, for former NHLer Ben Clymer, all it took was a move to Dynamo Minsk of the Kontinental League and a selection into the circuit's all-star game.

"Being American, to play hockey in such an important place in Russian culture was an experience I'll cherish along with my first NHL game, my first playoff game, playing in Game 7 of the Stanley Cup final and a handful of other events I'll remember in great detail years from now," said Clymer, who played nearly 450 NHL games with Washington and Tampa Bay and won a Stanley Cup with the Lightning in 2004.

Surrounded by cultural relics of a long-standing Slavic civilization, the experience of playing hockey in Red Square is like no other. With founding father Vladimir Lenin's mausoleum lurking in the shadows of the Kremlin walls and 16th-century ruler Ivan the Terrible's lively and carnival-like St. Basil's Cathedral dominating the horizon, a hockey game in the backyard of Moscow's political headquarters isn't at all like any outdoor game you'd find in North America.

However, that's not to say the unique experience won't jog memories of home for a veteran outdoor player.

"It was an incredibly cold day, something like minus-16 degrees Celsius," said Clymer, 31. "It was a little windy, but not too bad. The wind in your face from skating was far colder. Every intermission I took my skates off in the dressing room to try and warm them up, but at no point did my feet regain feeling until finally about half an hour after the game.

"It made me think about all the times when I was a boy skating outside in Minnesota and I would get frostbitten on my toes."

Clymer was part of Team Jagr – consisting of import players – in the all-star game. Making his experience all the more special was the fact he converted a goal off a pass from former Washington Capitals teammate Jakub Klepis in the first period. In the end, Team Yashin – made up of Russian players – made a valiant attempt at a comeback, but Clymer's import team walked away with a 7-6 victory.

An outdoor game unlike any other, partaking in a Red Square sub-zero skate should not only be a goal for the most dedicated and driven hockey fans, but also one of the greatest challenges to reach in a lifetime. ■

80. COMPREHEND THE COMPOSITE STICK

The days of the wooden stick are pretty much gone in hockey, but that doesn't mean the process of making the game's greatest offensive weapons is any less magical.

To be sure, the steps needed to turn carbon into a stick are different, not to mention fascinating. So if you ever get a chance to visit a hockey stick factory, definitely take the opportunity.

Easton, one of the leading names in the hockey equipment industry, makes its sticks just across the U.S. border in Tijuana, Mexico. Every summer, handfuls of NHL players sponsored by the company make the trip down to the sunny locale and talk shop with designers while they tour the facilities. Recent visitors to the Easton plant include snipers Dany Heatley, Marian Gaborik and Daniel Briere.

"They tell us what they're looking for, what kind of shot they're getting off and how to tweak it," said Mike Mountain, director of sticks and blades for Easton. "Certain players will request a heavier stick, so we'll add sand mixed in with resin. Some like them light, so we'll take everything out."

The main ingredients in today's pro sticks are quite high-tech.

"No. 1 is carbon," Mountain said. "The second is Kevlar, for impact absorption and feel…it gives the stick a wood sensation."

There's also foam in the blade, which, depending on the model, may be fused to the stick during the production process.

Modern stick shafts are molded and then heated in batches in an oven so big you can walk inside it. Sometimes, the oven is used to cure the sticks, while in other stages, the graphics are put on and seared in by the heat.

All in all, Mountain estimates it takes six to eight hours for a stick to be created these days. But the production of a hockey stick isn't the only thing to see at Easton's factory. Innovation is also on the menu in Tijuana: The company's research-and-development wing also operates out of the same building.

"It's a great way for those guys to be right there next to production," Mountain said.

The research department works like a laboratory, where extensive testing is done on prospective new sticks to ensure they work well and meet Easton's standards. Though the specifics of the tests are a company secret, Mountain said they function very much like automobile trials.

When it comes to hockey sticks, there are tests for impact, flex and shooting capabilities; in most cases, specialized machinery is used to conduct the experiments. And since this is a bastion of hockey we're talking about, there's also a net set up on a simulated ice surface so the team can see if a new stick passes the fun test.

"I've been down a couple times where I've had an idea for a stick in the morning and by the time I leave at the end of the day, that stick is in my hands," Mountain said. "I'll take it back across the border and use it in a game that night."

When it comes to occupations, some people have all the luck. ■

81. GROW A PLAYOFF BEARD WITH YOUR HOCKEY HAIR

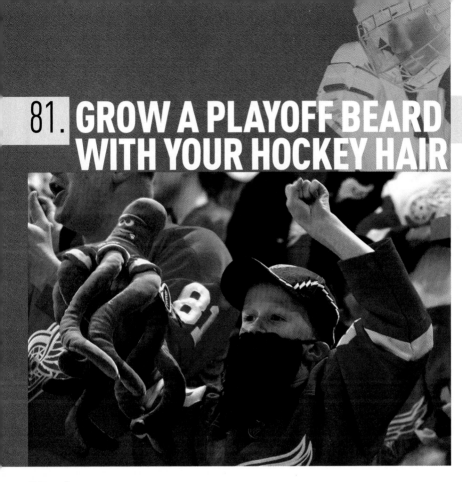

Much like the origin of hockey itself, nobody is sure when one of the game's quirkier traditions began.

The New York Islanders get most of the credit for inspiring the hairy superstition of the playoff beard, most notably the early '80s scruff of Butch Goring. The team didn't look particularly pretty, but on the other hand, they did win four consecutive Stanley Cups.

Today, the playoff beard thrives. Not only do NHLers and beer-leaguers alike grow out their facial hair come playoff time, but fans are also known for joining in on the craze. From the day their team kicks off its post-season journey to when it all ends in glory or defeat, dedicated hockey fans get grizzly.

The playoff beard is a superstition first and a sideshow second. The exception to this rule is stay-at-home defenseman Mike Commodore, who has gained a lot of notoriety in the past few years due to his playoff 'do. Taking the playoff beard concept one step further, Commodore didn't cut the hair on top of his head either, sprouting a red afro that made him a fan-favorite in Calgary in 2004 and Carolina in '06.

As someone who's had to manage those extra locks while also dealing with the added pressures of a deep playoff run, Commodore is wise beyond his years when it comes this particular aspect of hockey culture – and he said it's OK to make one key concession.

"I just grow it out," said Commodore of his beard technique. "Except I have to shave my neck, under my chin. It just gets too hot and uncomfortable in the summer weather away from the rink."

The playoff beard has become less comfortable over the years as the NHL playoffs dig deeper and deeper into June. And while that might be enough to deter someone from joining in, the whole idea behind the beard is to commit and dedicate yourself to the team with blind faith. Throwing a fake beard over your face won't cut it; you can't check this one off the list until you've gone ungroomed from start to finish.

The beauty of the beard is in how no two are exactly the same. On each and every playoff team, there are beards of varying degrees of thickness, length, color and design. While playoff-tested veterans Kris Draper and Scott Niedermayer cultivate thick rough every spring, younger stars such as Sidney Crosby and Jonathan Toews are still a little fuzzy on the whole concept.

But playoff beards aren't the only hairy hockey habit.

There's also the mullet, often simply called "hockey hair" because of its deep connection to the game. Jaromir Jagr, Al Iafrate, Ryan Smyth and Chris Simon all had fine manes of flowing locks that helped define them for a generation of young hockey fans.

For these guys it wasn't so much about the playoff beards, but the year-round mop top. It's such a singular hairstyle that even a non-hockey fan could take one look and say, "Yep, that guy's a hockey player."

If you've ever seen – or better yet, had – a mullet, you know the specifics: short on top and on the sides, and long and flowing in the back. ("Business up front and party in the back," is another way to describe it.)

So whether you grow out a mullet or try your chin at the playoff beard, remember hair – and a lot of it – has deep roots in the game and its fandom. Is it for you? The only way to find out is to throw away your razor and shaving cream and accept the fact you're a tried-and-true hockey fanatic.

With perfect hair and a fantastic beard. ▪

SEE PENGUINS MARCH AND PHILLY FLY

Philadelphia Flyers coach John Stevens put it best: "These two teams just don't like each other very much."

Well, if familiarity breeds contempt, then it's no wonder.

The Philadelphia Flyers and Pittsburgh Penguins have been in the same division since their expansion entrance into the NHL in 1967. The state rivals have faced off 242 times in the regular season over the past four decades, plus five playoff meetings (29 games) including in 2008 and '09.

The Flyers and Penguins played the third-longest game in NHL history in the 2000 playoffs, a marathon that stretched into a fifth overtime period before Philadelphia's Keith Primeau finally ended it.

Not only do these teams not like each other very much, but the hatred that runs through the veins of every player in both dressing rooms ultimately reaches the fans in the stands, too.

Anytime there's a Pittsburgh-Philadelphia matchup, there are bound to be some fireworks, in addition to the great hockey that usually occurs.

Specifically at the Wachovia Center in Philadelphia, where fans take pride in their reputation of being loud, rowdy and obnoxious. Even outside the arena, before the doors are opened, fans are getting pumped up, chanting, "Let's go Flyers!" and rooting their team on from the parking lot.

Inside the rink, a sea of orange appears, and the crowd noise is piercing. Lauren Hart sings the national anthem; later, Kate Smith appears on the scoreboard belting out her eternal "God Bless America," conjuring up images of a toothless Bobby Clarke and ecstatic Bernie Parent carrying the Stanley Cup off the Spectrum ice.

Every time, the crowd goes nuts for the Flyer icons.

"The fans are great in all areas," said Flyers TV broadcaster Jim Jackson. The faithful are passionate, Jackson continued, and there's an edge there, too. The proximity of Pittsburgh and Philadelphia adds to the animosity, but the present-day roots of the rivalry can be traced to one source.

"Two words," Jackson said, "Sidney Crosby."

While the Penguins and Flyers have always been divisional foes, the rivalry didn't truly take off until after the 2004-05 lockout. Problem was, the interstate enemies were rarely contenders at the same time. During Clarke's Broad Street Bullies era in the 1970s, when the Flyers won back-to-back Stanley Cups in '74 and '75, the Penguins were lingering at the bottom of the NHL standings and continued to do so throughout Philadelphia's success in the '80s. And when Mario Lemieux's Penguins won consecutive Cups in the early '90s, the Flyers were in the middle of a five-year playoff drought.

However, with both teams consistently competing for the Cup since 2005 – often against each other – the Battle of Pennsylvania is more meaningful than it's ever been. And, more than ever, it's worth a trip to the cheese-steak capital to take in a Pens-Flyers game.

On Nov. 10, 2007, the Penguins arrived in Philadelphia for one of their four trips that season to the City of Brotherly Love. During the game, Flyers captain Jason Smith slashed Crosby across the wrist, causing the Penguins captain to fall to the ice. Smith got away without a penalty, while Crosby skated briskly to the bench, gasping for air and clenching his hand in pain.

The jeers started.

"Brush it off, Sid, it's just a hangnail!" needled one Flyers fan.

"The 'C' on your jersey stands for cuticle!" another yelled.

Fans continued calling Crosby four-letter words suitable only for an R-rated rivalry. Classy or not, the fans and Flyers got their wish as Philadelphia pulled out the win.

Later, in December, the Penguins returned for another tilt, and the Flyers fans were hungry for more. As the game unfolded, it was clear Philadelphia was the better-prepared team; they jumped out to a huge lead before ultimately winning 8-2.

The score doesn't tell the whole story, though. There were four fights – officially – as well as multiple scrums after the whistle that led to numerous roughing penalties; just more gas for the rivalry fire.

When Crosby escaped undetected after tripping Flyers goalie Martin Biron with about 10 minutes left in the third period, the home fans leapt to their feet screaming for revenge. With the game out of reach, coach Michel Therrien left Crosby on the bench to prevent the possibility of injury, while Philadelphia fans around the arena chanted "We want Crosby!" in an effort to get the city's most reviled opponent back on the ice (to no avail).

Ultimately, the only thing the Flyers fans – and players – really want is to leave with a win, no matter what it takes. The fans' excitement fuels the players' emotions; the crowd voted "the NHL's most intimidating fans" by a players' poll in 2007-08 knows its job is to support the team and help the Flyers win.

When the Penguins come to town, the "Let's go Flyers!" chants are replaced by "Crosby sucks!" or "We want Crosby!" and other provocative phrases that clearly indicate the fans' loyalties.

The teams are oh-so-similar in many ways and there are great young players on both sides, from Crosby, Evgeni Malkin, Jordan Staal and Marc-Andre Fleury in Pittsburgh to Mike Richards, Jeff Carter, Braydon Coburn and Claude Giroux in Philadelphia.

Flyers fans are some of the toughest in the league, yet also among the most passionate. So when an arch-enemy comes to town, especially Crosby and the Penguins, the crowd support is relentless and remorseless.

The Battle of Pennsylvania is one of the most intense and tightly contested rivalries in the NHL today. If you're a fan of thrilling hockey featuring some of the league's most skillful players – with the scent of danger always hanging in the air – head to Philadelphia when there's a Pens-Flyers game on tap. ■

83. MASTER HOCKEY'S BIG THREE: AIR, BUBBLE AND VIDEO

The forward sees an opening and carries the puck deep into the offensive zone. He winds up for a shot, but the disc is swatted away by an alert defender. Both players battle in the corner – an awkward, stick-swinging dance – with neither able to gain control. Finally, the forward digs the puck out and feeds an open teammate in the slot for a lightning-fast one-timer that beats the helpless goalie.

The score is 1-0, but there is no time to celebrate. The players must scramble back into position at center ice before the puck comes popping up from a slot in the table for a "faceoff" and the game begins again.

Bubble hockey.

One of the holy trinity of off-ice hockey hobbies that every fan must master (or at least play), bubble hockey has withstood the test of time, despite its relative stone-age technology. The others, air hockey and video game hockey, though also noble in their quest for off-ice supremacy and bragging rights among friends, can only aspire to one day gain the level of awe and reverence that the game played under the plastic dome commands.

Although, they're definitely trying.

In recent years, the NHL series of video games from EA Sports has received rave reviews, wowing players with its high-definition graphics and revolutionary gameplay techniques, such as independent skating and stickhandling controls. Critics describe the series as a great gaming experience for casual and hardcore fans, with many reviewers proclaiming *NHL '08*, specifically, as the greatest sports video game ever.

While that may be true, those who remember the rise of video games in the early '90s might dismiss *NHL '08*, *'09* or *'10* in favor of classics such as *NHL '94* or *Blades of Steel*. But although your Xbox and PlayStation might put you "in the game," it's not always with the strict realism that more hands-on gamers desire.

Then there's air hockey, an arcade and rec-room staple since the early 1970s, when the U.S.-based Brunswick Company designed and built the prototype. The game is played on a slick, frictionless surface, often with tiny holes blowing air through to help the puck glide. Two players, standing at opposite ends, use hand-held plastic mallets (which basically look like enlarged pucks, with a knob/handle on top) to knock a flat, round disc back-and-forth across the table. The "net" is a slot at each end of the table that players defend, while simultaneously trying to score at the other end.

Air hockey might be the fastest of hockey's 'Big Three' games, with the disc whizzing back and forth at furious speeds – and players often breaking into an inglorious sweat as they attempt to keep up. It caught on quickly throughout North America; to this day, the U.S.A.A. (United States Air-Table Hockey Association) and other similar governing bodies around the world host highly competitive tournaments and crown national champions.

But when it comes to off-ice hockey games, the undisputed champion is bubble hockey. It's played in a manner similar to table soccer ("foosball" to the initiated), with "skaters" from the two teams moving end to end on the table via rods below the "ice." Each skater slides forward and back along its own narrow lane/slot when the player pushes or pulls on the appropriate rod at each end of the table. Skaters rotate to shoot or stickhandle when the player spins the rod. (If it sounds at all confusing, that's simply because it is. After all, there are five rods – one per skater – plus a knob to control the goalie, too.) As in the real on-ice product, bubble hockey at its best is a fast, free-flowing game that rewards quick thinking and split-second hand-eye coordination.

The quintessential hockey surrogate, bubble hockey is a must-have for games rooms, barrooms and arcades everywhere. Along with air hockey and video games, it makes for a memorable hockey experience – even if you can't skate to save your life. ◼

84. BUILD A HOCKEY SHRINE

Sure, every hockey fan loves their team, but how *much* do they love their team?

A garage's worth?

Four rooms' worth?

Collecting memorabilia is a great pastime for any hardcore fan and erecting a shrine to a favorite hockey player, team or era is a great way to remember the good times and have fun doing it. You can get pretty much anything with a hockey tie-in these days, from the obvious (jerseys, pucks, sticks) to the obscure (baseballs signed by hockey players, clocks, even official lineup cards from NHL games).

For Long Island, N.Y., collector Richard Poitras, an affection for the NHL's Original Six era has filled up four rooms in his house, plus the garage – but where else is he going to keep the actual scorekeeper's bench from the old Montreal Forum?

Along with the bench, some of Poitras' more impressive items include Lord Stanley's dinnerware (last used on Thanksgiving) and a handwritten letter from the Cup's original sponsor. As well, Poitras cherishes a picture of the 1945-46 Omaha Knights that is signed by the entire team. The most famous member of that squad was Gordie Howe, who played his one and only season of minor league hockey in Nebraska before departing for the Detroit Red Wings and NHL immortality.

"I'm not sure when it's going to stop," said Poitras of his collection addiction. "The lady I'm with, she's a saint."

While Poitras might not know when the end will come, he certainly remembers the beginning. When his son, Justin, began playing travel hockey in the early 1980s, Poitras sought to eliminate a lot of the waste created during games.

"Every time a kid broke a stick, they'd throw it away," he said. "I started collecting them and it became a joke with everyone."

Poitras would turn the sticks into furniture and other do-it-yourself projects, and that's all it took for the collection bug to bite. His hoard features more than 100 jerseys, approximately 10,000 hockey cards and, just to be different, a yo-yo from every team in the NHL. And thanks to his devotion, he even gets a little help from the league.

After the retired Citigroup employee won an auction for a Gibson Les Paul guitar signed by the 2008 Western Conference All-Stars, the NHL became aware of his impressive collection. A photographer spent nine-and-a-half-hours documenting every piece in Poitras' stockpile and the league even helped him acquire an All-Star Game official banner.

"The NHL was very nice," he said.

Most of Poitras' acquisitions come through auctions.

"You find some stuff on eBay," he said. "I started to get involved with auction houses as well."

And despite his vast variety of items, Poitras said the key to building your personal shrine is to be specific.

"Pick something you want to key on and stick with that," he said. "You'll find it more manageable. I always liked the Original Six because that's what I grew up with."

So whether it's international hockey or the old International League, Rocket Richard or Alex Ovechkin, focus is very important. From the NHL's official website to private collectors to auction houses such as Lelands and Gameworn.net, there's a unique collectible for the hockey nut in you. The only question is whether to weed out items when you run out of space and still want to collect more.

"That's the smart thing to do, but I'm stupid," Poitras laughed. "And I can always find space for a Stanley Cup ring." ∎

85. WITNESS THE FINAL GAME AT AN NHL RINK

There are two keys to completing this task:

Key No. 1: Purchasing one or more tickets for the final NHL game at one of the league's esteemed arenas. This may present a problem insofar as it requires the purchaser to (a) be rather patient, as building closings don't happen every season; and (b) be prepared to sell internal organs and/or family members in order to afford the asking price.

Key No. 2: Actually enjoying yourself once you're there. This also may present a problem, because there are more than a few distractions anytime thousands of fans gather for a final goodbye to a rink that holds millions of hockey memories.

"I remember it being a hectic night," said former Maple Leafs winger Kris King, who was in the lineup on Feb. 13, 1999, the night Toronto and the Chicago Blackhawks closed down Maple Leaf Gardens. "It wasn't a very memorable night for me, first of all because (Toronto) lost, but also because (Leafs coach) Pat (Quinn) lost me on the bench…I think I only played about four shifts all game.

"But everything surrounding that game was great. We had a big pre-game meal at a nearby hotel, and all the old Leafs players were there, so you got to mix and mingle with the greats. Just getting wrapped up in being with all the great stars was an amazing thing. But it was sad in a way, too, because I played junior hockey in that building and closing that chapter was a bit surreal.

"It was really a big open house that night. And it was important, because you understood how much that building meant to so many great hockey players – and also to so many great hockey fans as well. In a way it was actually quite somber. I wouldn't consider it a celebration by any means."

Former Montreal Canadiens coach Jacques Demers appreciated the chance to stand in a place where he had seen so much – first as a fan, then as the last bench boss to lead the Habs to a Stanley Cup championship in the fabled Montreal Forum – one final time before it closed in 1996.

"I've closed two buildings," Demers said. "First, the Detroit Olympia in 1979 (while coaching the Quebec Nordiques), when we couldn't leave the building afterwards because everybody wanted a piece of memorabilia, and also the Forum.

"Both times, it was chaos. The night they closed the Forum, the ovation they gave 'Rocket' Richard is something I'll always remember. It seemed like it never stopped."

A television analyst for Canadiens games, Demers would've loved to have been coaching the Habs for that final game at the Forum. But just being there was about as good as consolation prizes get.

"It was all good times that night," Demers said. "I was a little sad because I wasn't coaching, but they showed my picture with the Cup on the Jumbotron and I felt good about that."

Attending the final game at any particular arena provides boasting material for most fans and players. But if he were given the choice, Demers would prefer to still attend NHL games at his old stomping grounds.

"The Forum itself has so much history, you didn't want it to close," he said. "You hoped they could find a way to keep it open forever."

86. BURN A SNOWMAN AND RING A BELL

Giving it that ol' college try is something every sports fan needs to do, even if you're loyal to a pro team. The university fight songs, the distinctive team colors, the mascots, the rivalries – the entire experience is sensational and unique.

At Lake Superior State in Sault Ste. Marie, Mich., there are two must-see events for all fans, not just those who rabidly follow the two-time NCAA champion Lakers.

For starters, have you ever seen a snowman on fire? Here's your chance. Held every March as a way to chase away winter and raise students' spirits, the annual Snowman Burning is a ritual that was brought to the campus in 1971 by legendary Lakers PR man, W.T. Rabe. The snowman in question generally takes on a theme; in 2009, it took aim at corporate criminals and the economic downturn. Nemesis opponents used to be a frequent target in past burnings – until the Lakers kept losing to the effigied enemy and it was deemed bad luck. The massive snowman (it usually stands about 12 feet high, with plenty of straw-stuffed girth) is made out of paper and wire; in 1992, the tradition was halted due to environmental concerns, but the next winter was one of the worst in years. So, the burning began again.

One tradition the Lakers have never wavered on is the Hoholik Victory Bell run.

After every home-ice victory, the members of the Lakers hockey team take off their skates, put on running shoes and head over to the nearby Norris Center, where a Liberty-sized bell hangs outside the gymnasium.

For Lakers coach Jim Roque, who also played college hockey for the team, it's a sight-and-sound experience that can't be missed.

"The fans line up and make a tunnel for the players to run through," he said. "The band is there playing the school fight song…it's amazing."

Every player rings the bell once. They used to gong it with a hammer, but when the team won the national title in 1992, the Hoholik Victory Bell sustained so much damage it had to be replaced by a church bell that is pulled on.

The players also use the bell-ringing ceremony during games as a rallying point and will often motivate each other by saying, "Let's ring that bell tonight!"

Not a whole lot has changed in Lake Superior State hockey since Roque's days on the ice.

"Guys have always been charged up (about the Hoholik Victory Bell)," he said. "It kind of gets bred in you."

As a coach, Roque realizes there is some method to the madness in getting the pageantry just right. That is to say, it's necessary to give the fans enough time to *get* to the Norris Center.

"My first year, I let the players go too fast," he said.

Nevertheless, a win at Taffy Abel Arena clears out the crowd even faster than a loss.

"They get out of there quick," said Roque of the fans. "They want to get a good spot."

87. MEET YOUR HOCKEY HERO

Here's the funny thing about having a genuine personal experience with a hockey hero: You can never really plan for it.

Yes, there are surefire ways to meet an NHL player – autograph signings, charity fundraisers, open practices and other official events usually do the trick.

But to be frank, taking the tried-and-true route to achieve this particular item on your Puck-it List seems just a little too safe, a little too processed, a little too artificial. No, if you really want to catch a player with his guard down, it has to happen naturally.

That means you can't force the issue. However, there's nothing that should prevent you from maximizing the potential of such an encounter – or from being ready for the experience if and when it does go down.

First of all, make sure you spend some part of your day in a local gym, ice rink, golf course or, if you're of legal drinking age, a nightclub which players are known to frequent. (In the off-season, the list expands to include upscale warm-weather resorts and hunting and gaming lodges.)

Why? Because, again, that's where players hang out. To say most players lead sheltered lives wouldn't be completely fair – see the Niedermayer Bros. on top of a mountain with the Stanley Cup – but for the most part, the culture of the game leads players to certain stress releases during their down time. Being persistently present where one of these activities takes place will assuredly increase your shot at shaking hands with and chatting up a past or present-day idol.

Once you do cross paths with an NHLer, the main thing to remember is to play it cool. Remember, by the time players make it to the NHL, they've been dealing with overzealous fans and hangers-on for years and usually have social methods of slowly slipping away from the spotlight. If you can talk to the player without staring, screaming or hugging them, you'll be more likely to hold their attention for a few precious moments.

Finally, should the temptation for an autograph be too much to resist, be sure to have a writing utensil on hand. Nobody says you have to wear a Sharpie in your shirt pocket, but there is little that's more frustrating to players than to stand by idly while an autograph seeker asks around for a pen. ■

88. EUROPEAN REC-LEAGUE ROAD TRIP

Men's league hockey is a great tradition – adults who refuse to stop playing the game they love. While there are many who keep playing, few are part of a travel team. Even fewer travel to Europe.

Matt Johnson, 33, is one of the few. He plays regularly otherwise, but has also been part of a team – the Voyageurs – that travels to Europe each winter to take on rec-leaguers from across the Atlantic.

Johnson's squad is made up of real estate brokers, bankers and lawyers. Gus Prokos has been running the trip "for the love of the game, not for money" since the mid-1990s. It's been a fluid group of players (including some Americans, who heard about the trip through the grapevine) and the stories are plentiful.

"I look at these trips as a fantasy," said one of Johnson's teammates. "It's about being free and on the road with the team, pulling pranks on each other, staying out too late and overdoing it on the ice.

"Then you get home, covered with multiple minor cuts and bruises, and say to yourself: 'Self! I am too old for this crap!' Only to forget how you felt 10 days later when you send off your deposit cheque for the next year's trip."

Johnson, from Toronto, is one of the newbies. He's been on two trips, but already has stories to last a lifetime. In two years he's soaked up more than his share of European culture in countries such as the Czech Republic, Austria, Switzerland and Germany. Next year, they're heading to Hungary.

Along the way Johnson has played in a Soviet-era "bomb shelter" rink, complete with sheet-metal walls in disrepair and an air-raid siren to signal the end of periods; won a game on an outdoor rink with a skate-up bar in the heart of Vienna ("Pints on the bench!"); played on the same rink in Fussen, Germany, that Eric Lindros won world junior gold on; visited the arena in Davos, Switzerland, that's home to the Spengler Cup; and, bobsledded in Innsbruck with Olympians.

Everywhere he's been, Johnson said, everyone he's met is "looking to outdrink the Canadian hockey players." But one of his favorite stories – although it involves alcohol – is of a chance encounter with two other Canadians.

It was in a small Austrian border town, Lustenau, on the Rhine River. Population: 22,000. Scheduled to play a men's team after the local pro club practiced, Johnson and the boys were watching the training session. One player, from Newfoundland, overheard them talking and deserted the drills to engage in an English conversation.

"He literally ignored his practice," Johnson said, "which was hilarious in its own right."

Overjoyed by the presence of fellow Canadians in his sleepy Austrian town, the player told them what to do and where to go and even invited them all to the Saturday night game as his guests.

During that game, Johnson noticed one player with a decidedly un-Austrian name dominating. He recognized the name; it tweaked at his memory. So Johnson text-messaged a hockey friend, one of those guys who knows everyone and everyone knows. "Yeah," came the reply, "I played with that guy at university; he was great. That's the guy so-and-so stayed with on their European trip 10 years ago – without calling ahead. Get his attention."

"So I did," said Johnson matter-of-factly.

He had to wait until the game's end. Then he yelled the player's name and told him that they had a mutual friend during the presentation of the game's three stars. The player abandoned his honored position on the blueline. "You know him?" he asked. "Meet me in the arena bar after the game."

Johnson, excited and intrigued, led the Voyageurs into the bar, which, unbeknownst to them, closed the arena entrance and opened its back doors to the public post-game, becoming the town's lone nightclub.

"So we're in this ridiculous bar," he said, "when this little, bald, kind of funny-looking guy who didn't really speak English shows up and gets my attention. Next thing we know, we're standing in the hallway outside the pro team's dressing room."

Johnson and his 15 rec-league teammates waited while the Austrian fellow disappeared into the dressing room. He returned shortly. "Go," he announced.

As the boys entered the dressing room, they were greeted by Lustenau's pair of Canadian players. The first, the guy from practice (with a wife and two-week-old baby at home), was brandishing an oversized bottle of Screech, Newfoundland's version of moonshine. The second, the star of the game, was waiting in the middle of the room with "tons" of beer.

The European players on the team seemed oblivious to the appearance of 16 more Canadians; ignoring the interlopers, if in a somewhat knowing manner. The 18 Great White Northerners proceeded to talk hockey (turns out one of the Lustenau Canadians had played in the QMJHL as well as for the Canadian national team), life and Europe. They also polished off the alcohol – with a certain 16 of them continually postponing their bus out of town. (It was the final night of the trip, you see.)

"We ended up partying in the dressing room all night long." Johnson said. "And nobody else from the team participated. We were just 16 plus two in the middle of the room, partying. It was awesome."

By the wee hours of the morning, great times had been had by all, but the itinerary could wait no longer. It was off to the next destination – the airport – with another memory in tow.

Just goes to show, you never know what might happen when you take a rec-league road trip to Europe; good times are assured, great times are possible. ■

89. ROCK OUT, HOCKEY-STYLE

The game is played with speed and brute force, so why should the music be any different? To get the total arena experience of a hockey game, you really have to lose yourself in the spectacle.

And that's where music comes in. Rocking out at a hockey game is essential for any fan who wants to crank the fun knob up to 11.

The links between hockey and music have always been strong, since a lot of musicians wish they could play shinny, while a lot of jocks wish they could shred on the guitar.

Songs dedicated to the coolest game on earth have run from the traditional ol' chestnut "The Hockey Song" by Stompin' Tom Connors to the poignancy of The Tragically Hip's "Fifty-Mission Cap" to the silliness of Atom and his Package's "Goalie," which posits what occupation the world's fattest man should take up.

At the other end of the spectrum, Buffalo's Drew Stafford started a band with Zach Parise's brother Jordan while attending the University of North Dakota, and Tampa Bay winger Steve Downie once had his guitar smashed – at the World Junior Championship, no less – by teammates who weren't in the same groove.

But the true heroes of a rockin' game-night experience are those who pump the tunes through majestic arenas filled with feverish crowds; the ones who help rev up the home fans to blow the roof off the building.

In Pittsburgh, that duty is handled by DJ Vinny Karpuszka and game-night producer Billy Wareham, who pick the songs that shake the walls of Mellon Arena every time the Penguins take to the ice.

With an extensive catalog that leans heavily on the heavy – metal and hard rock, that is – Wareham knows what a Pittsburgh Penguins crowd wants to hear.

"We do our part to maintain the energy in our building," said the 25-year-old Wareham. "This city is a big rock 'n' roll city, so we play a lot of that. And why not? It's the right choice.

"You can't go wrong with metal and rock 'n' roll and hockey."

Wareham, who estimated that Karpuszka spins hundreds of different songs per game – a new track after every whistle – said the most recent Metallica album has been getting a lot of play, as well as Disturbed, a metal act favored by some of the Penguins. Other go-to artists include Van Halen, Motorhead and AC/DC, but less mainstream gems such as Mastodon, The Sword and Queens of the Stone Age are also popular picks.

Wareham and Karpuszka do their audio research using every form of media possible, from iTunes and YouTube to music magazines.

"We have our music sorted by situation and genre," Wareham said. "If we're in a position where we need to rally, we have our rally songs."

And despite the pre-game planning, which song gets played when is never mapped out specifically.

"If you plan things out," Wareham said, "you're going to fall into a trap of being predictable."

But a song without a crowd is nowhere near as effective and that's where raucous fans come in. Arena DJs obviously try to play songs that most of the audience will know, so when it's time to rally behind the team, it's your rock 'n' roll duty to belt out the tune in full throat. With upwards of 20,000 other fans singing along with you, it will be an unforgettable experience. ■

90. WALK THE RED MILE

Let's face it, it's all about the girls.

Calgary's Red Mile rose to prominence in the sporting world during the spring of 2004 – and not so much because of the hockey, the people or the street. Let's be frank. Celebrations are going to break out whenever you invite spectators to watch an event in which winners and losers are determined by a scoring system.

But combine avid hockey fans in an environment that's not accustomed to winning with nice weather, a strip of bars, alcohol and some pretty girls gone wild and you're going to get a memorable hockey experience.

It was often said during Calgary's run to within one win of the Stanley Cup in 2004 that the Red Mile, before and after games, was "Cup crazy." It was crazy, all right, even if the NHL's final series didn't end as anticipated. The Tampa Bay Lightning won it all that magical spring, but Calgary's Red Mile – an eight-block stretch of road along 17th Avenue Southwest – was a haven for fans to, er, hang out before and after games and bask in the success of the Flames.

The Red Mile began innocently enough in 2004. The 17th Avenue row of bars and restaurants was typically buzzing on game night as patrons eventually made their way to the Saddledome, which is at the east end of the strip. Fans in Calgary had waited a long time for a playoff breakthrough; prior to winning three rounds in '04, the Flames hadn't won a post-season series since winning the franchise's one and only Stanley Cup back in 1989.

"The first round (of the playoffs), the bars were busy, but not packed," said Glen Scott, a Calgary lawyer who is also co-owner of Bob The Fish, a popular watering hole that still anchors one end of the Red Mile. "By the second round, you had to reserve a table before games and after a win you'd have trouble getting in."

By the third round, the bars were packed, so happy fans just strolled along the Red Mile, half of them trying to find an establishment they could get into and half just walking around having a good time. By that time, police had shut down 17th Avenue to motorists, making it a pedestrian-only strip before and after games. If that wasn't an invitation to come on by and celebrate, nothing was. Good ol' Western hospitality.

As for the gratuitous topless nudity that could be glimpsed now and again along the Red Mile, call it a byproduct of the good times and spring being in the air.

"During one game early in the playoffs," Scott said, "I was at a bar in the Saddledome when this gorgeous girl at a table next to us just lifted her top. I think she was celebrating a goal. Then before you know it, they're doing it on the street. It was like Mardi Gras."

Before long, the Red Mile was the place to be and top-doffing was the thing to do. Upwards of 50,000 people turned the Red Mile into pedestrian gridlock after games.

It was paradise for the male hockey fan. Where else could you get away with spouting cheap lines such as "Shirts off for Kiprusoff," a tribute to Calgary's goalie?

University of Calgary professor Mary Valentich told the *Globe and Mail* in 2006 the nudity and exhibitionism that occurred along the Red Mile was the result of a "complex set of factors, including a desire to celebrate the Flames' victories, a desire to break the rules, feelings of stardom and a sense of history."

In short order, the website flamesgirls.com – which no longer exists – was getting millions of hits across the world and the Red Mile was an entity.

Thanks to the NHL lockout in 2004-05 and first round exits in four successive playoffs, the Red Mile hasn't regained its popularity.

"It'll be back," Scott said. "As long as there are hockey fans and girls, it'll be back (when the Flames win.)"

Celebrations also took to the Alberta streets in Edmonton during the Oilers' march to within one win of the 2006 Stanley Cup.

Thousands of fans flocked to Whyte Avenue and it was dubbed the Blue Mile by local media. While there were few reports of violence and police activity in Calgary, there were two stabbings during Edmonton's 2006 run, which ended with a Game 7 loss in Carolina.

"I was in Edmonton for those games as well," said Scott, a friend of Oilers owner Daryl Katz. "It was a very different atmosphere because Whyte Avenue is at one end of the University of Alberta campus and many of the young people involved were students. You didn't get many people who were at the game because it's not near Rexall Place.

"I'm an Oilers fan through and through because of Daryl and all their Cups in the '80s, but no place beats the Red Mile for celebrating."

Keep that in mind the next time Calgary advances to the Stanley Cup final. ■

91. TAKE A TOUR, MUSE A MUSEUM

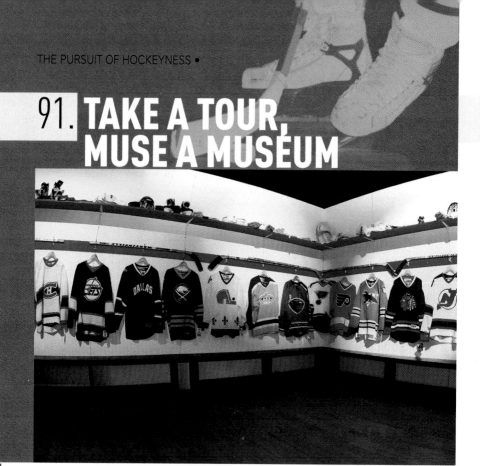

The Metropolitan Museum of Art. The Smithsonian. The British Museum. The Royal Ontario Museum. The Museum of Modern Art. The Louvre.

All great places to visit, for sure. But if you're a hockey fan, there are other options.

For most fans, a hockey museum tour begins and ends with the Hockey Hall of Fame in Toronto. The Hall is home to the single-largest collection of memorabilia and hockey history in the world. There is actually so much stuff it can't all be displayed at once (despite 50,000-plus square feet of space); rotating various exhibits is a full-time job in itself.

Beyond the Hall of Fame, though, there are plenty of other places to see a slice of hockey history. For starters, there's the International Hockey Hall of Fame in Kingston, Ont., which is one of the locales that claims to be hockey's birthplace (the other leading contenders are Montreal and Windsor, N.S.). The International Hall of Fame is where you can find a Don Cherry Exhibit – he's a "good Kingston boy" who grew up just around the corner from the Hall – along with displays devoted to each of the Original Six teams. And the Bobby Orr Hall of Fame in Parry Sound, Ont., is where visitors can learn about the early days and rise to stardom of the city's favorite son and view Orr memorabilia, including his original dressing room stall from the old Boston Garden.

Most puck-playing countries have their own hockey museums dedicated to their nation's on-ice history. In Eveleth, Minn., dubbed "The Capital of American Hockey," you can find the U.S. Hockey Hall of Fame, the "National Shrine of American Hockey." The U.S. Hall of Fame has been honoring players, builders and teams since 1973 and highlights such subjects as U.S. Olympic hockey and the history of the game in the lower 48.

In Tampere, Finland, there's the Jaakiekkomuseo, more easily called the Finnish Hockey Hall of Fame, which is housed in an old factory.

"Just entering the old Tampella factory area takes you to a different time," said Finnish hockey writer and THN correspondent Risto Pakarinen. "The actual museum is not huge, but it covers Finnish hockey history well, from the very early days – the first official game was in 1928 – to the present day.

"You probably won't spend all day there, an hour or two if you're a hockey nerd, but the visit will stay with you for a long time."

That sentiment is true of any museum, especially hockey museums. It's one thing to visit an Egyptian mummy or a dinosaur exhibit, but unless you're an expert in those fields it can be difficult to fully appreciate them. Most hockey fans, though, have skated on ice, felt the weight of a stick in their hands, pulled a musty sweater over their heads, and watched game after game after game. They can appreciate a hockey museum more than the average person might celebrate old Egyptian kings or extinct giant reptiles.

For a niche hockey museum, check out Hockey Heritage North in Kirkland Lake, Ont., about 300 miles due north of Toronto. Opened in early 2006, it pays homage to the history of hockey in northeastern Ontario, a history that is rich in players, teams and cultural significance.

"Up here in Northern Ontario, we only have one arena in town sometimes," said Kelly Gallagher, the museum's curator. "The local hockey rink is usually the heart and soul of the community and often one of the first buildings to be built after the school and hospital."

Mining towns across northeastern Ontario iced professional teams and vied for the Stanley Cup during the early 20th century, with some of hockey's most famous names as hired guns.

"With mining companies and their willingness to pay as much as they wanted for the best players, they would have great games between different mines," Gallagher said.

About 50 miles south, in Cobalt, Ont., legendary Cy Denneny played for the Mines in 1913-14, while Art Ross – for whom the NHL trophy is named – played for the Silver Kings in 1908-09. Ross also skated for the Haileybury Hockey Club, as did Newsy Lalonde, one of the NHL's original superstars.

In all, there are more than 300 former NHLers from northeastern Ontario honored at Hockey Heritage North's Gold Hall, and exhibits pay homage to the role that hockey plays in small communities throughout the region.

"It's so much to cram into one building," Gallagher said. "It's such a huge story to tell.

"But we really want to honor not just our past and not just the NHL players, but those (from northeastern Ontario) who have come up through the ranks and those who just consider hockey a part of their lifestyle." ▪

Come on, you didn't think we'd have 99 chapters on the pursuit of hockeyness without a little self-indulgence, did you? But before you skip ahead, permit us to make a quick case for your continued perusal.

Time and circumstance have nudged The Hockey News along an evolutionary tack, taking it from a tabloid newspaper that leaned heavily on game happenings and statistics to today's feature-based magazine that leaves the day-to-day events to the electronic media.

One thing that hasn't changed since the publication launched in 1947 is its high standing in the hockey world. If anything – and we realize we may have a slight bias – it's grown.

It's what hockey insiders read to help stay connected with their universe. An NHL player survey conducted in 2007 found that 85 percent of NHLers peruse THN, including Pittsburgh Penguins superstar Sidney Crosby.

"I read pretty much every issue," Crosby said. "We've had a subscription at my house for a long time. My dad had it when he was a kid and I had one when I was young, too."

THN matters not only because it holds a mirror up to the hockey world and analyzes it in-depth, but because it helps shape public opinion on players, the game and its issues.

Case in point: When Toronto Maple Leafs GM Brian Burke was an NHL vice-president responsible for supplementary discipline in the mid-1990s, senior writer Mike Brophy once criticized him for being too lenient with some suspensions. Burke fired back with an angry phone call to the reporter.

"Broph," Burke said, "you've got to understand that when American reporters see what is written in The Hockey News, they take it as gospel and run with it. Whether it's opinion or fact, they believe it's so."

Don Cherry's a believer, too. When he was with Rochester in the 1970s, the controversial hockey icon was named coach of the year by THN and founder/publisher/editor Ken McKenzie wrote about it in the paper's pages.

"I was absolutely thrilled," Cherry recalled. "I really believe that gave me my start and why I got to coach the Boston Bruins."

Watch the NHL draft and you'll see the team tables dotted with copies of THN's *Draft Preview* issue. Similarly, franchises put great stock in the annual *Future Watch* edition, which rates hockey's best in-the-system prospects. The People of Power and Influence ranking has become a significant status symbol in the business, so much so that THN receives an increasing number of lobbies from camps to get their people on the list.

Aside from all that, we feel we're a fun, entertaining and engaging read.

And modest. ■

93. PAY IT FORWARD, LIKE WALTER GRETZKY

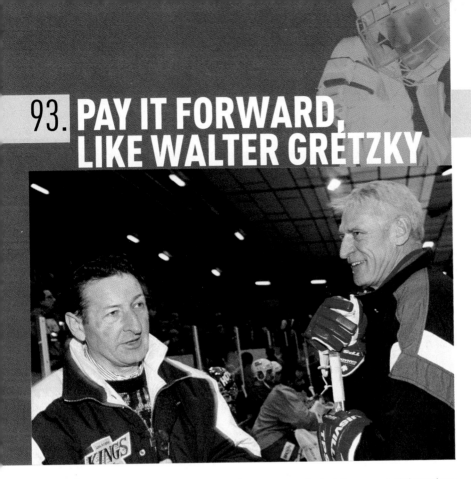

People generally remember where they were and what they were doing when they first heard about 9/11. Those old enough have similar recollections regarding President John F. Kennedy's assassination.

The people of Brantford, Ont., meanwhile, recall where they were and what they were doing on an October afternoon in 1991, when they heard a Toronto radio station report that Walter Gretzky, Wayne's father, had died.

An hour or so later, bulletins made it to the airwaves clarifying the initial reports. Walter was alive, but in critical condition in a Hamilton hospital.

Walter Gretzky, husband of Phyllis and father of five children, had suffered an aneurysm. The attack cost Walter his memory.

Pictures of each family member were hung on the wall of his hospital room. He didn't know his own children.

In fact, in his early days of recovery, Walter only spoke Ukrainian, his first language. He simply couldn't remember how to speak English.

Walter spent 10 months in the hospital under the care of Ian Kohler, a rehabilitation therapist.

Kohler had to teach Walter how to live life again.

"I didn't even know how to take a shower," Walter said. "Ian would shower me, brush my teeth and shave me each day."

The learning curve was slow, but progress was being made and when it came time for Walter to leave the hospital, the Gretzky family (ie. Wayne) hired Kohler to live in Brantford and continue working with Walter. And Kohler did, working with the Gretzky family patriarch for the next two-and-a-half years.

Walter did learn how to live again, the English language came back to him and he eventually remembered people he knew before the aneurysm. And he'll never forget Kohler's role in his recovery.

"He got me involved in society again," said Walter, who ended up with a new son-in-law from the ordeal as daughter Kim and Kohler fell in love, married and now have three children.

Kohler could only do so much, though. Walter has never regained some memories, such as Wayne's Stanley Cup victories with the Edmonton Oilers.

The Gretzky family, since Wayne signed his first NHL contract, has worked closely with the Canadian National Institute for the Blind; the W. Ross Macdonald School for the blind is located in Brantford. Wayne held tennis and fastball tournaments in Brantford to benefit the CNIB and the Walter Gretzky/CNIB Celebrity Auction and Golf Tournament in Brantford has raised more than $1 million to benefit blind adults.

Walter Gretzky/CNIB charity golf tournaments, seven in total, are held from Victoria to St. John's, with some of the proceeds from each tournament forwarded to the Wayne and Walter Gretzky Scholarship Fund (from which 25 blind students receive $3,000 university scholarships each year).

Walter, a spokesman for the Canadian Heart and Stroke Foundation as well, spends most of his time doing charitable work.

"I just volunteer my time," he said.

In 2002, Walter and Phyllis got involved with an Air Canada charitable promotion called Dreams Take Flight.

"They take terminally ill children to Disney World," Walter said.

"Air Canada donates two planes, the pilots donate their time and the stewardesses donate their time. Parents are not allowed to go. One year, they called one plane Walter and the other Phyllis.

"We meet at 4 a.m. at Pearson (airport), have breakfast and then we're there all day and back at midnight. The last 10 minutes of the flight home, you can hear a pin drop because the kids know the end is coming."

Aside from playing in his own tournaments, Walter also plays in other charity events when he has the time.

"It's not because people want to see me golf, but there's always an auction," Walter said.

"They always say, 'Bring something signed by W. Gretzky,' and they don't mean this W. (Walter) Gretzky."

His charitable work hasn't gone unnoticed.

Walter was named the Ideal Father of the Year by Variety Village in 1999 and he has been awarded the Order of Ontario and the Order of Canada.

Walter has also received an honorary doctorate of laws from McMaster University in Hamilton, an honorary doctorate of education from Nipissing University in Brantford and he's been named the Lord Mayor of Brantford, the benefit of which is a reserved parking space at the Wayne Gretzky Sports Centre.

Walter, 70, has had quite a life for a man who started out making $27 a week working as a lineman on construction projects for Bell Canada in 1956. And whatever he's received, he's given back a hundred-fold. ■

94. KNOW YOUR HOCKEY NUMBERS

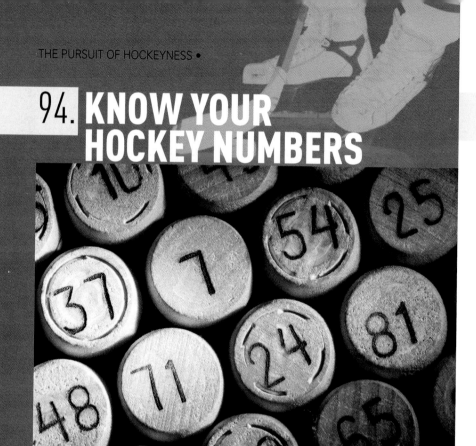

Name and number. It's all you need to know. OK, sure, there are other facts worth figuring, but if you can identify a player by the number on his back, you're practically on a first-name basis.

So, for every number from 0 to 99, here are our 'Three Star' selections. Some numbers – such as Nos. 1, 4, 7, 9 and 19 – have a surplus of stars, while others are very rarely worn; one-time Canadiens winger Jonathan Ferland is the only NHLer to ever don No. 86.

For popular numbers, some very notable names didn't make the 'Three Star' grade. Among No. 1-wearing goalies, Georges Vezina, George Hainsworth, Bernie Parent and Roberto Luongo, incredibly, didn't cut it. And then there's No. 9, the original hockey number. Traditionally, it's worn by the team's best player; as such, a long line of Hall of Famers have been No. 9s. Johnny Bucyk, Ted Kennedy, Lanny McDonald, Clark Gillies and Glenn Anderson all had their No. 9 retired by their respective NHL teams – but they couldn't bump Gordie Howe, Maurice Richard and Bobby Hull out of the 'Three Star' spots.

Here are our 'Three Star' selections, number by number by number. And let the debate begin.

No. 0 Martin Biron, John Davidson, Neil Sheehy

No. 1 Terry Sawchuk, Jacques Plante, Glenn Hall

No. 2 Doug Harvey, Eddie Shore, Brad Park

No. 3 Pierre Pilote, Lionel Hitchman, Barry Beck

No. 4 Bobby Orr, Jean Beliveau, Newsy Lalonde

No. 5 Bernie Geoffrion, Nicklas Lidstrom, Denis Potvin

No. 6 Toe Blake, Babe Dye, Phil Housley

No. 7 Phil Esposito, Ted Lindsay, Howie Morenz

No. 8 Alex Ovechkin, Cam Neely, Teemu Selanne

No. 9 Gordie Howe, Maurice Richard, Bobby Hull

No. 10 Guy Lafleur, Ron Francis, Syl Apps

No. 11 Mark Messier, Gilbert Perreault, Sweeney Schriner

No. 12 Sid Abel, Jarome Iginla, Dickie Moore

No. 13 Mats Sundin, Pavel Datsyuk, Ken Linseman

No. 14 Dave Keon, Brendan Shanahan, Theoren Fleury

No. 15 Jack Adams, Milt Schmidt, Dany Heatley

No. 16 Bobby Clarke, Brett Hull, Marcel Dionne

No. 17 Jari Kurri, Earl Seibert, Wendel Clark

No. 18 Serge Savard, Denis Savard, Dave Taylor

No. 19 Joe Sakic, Bryan Trottier, Larry Robinson

No. 20 Ed Belfour, Luc Robitaille, Mickey Redmond

No. 21 Peter Forsberg, Stan Mikita, Borje Salming

No. 22 Mike Bossy, Dino Ciccarelli, Steve Shutt

No. 23 Bob Gainey, Bob Nystrom, Eddie Shack

No. 24 Chris Chelios, Bernie Federko, Terry O'Reilly

No. 25 Joe Nieuwendyk, Yvan Cournoyer, Thomas Steen

No. 26 Peter Stastny, Martin St-Louis, Brian Propp

No. 27 Scott Niedermayer, Frank Mahovlich, Darryl Sittler

No. 28 Steve Larmer, Brian Rafalski, Robyn Regehr

No. 29 Ken Dryden, Mike Vernon, Mike Palmateer

No. 30 Martin Brodeur, Henrik Lundqvist, Rogie Vachon

No. 31 Billy Smith, Grant Fuhr, Curtis Joseph

No. 32 Dale Hunter, Steve Thomas, Kelly Hrudey

No. 33 Patrick Roy, Zdeno Chara, Dirk Graham

No. 34 Miikka Kiprusoff,
John Vanbiesbrouck,
Bryan Berard

No. 35 Tom Barrasso, Tony Esposito,
Mike Richter

No. 36 Jarret Stoll, Jussi Jokinen,
J-J Daigneault

No. 37 Chris Drury, Eric Desjardins,
Trevor Kidd

No. 38 Robbie Ftorek, Pavol Demitra,
Cristobal Huet

No. 39 Dominik Hasek, Doug Weight,
Dan Cloutier

No. 40 Henrik Zetterberg,
Vaclav Prospal, Patrick Lalime

No. 41 Jason Allison, Eddie Mio,
Martin Skoula

No. 42 Tom Preissing, Kyle Wellwood,
Robert Esche

No. 43 Al Iafrate, Martin Biron,
Darren Helm

No. 44 Chris Pronger, Todd Bertuzzi,
Kimmo Timonen

No. 45 Dmitri Kalinin, Arron Asham,
Brad Ference

No. 46 Andrei Kostitsyn, David Booth,
Zack Stortini

No. 47 John Grahame, Alexander
Radulov, Aaron Downey

No. 48 Daniel Briere, Scott Young,
Anton Babchuk

No. 49 Dan Fritsche, Mathieu Darche,
Eric Godard

No. 50 Joe Dipenta, Trevor Letowski,
Dany Sabourin

No. 51 Valtteri Filppula, Brian Campbell,
Francis Boullion

No. 52 Mike Green, Dustin Byfuglien,
Jonathan Ericsson

No. 53 Brett McLean, Derek Morris,
Denis Tolpeko

No. 54 Bobby Ryan, Paul Ranger,
Teddy Purcell

No. 55 Sergei Gonchar, Darryl Sydor,
Niklas Kronwall

No. 56 Sergei Zubov, Steve Bernier,
Kris Beech

No. 57 Steve Heinze, Shawn Heins,
Marcel Goc

No. 58 Kris Letang, Steve Montador,
Cody Bass

No. 59 Chad Larose, Travis Moen,
Sergei Krivokrasov

No. 60 Jose Theodore, Vladimir Sobotka,
Mikael Backlund

No. 61 Rick Nash, Maxim Afinogenov,
Byron Bitz

No. 62 Steve Webb, Scott Barney,
Kris Chucko

No. 63 Josef Vasicek, Patrick Traverse,
Warren Peters

No. 64 Wyatt Smith, Jamie McGinn,
Stefan Meyer

No. 65 Ron Hainsey, Brett Harkins,
Chris Conner

No. 66 Mario Lemieux, Gino Odjick, Milan Novy

No. 67 Michael Frolik, Alex Goligoski, Gilbert Brule

No. 68 Jaromir Jagr, Zigmund Palffy, Milan Jurcina

No. 69 Mel Angelstad

No. 70 Oleg Tverdovsky, Dave Steckel, Greg Stewart

No. 71 Evgeni Malkin, Lubomir Visnovsky, Mike Ribeiro

No. 72 Ron Hextall, Mathieu Schneider, Eric Meloche

No. 73 Michael Ryder, Jarkko Ruutu, Steven Goertzen

No. 74 Jay McKee, Sergei Kostitsyn, T.J. Oshie

No. 75 Brett Lindros, Colton Orr, Yann Danis

No. 76 Wayne Primeau, Evgeny Artyukhin, Dustin Penner

No. 77 Ray Bourque, Adam Oates, Cliff Ronning

No. 78 Pavol Demitra, Mike York, Marc-Antoine Pouliot

No. 79 Alexei Yashin, Andrei Markov, Vladimir Vujtek

No. 80 Nik Antropov, Geoff Sanderson, Kevin Weekes

No. 81 Marian Hossa, Miroslav Satan, Phil Kessel

No. 82 Martin Straka, Donald Audette, Tomas Kopecky

No. 83 Ales Hemsky, Domenic Pittis, Matt Foy

No. 84 Mikhail Grabovski, Guillaume Latendresse

No. 85 Petr Klima, Rostislav Olesz, Liam Reddox

No. 86 Jonathan Ferland

No. 87 Sidney Crosby, Pierre Turgeon, Donald Brashear

No. 88 Eric Lindros, Patrick Kane, Peter Mueller

No. 89 Alexander Mogilny, Mike Comrie, Sam Gagner

No. 90 Clark Gillies, Joe Juneau, Enver Lisin

No. 91 Sergei Fedorov, Brad Richards, Marc Savard

No. 92 Rick Tocchet, Michael Nylander, Jeff O'Neill

No. 93 Doug Gilmour, Johan Franzen, Petr Nedved

No. 94 Ryan Smyth, Yanic Perreault, Stan Neckar

No. 95 Aleksey Morozov, Danny Markov, Sergei Berezin

No. 96 Tomas Holmstrom, Pierre-Marc Bouchard, Fabian Brunnstrom

No. 97 Jeremy Roenick, Esa Tikkanen, Rotislav Klesla

No. 98 Brian Lawton

No. 99 Wayne Gretzky, Rick Dudley, Wilf Paiement

95. EAT, DRINK AND EAT HOCKEY

Every hockey town has its own atmosphere and unique charm, from pre-game festivities to the echoes in the arena to the mania of the fans who gather every game night.

This is especially true when traveling to a new city. Whether it's cheering on your favorite team on the road or simply taking in a game in a new locale, the hockey road trip is a time-honored tradition and allows for more treats than simply the game itself.

One way to get a little taste of a city's charm is through its cuisine. Even in an age where every highway stop has a McDonald's and every big-box shopping complex offers East Side Mario's or P.F. Chang's, most hockey towns still have a specialty dish awaiting tourists of the game.

Fans of the Carolina Hurricanes have become famous for their tailgating skills, so if you're heading down to Raleigh, grab some melt-in-your-mouth ribs or a pulled-pork sandwich.

Similarly, some dishes are so directly related to a city that any visit warrants a bite of the local delicacy; you can't go to Philadelphia without taking on a cheese-steak sandwich, while Chicago is the land of deep-dish pizza.

But one of the most storied teams in the NHL also has one of the richest culinary histories: Montreal.

For outsiders, the famous party town has its fair share of adult beverages available, but wonderfully bad-for-you staples such as poutine (french fries and cheese curds covered in gravy), smoked meat sandwiches and steamed hot dogs are also on many a menu.

In fact, for the total Montreal experience, it's tough to beat a trip to fast-food joints such as Lafleur's or La Belle Province.

The 2009 NHL all-star weekend in Montreal provided the perfect setting for a pilgrimage to the city's best (and cheapest) offerings. With the temperature absolutely frigid and the winds whipping around the downtown core, a trip into La Belle Province offered a wonderful respite from the weather. Plumes of condensation from the steamer wafted in the air every time hot dogs were ordered, mimicking the steam that would rise off the patrons as soon as they trudged back out into the frosty outdoors.

Like most of the city, the restaurant was heavily flavored with Habs gear, from the diners in their jerseys to the cooks behind the counter sporting Montreal Canadiens T-shirts as they worked the fryers.

In spartan booths, diners could enjoy steamed hot dogs – just like hockey fans do in rinks across the continent – gloriously greasy fries and that unique staple of Quebec, Pepsi, instead of the usually dominant Coca-Cola.

Hanging on the wall at La Belle Province is a banner featuring the winning Stanley Cup years of Montreal's past. In either a hopeful bit of forecasting or simply a drunken whim, someone had scrawled "2008" in black marker amidst the official silk-screened years. Of course, that never came to pass, but it's a pretty clear example of the confidence and pride Montrealers have in their Canadiens when times are good.

And considering they always have the option of loading up on a belly-full of protein, caffeine and deep-fried starches before each game, it's no wonder the passion burns so strongly in Montreal – that's a lot of calories to work off.

96. MAKE IT TO THE MINNESOTA HIGH SCHOOL

Ringing the concourse of the Xcel Energy Center in St. Paul, Minnesota, is a wonderful collection of sweaters in a rainbow of colors. Each one represents a high school hockey team in the state, each one a collective dream of kids from the suburbs of Minneapolis up to the Iron Range in the north.

And once a year in March, those kids get to take center stage.

With major junior teams consistently suiting up 16-year-olds and college prep teams snagging many other talented youngsters, Minnesota high schools remain a bastion for skilled skaters waiting to move on to the NCAA. In fact, it's rare for the first round of an NHL draft to unfold without a player from a Minnesota secondary school being selected. In 2008, Anaheim took Minnetonka defenseman Jake Gardiner with the 17th pick. In 2007, it was Cretin-Derham blueliner Ryan McDonagh going to Montreal 12th overall.

In the summer of '09, it was Nick Leddy's turn to be a high pick. Another defenseman, Leddy led his Eden Prairie Eagles to the 2008-09 state championship and was named 'Mr. Hockey,' the title given annually to the state's most valuable high school player. Leddy is one of the latest reasons why the state tournament is a must-see for any hockey fan who loves the passion that burns in the grassroots of the game.

"It's an unbelievable experience," Leddy said. "The atmosphere…you have to be there to really understand it."

The tournament is broken down into Class A and AA divisions, depending on school size (some powerhouse teams such as small-town Roseau, though, have opted up to AA). In each bracket, eight teams qualify for the tournament by winning sectional showdowns. Perhaps the most intriguing element of the tournament is that since the schools come from all over the state, matchups between very different programs are inevitable. Teams from the Twin Cities and the surrounding suburbs are usually targeted by fans from outside that region and vice versa.

But no matter who ends up playing in the A and AA championship games, a packed house of more than 18,000 fans is guaranteed. For most of the teams in the tournament, that dwarfs their usual attendance by at least a factor of 10. Plus, the media is out in full force, giving the event even more of a professional feel.

"After we won, there was a press conference with 10 or 15 reporters," Leddy said. "It was pretty cool."

For all the participants, the showdown also represents the finality of their high school season. Teams stay at hotels and some, like Leddy's Eden Prairie squad, even rent out the luxury suites at Xcel to watch other games when they're not on the ice themselves.

If you want to see the best high school hockey in the world, Minnesota is still the place where they do it right. And who knows? Depending on the draw, you might see the next Neal Broten or Blake Wheeler out there.

97. GO ON THE ULTIMATE HOCKEY ROAD TRIP

Apparently, Ramses II took the first road trip in recorded history. In fact, get this, one time he came down on the Medeans in his chariot after driving all night from Memphis.

Must have been a Predators fan.

Anyway, you have to admire the guy, or at least his willingness to drop everything and jump in the chariot with a few of his buddies to go and kill people.

The spirit of Ramses is alive and well when it comes to hockey fans. The road trip is a rite of passage for any serious watcher of the game. At some point in every hockey fan's life, it's necessary to hit the road and watch as much hockey in as many leagues as humanly possible.

With that in mind, we're suggesting four different hockey road trips in four different geographical areas, that will have you seeing one game in the NHL, the American League, the ECHL, one of Canada's three major junior leagues, a U.S. college game and a game in the low minors. That pretty much covers the hockey spectrum, at least at the pro and prospect levels.

You might want to plan your trip a little more extensively than we've outlined, perhaps by going to one of those websites that gives you directions right from your driveway all the way to your destination.

If you're a bunch of guys, pack an unhealthy amount of junk food and a few changes of clothes and worry about the details as you go along. (OK, you might want to look into ticket availability before you leave the house.)

And be prepared to drive. Carbon footprint, schmarbon schmootprint…

Here they are, courtesy of Ron Hutchinson of the Canadian Automobile Association, who did all the heavy lifting when it came to planning our routes.

Thanks, Ron. We'll take care of the cheeseballs.

ROAD TRIP NO. 1

"From Detroit to eternity"

Overview: Start in Detroit and finish up in Fort Wayne, Indiana.

Distance: 553 miles.

• Start your trip at Joe Louis Arena with a game featuring the 11-time Stanley Cup champions. After the Wings win, cross the bridge to Windsor to take in the Canadian ballet.

• Then it's on to Plymouth, Mich., to see the Ontario League's Whalers at the Compuware Arena, where they sell earplugs in the gift shop. (True story.) Take the I-96 West toward Lansing for about 18 miles, then jump on the M-14 West for four miles into Plymouth. If you're there in January, check out the International Ice Spectacular, where you'll see some impressive ice sculptures that take longer to melt than the Islanders' playoff hopes.

• From here, we move on to Ann Arbor and the Yost Arena at the University of Michigan, where those earplugs might still come in handy, particularly if your ears are sensitive to drunken college profanity. Get back on M-14 West toward Ann Arbor for 12 miles, then take Exit 45 and you're basically there. Unfortunately, you've missed the Michigan Brewers Guild Summer Beer Festival in nearby Ypsilanti.

• Now get ready to do some serious driving, because we're off to the Ervin J. Nutter Center, home of the Dayton Bombers of the ECHL. To get there, get on the I-94 East toward Detroit and take Exit 180 and get on US-23/Toledo/Flint for about 50 miles. Then take Exit 1A to the I-75 South to Dayton for 135 miles. Not only do you get to see an ECHL game, you might bump into Bombers owner

Costa Papista (and then you can tell all your friends you talked to someone named Costa Papista). While you're there, you can get in free to the National Aviation Hall of Fame.

• Next stop is the Allen County War Memorial Coliseum, home of the two-time Turner Cup champion Fort Wayne Komets of the International League. Get on I-75 North toward Toledo and drive about 55 miles. Go from there to US-33 West to Fort Wayne for a whole bunch of miles. When you're not at the game, drop into Science Central, which bills itself as "Indiana's amusement park for the mind."

• We started our trip with the Red Wings and we end it with the future Red Wings at Van Andel Arena, home to the American League's Grand Rapids Griffins. Jump on the I-69 North toward Lansing and keep your foot on the gas for about 85 miles. Make your way to US-131 North for another 50 miles to Grand Rapids. If you need a break from all that hockey, Grand Rapids has its own professional ballet company. The real kind.

ROAD TRIP NO. 2

"Devil of a drive"

Overview: Start in Newark, N.J., and make your way to Lewiston, Maine.

Distance: 854 miles.

• Our trip starts at the Prudential Center, where we'll catch the New Jersey Devils in action on a weeknight. (That way, we don't need to buy tickets in advance.) While in Newark, go to nearby Hoboken. Not only does Hoboken really begin to sound funny when you repeat it a bunch of times, it's where Frank Sinatra was born.

• Next stop is the Sovereign Bank Arena in Trenton, home of the Trenton Devils of the ECHL. You'll want to get on the I-95 South, which becomes the New Jersey Turnpike, for about 40 miles, then get on the I-195 West to Trenton. Since you're in the state capital, you might want to visit State House.

• Next, it's off to the Aviator Arena to watch the Brooklyn Aces of the Eastern Professional League. Get back on the New Jersey Turnpike and go north for about 13 miles, then take the I-95 North for another 25 miles. Finally, take the I-278 East for 11 miles to the Belt Parkway East onto Flatbush Avenue in Brooklyn.

• Next stop is the Tate Rink, home of the, well, Army at West Point. In order to get there, make your way to the I-95 South toward Trenton and from there, take Exit 74 and drive for 40 miles. Once you've arrived, be nice – the U.S. has a pretty good army.

• The next leg takes us to Hartford, where you can watch the AHL's Wolf Pack. Wind your way through West Point until you reach the I-84 East toward Danbury and go east for 65 miles. Take Exit 50 and make your way to the XL Center. The arena is named after – what else? – an insurance company, but it could just as well stand for Extra Large, since it seats 15,635 for hockey.

• After you update your insurance policy, jump in the car and head to the Androscoggin Bank Colisee, home of the Quebec League's Lewiston Maineiacs. Take the I-84 East for 45 miles and follow the signs to New Hampshire-Maine-Boston for another 27 miles. From there, get on the I-495 North for another 60 miles and go to the I-95 North for another 100 miles. If you've managed to do all that without a pee break, stop somewhere in Lewiston and hit a restroom.

ROAD TRIP NO. 3

"The Maple Leaf marathon"

Overview: Start in Toronto and finish in Cincinnati.

Distance: 541 miles.

• Our first couple of games on this trip begin in the Center of the Universe™ in two rinks that are separated by fewer than two miles. And the best thing is, on most Saturdays you can catch a Toronto Marlies game in the afternoon and a Toronto Maple Leafs game at night, thereby restricting your actual days of bad hockey to a bare minimum.

• Your day can start at the Ricoh Coliseum, which is home to the AHL's Marlies. Unlike a Maple Leafs game, tickets are plentiful and won't cost your firstborn child. After the Marlies game, go East, young man, go East, until you reach the Air Canada Centre. While there, watch as the money mysteriously gets sucked out of your wallet.

• On most Sunday afternoons, you can catch an afternoon OHL game either at the Hershey Center in Mississauga for the St. Michael's Majors or at the Powerade Center for the Brampton Battalion. You may have missed the chance to see John Tavares play junior, but don't fret: Another 'Next One' always comes along.

• From there, it's on to McMorran Arena, home of the IHL's Port Huron Ice-hawks. Take Highway 401 West toward London for about 100 miles, then make your way to Highway 402 West going toward Sarnia and drive for 65 miles. Remember, you need a valid passport now to cross the border from Canada into the U.S. The 402 becomes I-69 West at the border and takes you into Port Huron. If you want to kill some time after you arrive, check out the Edison Depot Museum, which chronicles the formative years of one of the world's most important inventors, Thomas Edison.

• Good news: You're going to visit the University of Michigan's Yost Arena on this trip, too. Get on the I-94 West and drive for about 45 miles to the I-696 West to Lansing for another 26 miles. Then make your way toward M-14 West to Ann Arbor.

• The last stop on this journey is the U.S. Bank Arena, home of the Kelly Cup-champion Cincinnati Cyclones of the ECHL. You want to get on the I-94 toward Detroit, then turn right for US-23 South toward Toledo. Get on the I-75 South toward Dayton and drive for about 190 miles until you reach Cincinnati.

ROAD TRIP NO. 4

"The infinite journey"

Overview: OK, this one takes some real dedication. It starts in Anchorage, Alaska, and ends in Prescott Valley, Arizona.

Distance: 3,951 miles.

• Things start in Anchorage, where we don't even have to change arenas to see our first two games. The Alaska Aces of the ECHL and the University of Alaska-Anchorage Seawolves play out of the Sullivan Center, which happens to have an international-sized ice sheet that is 200-by-100 feet.

• All right, the easy part is over. Now leave the arena and get yourself onto the Alaska Highway and drive for about 90 miles. You then leave the United States and enter Canada, where you will continue for the next 1,100 miles (no typo). Get to Highway 29 for another 85 miles and then to Highway 97 South for another 180 miles until you get to Prince George, home of the Cougars of the WHL. You might want to break this part of the trip up with a couple of stops. We're just sayin'…

• This next leg will be a relatively easy drive – only 300 miles, making your way to Highway 97 and then Highway 1 West, which is the Trans-Canada Highway, until you reach Vancouver. There, you can catch the Canucks and the Western

League's Giants, not to mention some great games in the B.C. Jr. A League. Just for fun, while you're there, stand at any spot in the city, swing a dead cat and see how many Starbucks you hit.

• Let's get back on the road. As we head to the U.S. border, we'll stop in Abbotsford, where we can witness the inaugural season of the Abbotsford Heat of the AHL, the Calgary Flames' new farm team.

• Once in the U.S., take I-5 South for 260 miles, then jump on the I-205 South for about 35 miles and back to the I-5 South for another, oh, 600 miles or so until you get to the Stockton Arena, home of the ECHL's Stockton Thunder.

• All right, now we're going to travel a really long way to see some, well, really not-so-great hockey. We won't blame you if you want to turn around and go home without seeing a game in the low minors. But as long as you have way too much time on your hands…

• Take the CA-99 South toward Fresno for about 225 miles to the Bakersfield Tehachapi Highway for another 100 miles. Get on the I-40 East for another 150 miles. Then, go figure, the I-40 East becomes the I-40 West and you drive on that for another 130 miles. From there, get on the AZ-89 for about 45 miles until you reach Tim's Toyota Center, home of the Arizona Sundogs of the Central League.

After this trip, you'll probably want to take the RV in for a tune-up. ■

98. FACE OFF AGAINST NHL OLDTIMERS

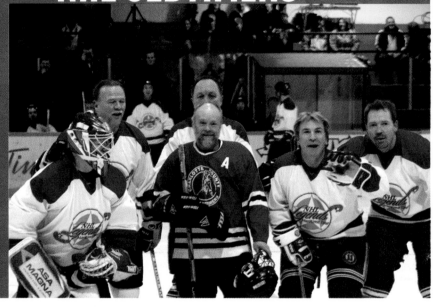

They are slower, often fatter, always grayer or balder. They're less lean and less mean. But they have, as the old cliche says, something that no one can take away from them.

They are professional hockey players. Always will be. They don't play in the NHL anymore, but there is nothing "former" about the guys who continue to lace them up to skate in charity games and alumni contests and there is nothing quite like watching – or for the lucky few, skating with or against – some of hockey's biggest legends.

"You really notice right away, in the first couple of shifts, that there is something special going on," said Saint John, N.B., businessman Steve Walton, who loves to play the off-ice game of hockey management.

When he isn't trying to keep a local team afloat in the region's senior league, Walton dreams up ways to bring some of the NHL's biggest names to some of Canada's smaller communities. Sure, you can count yourself a fan if you've been to the Montreal Forum or any of the Gardens, if you can say you saw Wayne Gretzky or Mario Lemieux or Bobby Orr in their prime, or if you can pull out an autographed Joe Sakic rookie card.

But no achievement could possibly equal facing off against Bryan Trottier and then skating into the corner against Terry O'Reilly.

In the winter of 2009, Walton brought those two and five other players – including three Hall of Famers, 21 Stanley Cup rings, thousands of NHL points and dozens of honors, awards and all-star appearances – to tiny Border Arena in the tiny border town of St. Stephen, N.B. A couple thousand fans huddled on the arena's benches (no stadium seating) or stood, noses nearly pressed against the glass, to watch a team of locals from the ranks of industrial and oldtimer leagues go up against some of the greatest names in hockey history.

Trottier brought his Islanders mates Billy Smith and Butch Goring, while O'Reilly and big, bad Bruins buddy Rick Middleton car-pooled up from Boston. Ex-Oiler Glenn Anderson, his Hall of Fame award still bearing that new-plaque smell, and Gary Leeman, whose star shone brightly but briefly during some of the darkest years in Toronto Maple Leafs lore, rounded out the lineup.

Before the game, Trottier has a pep talk for the local boys, explaining that this would be a no-checking-and-for-God's-sake-no-backchecking affair. If someone has a scoring chance, said the old Isles captain, let him go and we'll do the same. Oh, and don't piss off Smitty: He's old, but he can still swing his goal stick.

It's a surreal moment for the locals, who are fixated on Trottier and sweating almost as much about the full house as the high-caliber competition.

Walton had brought Trottier to New Brunswick a few times previously for exhibitions and to meet-and-greet the beer-leaguers who turn into hockey-card-collecting, road-hockey-playing kids in the presence of greatness.

"It's like being in a room full of 10-year-olds," said Walton of the reaction Trottier garners in the local team's dressing room. "They were mesmerized."

On the ice, the old guys always put on a show. At half-speed – heck, at one-tenth speed – they outpace and outclass any and all comers. They were professionals. They are professionals. They play tic-tac-toe and keep-away. They pull off moves the rest of the players, and fans, have never seen before. They don't always score, even on breakaways, but anyone who has played the game instantly recognizes the hockey magic that is unfolding.

"These guys have the edge when they want to show it," Walton said. "They could turn it into a Harlem Globetrotters thing real fast."

On a grander scale, there's the annual Baycrest International Pro-Am tournament that draws dozens of NHL legends to Toronto's York University, where they raise millions of dollars for Alzheimer's research while putting Average Joes on the ice with some of their idols.

But the highlight of any NHL oldtimers game usually happens off the ice. After the St. Stephen game, all the legends hung around the rink to meet and greet players, fans and kids. They signed autographs until there was nothing left to sign, then headed to a local pub for a meal and a drink. They told stories, let people hold their Cup rings, even let them try them on and pose for pictures with them. They are ambassadors of the game, old guys who love to play and talk hockey – except their stories involve way cooler stuff, like Billy Smith laughing about a well-documented scrap with Lanny McDonald, a bout that was sparked, naturally, by Smith's stick.

"I never did that again," said Smith to the small group gathered around him for one last story before last call.

"Do what? Spear McDonald?" someone asked.

Smith feigns offense.

"No…I speared him plenty more times. But I never fought him again."

Trottier is the de facto captain of the legends and genuinely enjoys what he's doing.

"It brings back some memories," he said. "We have a lot of fun on the ice."

And Trottier has a secret – the same one that's shared by every kid taking slapshots under the streetlights and every adult who still goes out in the dark of night to play the game they love.

"I would have played for free," Trottier said.

As the promoter, Walton has helped put dozens of New Brunswick players on the ice with some of their idols. The businessman knows the experience is priceless.

"It's one of those memories that will last a lifetime," Walton said. ■

99. COMPLETE YOUR PERSONAL ULTIMATE HOCKEY CHECKLIST

First of all, at some point in your life, see a game at every level of hockey: the pros (NHL, AHL, ECHL, low minors); college (NCAA, Canadian university); Europe (senior and junior); major junior (QMJHL, OHL, WHL); women's hockey; Jr. A and the U.S. Jr. League; high school; men's league; and, of course, the kids (midget, bantam, pee-wee, novice and atom). Preferably standing by the glass, with a drink in one hand and a hot dog in the other. And always cheer loudly: You're at a hockey rink, not a library.

Watch the World Junior Championship over the holidays and the NHL playoffs every spring. Watch *Hockey Night In Canada* on CBC on Saturday night; definitely the early game, plus the late game if you can handle it. Watch hockey highlights every night. Watch the Olympics every four years. Watch your favorite old games again and again, like 1972 and '87 and the last time your team won the Stanley Cup.

Pick a favorite team and stick with them. Know everything about them; their past glories and failures, their present challenges, their future glories (don't predict any failures). Watch them play. Every game. Smile like the owner when they win and frown like the coach when they lose. Own a team jersey or ball cap or keychain or bed sheets. Get a tattoo…or at least a bumper sticker. Defend the team in public, deride them in private. Know their stats. All of them. At least once in your life, see the team play in person. Save the ticket stub. Stand and cheer and yell and scream. Toss your cap on the ice when a hat trick is scored. Grow a beard when they make the playoffs; go golfing when they don't. Cry tears of joy when they finally win the Stanley Cup. And be there for the parade.

Carefully – or emotionally – select a favorite player and know more about him than you do your own family members. Keep the same favorite player your entire life. (You can add new ones as the older ones retire, but never forsake a fave.) Meet the player and try to make friends; if that fails, settle happily for a moment to remember.

Buy a pack of hockey cards. Look through your old hockey cards at least once a year. If you can't find them, blame your mother for throwing them out. (Just kidding, Mom.) Take a good, long look at some old black-and-white hockey photos, and wonder about the lives of those long-ago players. Keep a hockey reference book handy. Give away equipment you don't use. Set up a road hockey game for the kids on your street. Have a favorite childhood hockey memory, whether it's skating with your father for the first time or all those early morning 5 a.m. practices.

Own a stick, a puck and a pair of skates. And a helmet, gloves and shin pads. Use your equipment at least once a year. (Better yet, once a week.) Always carry your own gear, but never wash it. Tie a kid's skates for them, like someone used to do for you. Feel the wind in your hair as you skate. Hear the crunch of your blade biting into the ice. See the joy on the faces of people skating around you. Tape your own stick. Smell the rink. Score a goal. Go five-hole and blast a slapshot and roof one upstairs. Win a faceoff. Go hard to the net. And pass the puck, too, and hit the crossbar and score an empty-netter and break up a 3-on-1 and ring the puck around the boards. But never, never, never pull any flamingo stuff when you're trying to block a shot. Line up for handshakes after games. Grimace as your frozen feet finally start to thaw out. Have a hot chocolate.

Learn the lyrics to "The Hockey Song" by Stompin' Tom Connors. And at least the chorus to "Big League" by Tom Cochrane. Learn the locale of your nearest sports bar. Learn how to shoot a backhander like Mats Sundin (or at least how to raise the puck). Learn how to skate backwards. Learn why numbers such as 50, 92, 215, 544 and 801 are so significant in the world of hockey.

Watch a first-time Stanley Cup champion lift the trophy over his head. Look at his face while he's doing it.

Keep your head up, your stick on the ice and your feet moving. And remember that it's just a game. ■

PHOTO CREDITS

55. Courtesy of Mark Rogers

56. Courtesy of Francis Lessard

57. Steve Babineau/Getty Images

58. Courtesy of Alex Kunawicz

59. Screen capture

60. Dave Sandford/Getty Images

61. Steve Babineau/Getty Images

62. Bruce Bennett/Getty Images

63. Al Bello/Getty Images

64. All rights reserved

65. Grant Halverson/Getty Images

66. Dave Reginek/Getty Images

67. Bruce Bennett/Getty Images

68. Steve Babineau/Getty Images

69. Courtesy of Scott R. Galvin

70. Courtesy of David Connell

71. Gregory Shamus/Getty Images

72. Bruce Bennett/Getty Images

73. All rights reserved

74. Jamie Sabau/ Getty Images

75. Richard Wolowicz/Getty Images

76. Dave Sandford/Getty Images

77. Steve Powell/Getty Images

78. Bruce Bennett/Getty Images

79. Getty Images

80. Eliot J. Schechter/Getty Images

81. Dave Reginek/Getty Images

82. Len Redkoles/Getty Images

83. Bruce Bennett/Getty Images

84. Mike Stobe/Getty Images

85. Jad Gundu/Getty Images

86. John Shibley/LSSU

87. Brian Bahr/ALLSPORT

88. Courtesy of Michael Bevan

89. Chris Trotman/Getty Images

90. Dave Buston/Getty Images

91. Phillip MacCallum/Getty Images

92. The Hockey News

93. Bruce Bennett/Getty Images

94. Shutterstock

95. Craig Jones/Getty Images

96. Tom Carothers/VYPE High School Sports Magazine

97. Courtesy of Darren Abate

98. Courtesy of Chuck Brown

99. Gregg Forwerck/Getty Images